World Economic Situation and Prospects 2018

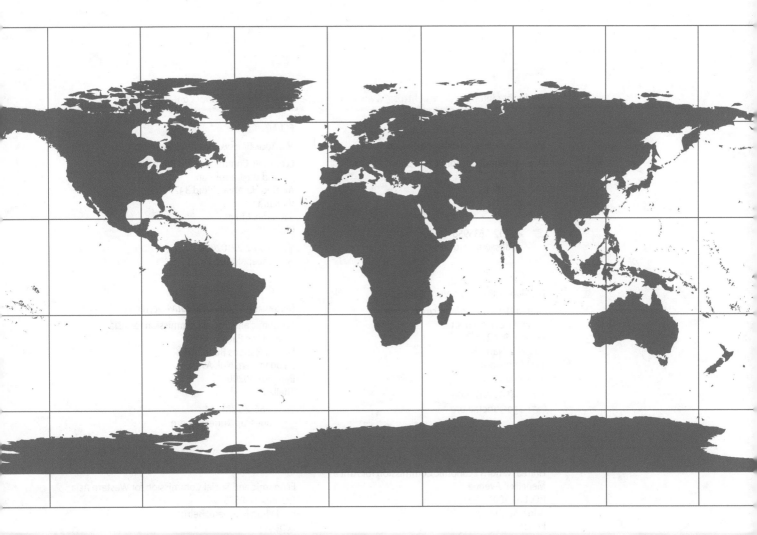

United Nations
New York, 2018

The report is a joint product of the United Nations Department of Economic and Social Affairs (UN/DESA), the United Nations Conference on Trade and Development (UNCTAD) and the five United Nations regional commissions (Economic Commission for Africa (ECA), Economic Commission for Europe (ECE), Economic Commission for Latin America and the Caribbean (ECLAC), Economic and Social Commission for Asia and the Pacific (ESCAP) and Economic and Social Commission for Western Asia (ESCWA)). The United Nations World Tourism Organization (UNWTO) also contributed to the report.

For further information, visit https://www.un.org/development/desa/dpad/ or contact:

DESA

MR. LIU ZHENMIN, *Under-Secretary-General*

Department of Economic and Social Affairs
Room S-2922
United Nations
New York, NY 10017
USA

☎ +1-212-9635958
✉ undesa@un.org

UNCTAD

DR. MUKHISA KITUYI, *Secretary-General*

United Nations Conference on Trade
  and Development
Room E-9042
Palais de Nations
1211 Geneva 10
Switzerland

☎ +41-22-9175806
✉ sgo@unctad.org

ECA

MS. VERA SONGWE, *Executive Secretary*

United Nations Economic Commission for Africa
Menelik II Avenue
P.O. Box 3001
Addis Ababa
Ethiopia

☎ +251-11-5511231
✉ ecainfo@uneca.org

ECE

MS. OLGA ALGAYEROVA, *Executive Secretary*

United Nations Economic Commission for Europe
Palais des Nations
CH-1211 Geneva 10
Switzerland

☎ +41-22-9174444
✉ info.ece@unece.org

ECLAC

MS. ALICIA BÁRCENA, *Executive Secretary*

Economic Commission for Latin America
  and the Caribbean
Av. Dag Hammarskjöld 3477
Vitacura
Santiago, Chile
Chile

☎ +56-2-22102000
✉ secepal@cepal.org

ESCAP

DR. SHAMSHAD AKHTAR, *Executive Secretary*

Economic and Social Commission for Asia
  and the Pacific
United Nations Building
Rajadamnern Nok Avenue
Bangkok 10200
Thailand

☎ +66-2-2881234
✉ unescap@unescap.org

ESCWA

MR. MOHAMED ALI ALHAKIM, *Executive Secretary*

Economic and Social Commission for Western Asia
P.O. Box 11-8575
Riad el-Solh Square, Beirut
Lebanon

☎ +961-1-981301
@ http://www.escwa.un.org/main/contact.asp

ISBN: 978-92-1-109177-9
eISBN: 978-92-1-362882-9
Print ISSN: 1995-2074
Online ISSN: 2411-8370
United Nations publication
Sales No. E.18.II.C.2
Copyright @ United Nations, 2018
All rights reserved

Acknowledgements

The *World Economic Situation and Prospects 2018* is a joint product of the United Nations Department of Economic and Social Affairs (UN/DESA), the United Nations Conference on Trade and Development (UNCTAD) and the five United Nations regional commissions (Economic Commission for Africa (ECA), Economic Commission for Europe (ECE), Economic Commission for Latin America and the Caribbean (ECLAC), Economic and Social Commission for Asia and the Pacific (ESCAP) and Economic and Social Commission for Western Asia (ESCWA)).

The United Nations World Tourism Organization (UNWTO), and staff from the United Nations Office of the High Representative for the Least Developed Countries, Landlocked Developing Countries and Small Island Developing States (UN-OHRLLS) and the International Labour Organization (ILO) also contributed to the report. The report has benefited from inputs received from the national centres of Project LINK and from the deliberations in the Project LINK meeting held in Geneva on 3-5 October 2017. The forecasts presented in the report draw on the World Economic Forecasting Model (WEFM) of UN/DESA.

Under the general guidance of Liu Zhenmin, Under-Secretary-General for Economic and Social Affairs, and the management of Pingfan Hong, Director of Development Policy and Analysis Division (DPAD), this publication was coordinated by Dawn Holland, Chief of Global Economic Monitoring Unit of DPAD.

The contributions of Grigor Agabekian, Helena Afonso, Peter Chowla, Ian Cox, Andrea Grozdanic, Arend Janssen, Shanlin Jin (intern), Leah C. Kennedy, Matthias Kempf, Poh Lynn Ng, Ingo Pitterle, Michał Podolski, Gabe Scelta, Krishnan Sharma, Shari Spiegel, Nancy Settecasi, Anya Thomas, Alexander Trepelkov, Thet Wynn, Sebastian Vergara and Yasuhisa Yamamoto from **UN/DESA**; Bruno Antunes, Stefan Csordas, Taisuke Ito, Mina Mashayekhi, Nicolas Maystre, Janvier D. Nkurunziza, Bonapas Onguglo and Julia Seiermann from **UNCTAD**; Yesuf Mohammednur Awel, Hopestone Chavula, Adam Elhiraika, Khaled Hussein, Allan Mukungu, Sidzanbnoma Nadia Denise Ouedraogo from **ECA**; José Palacín from **ECE**; Claudia De Camino, Michael Hanni, Esteban Pérez-Caldentey, Ramón Pineda, Daniel Titelman, Cecilia Vera, Jurgen Weller from **ECLAC**; Hamza Ali Malik, Jose Antonio Pedrosa Garcia, Sara Holttinen, Jeong-Dae Lee, Kiatkanid Pongpanich and Vatcharin Sirimaneetham from **ESCAP**; Seung-Jin Baek, Moctar Mohamed El Hacene, Mohamed Hedi Bchir and Ahram Han from **ESCWA**; Michel Julian, John Kester and Javier Ruescas from **UNWTO**; Miniva Chibuye from **UN-OHRLLS**; Sheena Yoon, Stefan Kühn and Steven Tobin from **ILO** are duly acknowledged.

The report was edited by Carla Drysdale.

Explanatory notes

The following symbols have been used in the tables throughout the report:

.. **Two dots** indicate that data are not available or are not separately reported.

— **A dash** indicates that the amount is nil or negligible.

- **A hyphen** indicates that the item is not applicable.

- **A minus** sign indicates deficit or decrease, except as indicated.

. **A full stop** is used to indicate decimals.

/ **A slash** between years indicates a crop year or financial year, for example, 2017/18.

– **Use of a hyphen between years**, for example, 2017–2018, signifies the full period involved, including the beginning and end years.

Reference to **"dollars"** ($) indicates United States dollars, unless otherwise stated.

Reference to **"billions"** indicates one thousand million.

Reference to **"tons"** indicates metric tons, unless otherwise stated.

Annual rates of growth or change, unless otherwise stated, refer to annual compound rates.

Details and percentages in tables do not necessarily add to totals, because of rounding.

Project LINK is an international collaborative research group for econometric modelling, coordinated jointly by the Development Policy and Analysis Division of UN/DESA and the University of Toronto.

For **country classifications**, see Statistical annex.

Data presented in this publication incorporate information available as at **11 November 2017**.

The following abbreviations have been used:

AAAA	Addis Ababa Action Agenda	IEA	International Energy Agency
BIS	Bank for International Settlements	IIF	Institute of International Finance
BoJ	Bank of Japan	ILO	International Labour Organization
bpd	barrels per day	IMF	International Monetary Fund
CIS	Commonwealth of Independent States	IMO	International Maritime Organization
CO_2	carbon dioxide	LDCs	least developed countries
ECA	United Nations Economic Commission for Africa	MDBs	multilateral development banks
ECB	European Central Bank	NAFTA	North American Free Trade Agreement
ECE	United Nations Economic Commission for Europe	ODA	official development assistance
ECLAC	United Nations Economic Commission for Latin America and the Caribbean	OECD	Organisation for Economic Co-operation and Development
ESCAP	United Nations Economic and Social Commission for Asia and the Pacific	OPEC	Organization of the Petroleum Exporting Countries
		PPP	purchasing power parity
ESCWA	United Nations Economic and Social Commission for Western Asia	SDGs	Sustainable Development Goals
		SIDS	small island developing States
EU	European Union	TFP	total factor productivity
FDI	foreign direct investment	UN/DESA	Department of Economic and Social Affairs of the United Nations Secretariat
Fed	United States Federal Reserve		
G20	Group of Twenty	UNCTAD	United Nations Conference on Trade and Development
GCC	The Cooperation Council for the Arab States of the Gulf		
GDP	gross domestic product	UNEP	United Nations Environment Programme
GHG	greenhouse gas	UNWTO	United Nations World Tourism Organization
GNI	gross national income	VAT	value-added tax
GVCs	global value chains	WESP	World Economic Situation and Prospects
ICAO	International Civil Aviation Organization	WGP	world gross product
ICT	information and communications technology	WTO	World Trade Organization

Foreword

The 2008 financial crisis laid bare the inadequacies in the rules we need for a stable and prosperous global economy. After a long period of stagnation, the world economy is finally strengthening. In 2017, global economic growth approached 3 per cent — the highest rate since 2011. As the *World Economic Situation and Prospects 2018* demonstrates, current macroeconomic conditions offer policymakers greater scope to address some of the deep-rooted systemic issues and short-term thinking that continue to hamper progress towards the Sustainable Development Goals.

While acknowledging that many cyclical and longer-term risks and challenges persist, the report notes that, in many parts of the world, conditions have improved to support the significant investment necessary for delivering the goods and services a growing population needs. This paves the way to reorient policy towards longer-term issues, such as rehabilitating and protecting the environment, making economic growth more inclusive and tackling institutional obstacles to development.

Reorienting policy to address these more fundamental drivers of growth and sustainability can underpin a virtuous circle. Investment in areas such as education, health-care, resilience to climate change and building financial and digital inclusion, supports economic growth and job creation in the short-term and promotes long-term sustainable development.

I commend the efforts of the United Nations Department of Economic and Social Affairs, the United Nations Conference on Trade and Development (UNCTAD) and the five United Nations regional commissions on the production of this joint report.

António Guterres
Secretary-General of the United Nations

Executive summary

Prospects for global macroeconomic development

As headwinds from the global financial crisis subside, policymakers have more scope to tackle longer-term issues that hold back sustainable development

The last decade has been punctuated by a series of broad-based economic crises and negative shocks, starting with the global financial crisis of 2008–2009, followed by the European sovereign debt crisis of 2010–2012 and the global commodity price realignments of 2014–2016. As these crises and the persistent headwinds that accompanied them subside, the world economy has strengthened, offering greater scope to reorient policy towards longer-term issues that hold back progress along the economic, social and environmental dimensions of sustainable development.

In 2017, global economic growth is estimated to have reached 3.0 per cent, a significant acceleration compared to growth of just 2.4 per cent in 2016, and the highest rate of global growth recorded since 2011. Labour market indicators continue to improve in a broad spectrum of countries, and roughly two-thirds of countries worldwide experienced stronger growth in 2017 than in the previous year. At the global level, growth is expected to remain steady at 3.0 per cent in 2018 and 2019.

Stronger economic activity has not been shared evenly across countries and regions

The recent acceleration in world gross product growth stems predominantly from firmer growth in several developed economies, although East and South Asia remain the world's most dynamic regions. Cyclical improvements in Argentina, Brazil, Nigeria and the Russian Federation, as these economies emerge from recession, also explain roughly a third of the rise in the rate of global growth between 2016 and 2017. But recent economic gains remain unevenly distributed across countries and regions, and many parts of the world have yet to regain a healthy rate of growth. Economic prospects for many commodity exporters remain challenging, underscoring the vulnerability to boom and bust cycles in countries that are overly reliant on a small number of natural resources. Moreover, the longer-term potential of the global economy carries a scar from the extended period of weak investment and low productivity growth that followed the global financial crisis.

Investment conditions have improved, but elevated policy uncertainty and rising levels of debt may prevent a more widespread investment rebound

Conditions for investment have generally improved, amid low financial volatility, reduced banking sector fragilities, recovery in some commodity sectors and a more solid global macroeconomic outlook. Financing costs generally remain low, and spreads have narrowed in many emerging markets, reflecting a decline in risk premia. This has supported rising capital flows to emerging markets, including a rise in cross-border lending, and stronger credit growth in both developed and developing economies.

Improved conditions have supported a modest revival in productive investment in some large economies. Gross fixed capital formation accounted for roughly 60 per cent of the acceleration in global economic activity in 2017. This improvement is relative to a very low starting point, following two years of exceptionally weak investment growth, and a prolonged episode of lacklustre global investment overall. A firmer and more broad-based rebound in investment activity, which is needed to support stronger productivity growth and accelerate progress towards the Sustainable Development Goals, may be deterred by elevated levels of trade policy uncertainty, considerable uncertainties regarding the impact of balance sheet adjustment in major central banks, as well as rising debt and a build-up of longer-term financial fragilities.

Rebound in world trade could face a setback if protectionist tendencies increase

Global trade rebounded in 2017. In the first eight months of the year, world merchandise trade grew at its fastest pace in the post-crisis period. The rebound springs predominantly from stronger import demand in East Asia, as domestic demand picked up in the region, supported by accommodative policy measures. In several major developed economies, imports of capital goods have rebounded, as firms respond to improving conditions for investment.

Recent course adjustments in major trade relationships, such as the United Kingdom of Great Britain and Northern Ireland's decision to withdraw from the European Union and the United States of America's decisions to renegotiate the North American Free Trade Agreement and to reassess the terms of its other existing trade agreements, have raised concerns over a potential escalation in trade barriers and disputes. These could be amplified if met by retaliatory measures by other countries. An increasingly restrictive trade environment may hinder medium-term growth prospects, given the mutually reinforcing linkages between trade, investment and productivity growth. In this regard, policies should focus on upholding and revitalizing multilateral trade cooperation, emphasizing the possible benefits from trade in services.

Progress towards sustainable development

Weak growth in per capita income poses setbacks to sustainable development targets in several regions

The uneven pace of global economic recovery continues to raise concerns regarding prospects for achieving the Sustainable Development Goals. Many countries have even suffered recent setbacks, as average incomes declined in four major developing regions in 2016.

In 2017–2019, further setbacks or negligible growth in per capita gross domestic product (GDP) is anticipated in Central, Southern and West Africa, Western Asia, and Latin America and the Caribbean. These regions combined are home to 275 million people living in extreme poverty. This underscores the importance of addressing some of the longer-term structural issues that hold back more rapid progress towards sustainable development and to ensure that the targets of eradicating poverty and creating decent jobs for all are not pushed further from reach. Failure to address these issues may leave a quarter of the population of Africa in extreme poverty by 2030.

Supporting growth in LDCs requires both financial resources and progress towards addressing institutional deficiencies and security concerns

Very few of the least developed countries (LDCs) are expected to reach the Sustainable Development Goal target for GDP growth of "at least 7 per cent" in the near term. Approaching this target will require higher levels of investment in many LDCs. Mobilizing necessary financial resources may be approached through various combinations of domestic and international, public and private sources of finance. However, more rapid progress in many of the LDCs is hindered by institutional deficiencies, inadequate basic infrastructure, high levels of exposure to weather-related shocks and natural disasters, as well as challenges related to security and political uncertainty. These barriers must be addressed to ensure that available finance is channelled efficiently towards productive investment.

Accelerated economic growth increases need to consider links to environmental sustainability

The acceleration in economic growth also bears an environmental cost. The frequency of weather-related shocks continues to increase, highlighting the urgent need to build resilience against climate change and contain the pace of environmental degradation. While the level of global energy-related carbon emissions remained flat between 2013–2016, the return to stronger GDP growth is likely to result in higher emission levels.

International shipping and aviation emissions do not fall under the purview of the Paris Agreement, and emissions from these two sectors have grown faster than those from road transport over the past 25 years, and have continued to rise unabated since 2013. While air pollution measures have been strengthened in both shipping and aviation industries, it is not clear that current policies will be sufficient to reduce emissions to levels consistent with the objectives of the Paris Agreement.

Transition towards sustainable energy remains gradual

Transition towards sustainable energy is advancing at a gradual pace. Renewables account for more than half of all recently installed power capacity, but still provide only about 11 per cent of global power generation. China remains the world's biggest investor in renewables, and renewable investment in 2017 will be supported by massive wind projects in Australia, China, Germany, Mexico, the United Kingdom and the United States. At a time when many countries, notably in Africa, continue to suffer from severe shortages of energy supply, there is enormous potential to lay the basis of environmentally sustainable growth in the future through smart policies and investments today.

Uncertainties and risks

Economic prospects remain vulnerable to changes in trade policy, a sudden deterioration in global financial conditions and rising geopolitical tensions

While many of the overhanging fragilities from the global financial crisis have eased, a number of uncertainties and risks loom on the horizon. Elevated levels of policy uncertainty continue to cloud prospects for world trade, development aid, migration and climate targets, and may delay a more broad-based rebound in global investment and productivity. Rising geopolitical tensions could intensify a tendency towards more unilateral and isolationist policies. The prolonged period of abundant global liquidity and low borrowing costs has contributed to a further rise in global debt levels and a build-up of financial imbalances. It is also linked to the current high levels of asset prices, which suggest an under-pricing of risk.

Many developing economies—especially those with more open capital markets—remain vulnerable to spikes in risk aversion, a disorderly tightening of global liquidity conditions, and sudden capital withdrawal. Monetary policy normalization in developed economies could trigger such a spike. Central banks in developed economies are currently operating in largely unchartered territory, with no historical precedent as guidance. This makes any adjustment of financial markets less predictable than during previous recoveries and amplifies the risks associated with policy errors.

Policy challenges and the way forward

Synchronized upturn among major economies, stable financial market conditions and the absence of major negative shocks offer opportunities to reorient policy

While a number of risks and uncertainties remain, what stands out in the current economic environment is the alignment of the economic cycle among major economies, stability in financial market conditions and the absence of negative shocks such as commodity price dislocations.

As conditions for more widespread global economic stability solidify, the need to focus policy actions on economic crisis consequences and short-term macroeconomic stabilization has eased. Coupled with improving investment conditions, this creates greater scope to reorient policy towards longer-term issues, such as strengthening the environmental quality of economic growth, making it more inclusive, and tackling institutional deficiencies that hinder development.

Reorienting policy to address these challenges and maximizing co-benefits between development objectives can generate stronger investment, higher job creation and more sustainable medium-term economic growth. Current investment in areas such as education, expanding access to healthcare, building resilience to climate change, improving the quality of institutions, and building financial and digital inclusion, will support economic growth and job creation in the short-term. It will also accelerate progress towards social and environmental goals and raise the longer-term potential for sustainable growth.

Policy reorientation should encompass four concrete areas: increasing economic diversification, reducing inequality, strengthening financial architecture and tackling institutional deficiencies

Policymakers should use the current macroeconomic backdrop to focus on four concrete areas. First, the long-standing need for economic diversification in countries that remain heavily dependent on a few basic commodities cannot be overstated. The heavy economic costs related to recent commodity price realignments proves the point.

Stemming and redressing the rise in inequality is also crucial for ensuring balanced and sustainable growth going forward. This requires a combination of short-term policies to raise living standards among the most deprived, and longer-term policies that address inequalities in opportunity, such as investment in early childhood development, broadening access to healthcare and education, and investment in rural roads and electrification.

A third crucial area is realigning the global financial architecture with the 2030 Agenda for Sustainable Development and the Addis Ababa Action Agenda. This requires creating a new framework for sustainable finance and shifting gradually from the current focus on short-term profit towards a target of long-term value creation, in a socially and environmentally responsible manner. Macroprudential policies, well coordinated with monetary, fiscal and foreign exchange policies, can support these goals by promoting financial stability and containing the build-up of financial risks.

Finally, weak governance and political instability remain fundamental obstacles to achieving the 2030 Agenda for Sustainable Development. At the same time, stronger global economic growth can do little on its own to help those afflicted by conflict situations, where there is little scope for meaningful progress towards sustainable development. Policy priorities must include redoubling efforts to support conflict prevention and resolution and tackling the institutional deficiencies underpinning many of these obstacles.

Table of contents

Page

Chapter I
Global economic outlook

Prospects for the world economy in 2018–2019

Global growth has strengthened

The past decade has been characterized by fragile growth, high investor uncertainty and periodic spikes in global financial market volatility. As crisis-related fragilities and the adverse effects of other recent shocks gradually subside, the world economy has strengthened. Towards the end of 2016, global economic activity began to see a modest pickup, which extended into 2017.

World industrial production has accelerated, in tandem with a recovery in global trade that has been predominantly driven by stronger demand in East Asia. Confidence and economic sentiment indicators have also generally strengthened, especially in developed economies. Investment conditions have improved, amid stable financial markets, strong credit growth, and a more solid macroeconomic outlook.

In 2017, global economic growth is estimated to have reached 3.0 per cent when calculated at market exchange rates, or 3.6 per cent when adjusted for purchasing power parities[1] — the highest growth rate since 2011 (figure I.1). Currently, all major developed economies are experiencing a synchronized upturn in growth. Compared to the previous year, growth strengthened in almost two thirds of countries worldwide in 2017.

> As lingering fragilities following the global financial crisis subside, the world economy has strengthened

Figure I.1
Growth of world gross product

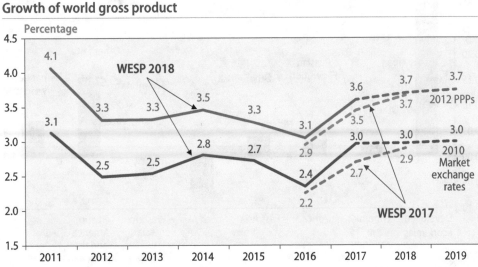

Source: UN/DESA.

---

1   Purchasing power parities (PPPs) adjust for differences in the cost of living across countries. Developing countries have a higher weight in PPP exchange rate-based aggregations than when using market exchange rates. Since developing countries have been growing significantly faster than developed countries, the rate of global growth is higher when using PPP exchange rates.

At the global level, world gross product (WGP) is forecast to expand at a steady pace of 3.0 per cent in 2018 and 2019 (table I.1).[2] Developing economies remain the main drivers of global growth. In 2017, East and South Asia accounted for nearly half of global growth, as both regions continue to expand at a rapid pace. The Chinese economy alone contributed about one-third of global growth during the year.

However, stronger economic activity has not been shared evenly across countries and regions, with many parts of the world yet to regain a healthy rate of growth. Moreover, the longer-term potential of the global economy continues to bear a scar from the extended period of weak investment and low productivity growth that followed the global financial crisis. Widespread weakness in wage growth, high levels of debt and elevated levels of policy uncertainty continue to restrain a firmer and more broad-based rebound in aggregate demand. At the same time, a number of short-term risks, as well as a buildup of longer-term financial vulnerabilities, could derail the recent upturn in global economic growth.

The recent acceleration in WGP growth, from a post-crisis low of 2.4 per cent in 2016, stems predominantly from firmer growth in several developed economies (figure I.2). Cyclical improvements in Argentina, Brazil, Nigeria and the Russian Federation, as these economies emerge from recession, also explain roughly a third of the rise in the rate of global growth in 2017.

The composition of global demand has shifted more towards investment over the last year. Gross fixed capital formation accounted for roughly 60 per cent of the acceleration in global economic activity in 2017 (figure I.3). This improvement, however, is relative to a very low starting point, following two years of exceptionally weak investment growth, and a prolonged period of lacklustre global investment activity. Business investment contracted in a number of large economies in 2016, including Argentina, Australia, Brazil, Canada,

Figure I.2
Contributions to change in world gross product growth by country, 2017

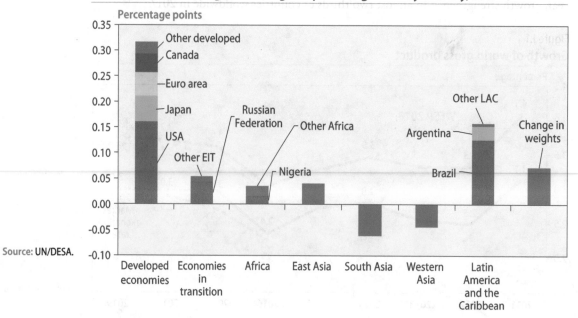

Source: UN/DESA.

---

2   Country-level forecasts underlying this summary table are reported in the Statistical annex. Unless otherwise specified, regional aggregations are based on 2010 market exchange rates.

Table I.1
Growth of world output, 2015–2019

Annual percentage change	2015	2016	2017[a]	2018[b]	2019[b]	Change from WESP 2017	
						2017	2018
World	2.7	2.4	3.0	3.0	3.0	0.3	0.1
Developed economies	2.2	1.6	2.2	2.0	1.9	0.5	0.2
United States of America	2.9	1.5	2.2	2.1	2.1	0.3	0.1
Japan	1.1	1.0	1.7	1.2	1.0	0.8	0.3
European Union	2.2	1.9	2.2	2.1	1.9	0.4	0.3
EU-15	2.1	1.8	2.0	1.9	1.8	0.4	0.2
EU-13	3.8	2.9	4.2	3.6	3.5	1.0	0.3
Euro area	2.0	1.8	2.1	2.0	1.9	0.4	0.3
Other developed countries	1.6	1.8	2.5	2.4	2.2	0.5	0.2
Economies in transition	-2.2	0.4	2.2	2.3	2.4	0.8	0.3
South-Eastern Europe	2.0	2.9	2.5	3.2	3.3	-0.6	-0.1
Commonwealth of Independent States and Georgia	-2.4	0.3	2.2	2.3	2.4	0.8	0.3
Russian Federation	-2.8	-0.2	1.8	1.9	1.9	0.8	0.4
Developing economies	3.9	3.8	4.3	4.6	4.7	-0.1	-0.1
Africa	3.1	1.7	3.0	3.5	3.7	-0.2	-0.3
North Africa	3.2	2.8	4.8	4.1	4.1	1.3	0.5
East Africa	6.7	5.4	5.3	5.8	6.2	-0.7	-0.5
Central Africa	1.7	0.6	0.7	2.1	2.5	-2.7	-2.1
West Africa	3.2	0.3	2.4	3.3	3.4	-0.7	-0.8
Southern Africa	1.9	0.6	1.2	2.3	2.5	-0.6	-0.3
East and South Asia	5.8	6.0	6.0	5.8	5.9	0.1	-0.1
East Asia	5.7	5.6	5.9	5.7	5.6	0.3	0.1
China	6.9	6.7	6.8	6.5	6.3	0.3	0.0
South Asia	6.2	7.7	6.3	6.5	7.0	-0.6	-0.4
India[c]	7.6	7.1	6.7	7.2	7.4	-1.0	-0.4
Western Asia	3.6	3.0	1.9	2.3	2.7	-0.6	-0.7
Latin America and the Caribbean	-0.6	-1.3	1.0	2.0	2.5	-0.3	-0.1
South America	-1.9	-2.7	0.4	1.8	2.4	-0.5	-0.2
Brazil	-3.8	-3.6	0.7	2.0	2.5	0.1	0.4
Mexico and Central America	3.1	2.5	2.5	2.6	2.6	0.1	0.3
Caribbean	0.2	-0.8	0.2	1.8	2.0	-1.2	0.0
Least developed countries	4.2	4.3	4.8	5.4	5.5	-0.3	-0.2
Memorandum items							
World trade[d]	2.9	2.2	3.7	3.5	3.6	1.0	0.2
World output growth with PPP weights[e]	3.3	3.1	3.6	3.7	3.7	0.1	0.0

Source: UN/DESA.
a Estimated.
b Forecast, based in part on Project LINK.
c Fiscal year basis.
d Includes goods and services.
e Based on 2012 benchmark.

the Russian Federation, South Africa, the United Kingdom of Great Britain and Northern Ireland and the United States of America.

While investment is no longer a drag on global growth, the recovery remains moderate and contained to a relatively narrow set of countries. A more entrenched recovery in investment growth is likely to be held back by elevated levels of uncertainty over future trade policy arrangements, the impact of balance sheet adjustments in major central banks, as well as high debt and a build-up of longer-term financial fragilities. Further details on prospects for investment and its links to productivity over the medium-term are discussed in the next section of this chapter.

Figure I.3
Contributions to change in world gross product growth by component, 2017

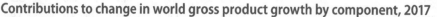

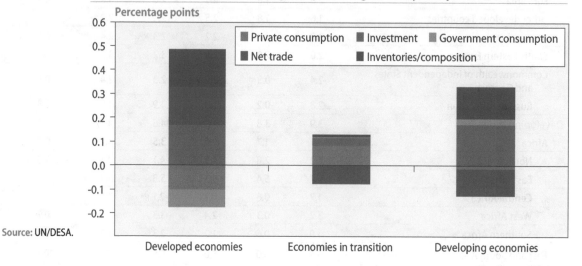

Source: UN/DESA.

Economic prospects for many commodity exporters remain challenging, reinforcing the need for economic diversification

Recent economic gains have not been evenly distributed across countries and regions. East and South Asia remain the world's most dynamic regions, benefiting from robust domestic demand and supportive macroeconomic policies. In contrast, economic conditions remain challenging for many commodity-exporting countries, underscoring the vulnerability to commodity boom and bust cycles in countries that are over-reliant on a narrow range of natural resources. Prospects in Africa, Western Asia and parts of South America remain heavily dependent on commodity prices (figure I.4).

Following the sharp global commodity price realignments of 2014–2016, commodity prices have not exhibited a common trend in 2017, but have been driven by sector-specific developments. As such, the economic performance of commodity exporters has diverged, with countries such as Chile starting to benefit from the upturn in copper prices, while the drop in cocoa prices has led to a deterioration in economic prospects in Côte d'Ivoire. For the most part, currency pressures associated with the steep price adjustments have eased, allowing some scope for policy easing in a number of countries. The moderate recovery in the price of oil from the lows seen in early 2016 has brought some respite to oil-exporting countries. However, given that oil prices stand at roughly half their average level in 2011–2014, growth prospects of the oil exporters will remain subdued over the forecast horizon, reinforcing the need for economic diversification.

Figure I.4
Commodity dependence of export revenue in developing countries, 2014–2015

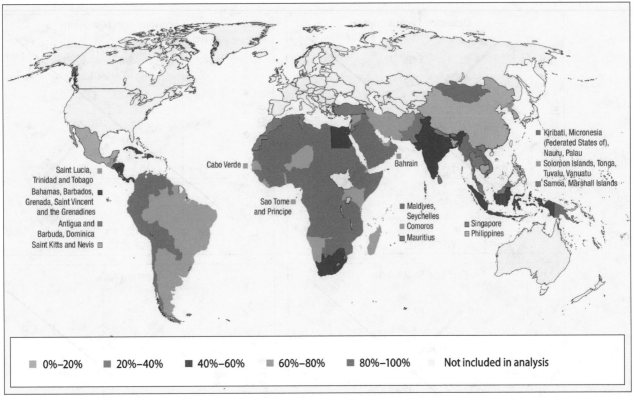

Source: UNCTAD (2017a).

Note: The figures represent commodity export value as share of merchandise export value. The boundaries and names shown and the designations used on this map do not imply official endorsement or acceptance by the United Nations.

The ongoing structural adjustments to commodity prices, coupled with political uncertainty or security challenges, explain much of the downward revision to GDP growth estimates in Africa and the Latin America and the Caribbean region for 2017 compared to forecasts reported in the *World Economic Situation and Prospects 2017* (United Nations, 2017) (figure I.5).[3] At the global level, the current estimate for WGP growth in 2017 of 3.0 per cent represents a small upward revision to forecasts released a year ago. This adjustment is noteworthy in itself, as it marks the first occasion since 2010 that the world economy will exceed rather than disappoint expectations. The extended spate of downward revisions to forecasts over the previous seven years reflects repeated failures to recognize the extent of fragilities remaining after the global financial crisis. In addition, unexpected shocks such as commodity price realignment and the impact of policy measures — notably fiscal tightening in developed economies — were also underestimated. These headwinds have now eased.

The upward revision to growth estimates for 2017 stems predominantly from firmer-than-expected growth in several developed economies — notably in Europe and Japan — as well as a faster-than-anticipated recovery in the Russian Federation, which is supporting a broader growth revival in the region.

Global economic growth is exceeding, rather than disappointing, expectations, for the first time since 2010. But many countries in Africa and Latin America and the Caribbean have underperformed relative to expectations.

---

3   In the case of Latin America and the Caribbean, a significant part of the downward revision is due to the deeper-than-expected recession in the Bolivarian Republic of Venezuela.

Figure I.5
Forecast revisions relative to WESP 2017, GDP growth in 2017

Percentage

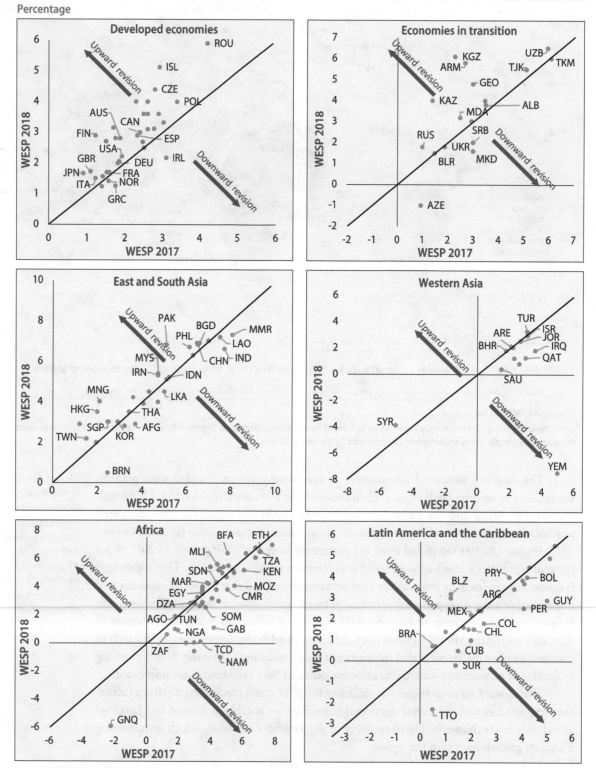

Source: UN/DESA.

Notes: Figures compare GDP growth forecasts for 2017 in WESP 2017 to GDP growth estimates for 2017 in WESP 2018. Libya and Venezuela (Bolivarian Republic of) are excluded from the figure. Only selected points are labelled for clarity. See Table J in the Statistical annex for definitions of country codes.

The uneven pace of global economic recovery continues to jeopardize prospects for achieving the Sustainable Development Goals (SDGs). While the overall growth prospects of the global economy may have improved, forecasts for a few regions, including some of the world's poorest countries, have been revised downward. Many of these countries have even suffered setbacks in progress towards the SDGs, as GDP per capita declined in four major developing regions last year (figure I.6). Further setbacks or negligible per capita growth is anticipated in Central, Southern and West Africa, Western Asia, and Latin America and the Caribbean in 2018–2019. These regions combined are home to nearly 20 per cent of the global population, and more than one-third of those living in extreme poverty. This pushes the targets of eradicating poverty and creating decent jobs for all further from reach, and poses risks to many of the other SDGs.

At the same time, according to preliminary data, the level of global carbon dioxide emissions from fossil fuel combustion and cement production increased in 2017, after having remained flat between 2013 and 2016 (Global Carbon Project, 2017). This suggests that the return to stronger economic growth may also result in rising emissions levels. These factors underscore the importance of addressing some of the longer-term structural issues that hold back more rapid progress towards sustainable development.

Only a small handful of the least developed countries (LDCs) are expected to reach the SDG target for GDP growth of "at least 7 per cent" in the near term. As a group, the LDCs are projected to grow by 4.8 per cent in 2017 and 5.4 per cent in 2018. These figures are a significant improvement compared to the growth rates seen in 2015 and 2016, reflecting more benign global conditions and gradually rising commodity prices. However, the achievement of more rapid progress in many of the LDCs is hampered by institutional deficiencies, inadequate basic infrastructure as well as high susceptibility to weather-related or commodity price shocks, given the lack of economic diversification. These challenges are exacerbated by security and political uncertainty in several countries (see Box I.1 for further discussion on LDCs).

Regions covering nearly 20 per cent of the global population are expected to see negligible growth in average incomes in 2018–2019

Economic growth in most of the least developed countries remains well below the SDG target of 7 per cent

Figure I.6
Average annual GDP per capita growth by region

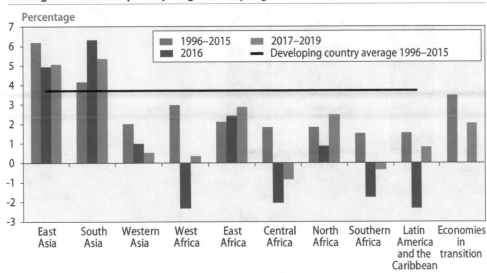

Source: UN/DESA, based on United Nations Statistics Division National Accounts Main Aggregates Database, United Nations Population Division World Population Prospects and UN/DESA forecasts.

Box I.1
Prospects for least developed countries

Growth in the least developed countries (LDCs)[a] is expected to rise modestly from an estimated 4.8 per cent in 2017 to 5.4 per cent and 5.5 per cent in 2018 and 2019, respectively. The acceleration is due mostly to more favourable external economic conditions and, in particular, firming commodity prices, which support trade, financial flows and investment in natural resource projects and infrastructure. GDP per capita grew by an estimated 2.5 per cent in 2017, which solidifies the recovery from the lows of 2015–2016, but remains subdued compared to the momentum reached before 2007. Prospects for the group are positive with per capita growth expected to accelerate to 3.0 per cent in 2018 and 3.2 per cent in 2019.

However, given the depth and extent of poverty and inequality among LDCs, tangible improvements in quality of life will remain limited. Structural challenges continue to hamper significant progress in economic and social development. This includes a lack of infrastructure and public services, political instability and institutional deficiencies and vulnerability to shocks from commodity revenue and extreme weather events.

Moreover, despite facing better prospects, the LDCs as a group will not accomplish SDG target 8.1 this year, which calls for "at least 7 per cent gross domestic product growth per annum" in the LDCs. Nonetheless, some countries in the group will achieve average growth above or close to 7 per cent in 2018–2019, and the majority will grow at a 5 per cent or higher rate by the end of 2019 (see figure I.1.1). Bangladesh is projected to be among the fastest growing LDCs in 2018 with expected real GDP growth of 7.1 per cent, supported by vigorous domestic demand, especially private investments.

Bhutan is also expected to grow by 7.1 per cent in 2018, benefitting from infrastructure investments. The fastest growing East Asian LDCs include Cambodia, the Lao People's Democratic Republic and Myanmar with growth rates forecast to be slightly above 7 per cent in 2018–2019, mainly as a result of export growth and infrastructure projects.

a South Sudan and Tuvalu are not included in the analysis due to insufficient data. Equatorial Guinea is excluded from the aggregation, as it became the fifth country to graduate from the least developed country category on 4 June 2017.

Figure I.1.1
Real GDP growth in the least developed countries group

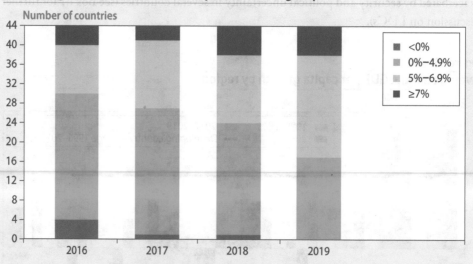

Source: UN/DESA forecasts.

(continued)

Box I.1 (*continued*)

In Africa, the fastest pace of growth is in countries in the eastern region, including Djibouti, Ethiopia, Rwanda and the United Republic of Tanzania, underpinned by infrastructure investments, resilient services sectors and the recovery of agricultural production. Senegal in West Africa has joined this group, spurred by greater competitiveness, progress in structural reforms and favourable external conditions, such as positive terms of trade, favourable climatic conditions and a stable security environment.

Some LDCs face prominent growth challenges. Conflict-afflicted Yemen has been in recession for the past several years. The ongoing armed conflict has inflicted significant damage to the agriculture sector and the crumbling institutional infrastructure is expected to prevent a significant rebound in the near future.

Following estimated growth of only 1.3 per cent in 2017, Haiti is forecast to see a moderate pickup in economic activity by 2019, amid continued reconstruction of infrastructure and recovery in the agricultural sector. However, severe macroeconomic imbalances, political unrest and natural disasters threaten to derail the recovery.

Strong public and private investment is a common feature among those LDCs that are growing at over 7 per cent per year. As explained in the *State of the Least Developed Countries 2017* (UN-OHRLLS, 2017), an additional investment of $24 billion per year would suffice to bring the group, on average, to 7 per cent GDP growth between 2016 and 2020.

Funding of such investment could come from a combination of sources. Domestic resource mobilization features prominently in the Istanbul Programme of Action and the Addis Ababa Action Agenda as a means to finance current investment gaps, namely in poverty alleviation and public service delivery.

As an analytical exercise, we can consider a scenario in which the additional investment of $24 billion is funded solely through domestic public resource mobilization. In this case, general government revenue in the LDCs would have to increase by approximately 13 per cent in 2018 and 2019.[b] As most of these countries struggle to raise tax revenue, which amounts to less than 15 per cent of GDP in half of the LDCs (ibid.), an increase in tax revenue of this magnitude would prove overly burdensome for some countries in the short term.

An alternative scenario to consider is financing the additional investment through international public finance. Should official development assistance (ODA) from OECD Development Assistance Committee (DAC) members fill the investment gap in the LDCs, it would have to roughly double as compared to 2016 levels.

This would represent a commitment by DAC members of providing 0.11 per cent of gross national income (GNI) in ODA to LDCs. This would be 0.04 percentage points below the lower end of the 2030 Agenda target of achieving 0.15 per cent to 0.2 per cent of ODA/GNI to LDCs. Other types of concessional international public finance could also help fund investment needs, including lending by multilateral development banks, although debt sustainability is a concern for many LDCs.

Mobilizing domestic or international private sector resources to finance investment needs can be considered as a third scenario. Foreign direct investment (FDI) to LDCs is estimated to have totalled $33.4 billion in 2017. In order to meet the additional investment needs entirely through FDI, inflows would have to increase by 50 to 60 per cent in 2018 and 2019. In practice, FDI in LDCs remains heavily concentrated in a few countries and in the extractive industries. Directing FDI towards the longer-term infrastructure and economic diversification needs across all LDCs remains an important policy challenge.

Only a few of the LDCs are expected to grow fast enough to progress substantially towards the SDGs, while the others urgently need developed countries to meet their targets for ODA. Amid imperfect institutional frameworks and business environments, efforts and incentives are necessary to bolster both FDI and domestic resource mobilization. Finally, policies to promote economic diversification are needed, in order to support long-term sustainability and more inclusive growth.

b For simplicity, the calculations in this section ignore linkages between financing sources.

Authors: Helena Afonso (UN/DESA/DPAD), Miniva Chibuye (UN-OHRLLS) and Michał Podolski (UN/DESA/DPAD)

Benign global inflation against a backdrop of stronger growth

In developed economies, the uptick in GDP growth has been associated with an easing of deflationary pressures, which posed a key policy concern in 2015–2016. In the first half of 2017, inflation dynamics in many countries were impacted by the steep year-on-year rise in energy prices relative to the lows seen in early 2016. While this transitory impact had largely dissipated by mid-year, longer-term inflation expectations in developed countries, as measured by the difference between nominal and inflation-indexed government bond yields, have edged upward relative to 2016 levels, suggesting that expectations of a return to deflation have diminished.

The upward shift in inflation led the President of the European Central Bank (ECB) to state in March 2017 that "the risks of deflation [in Europe] have largely disappeared". Subsequently, the ECB halved the pace of its asset purchases. In Japan, inflation has edged above zero, while in the United Kingdom and the United States headline inflation exceeded the central bank targets of 2 per cent for at least part of 2017. In aggregate, inflation in developed economies is expected to average 1.5 per cent in 2017, up from 0.7 per cent in 2016 (table I.2), but still well below central bank inflation targets.

By contrast, price pressures have eased in many large developing economies and economies in transition. This created space for several countries in South America, parts of Africa and the Commonwealth of Independent States (CIS) to cut interest rates in 2017, easing monetary conditions and providing more support to economic activity (see figure I.A.5 in Appendix). In countries such as the Russian Federation and South Africa, this partly reflects a recovery in exchange rates, following sharp depreciations in 2015–2016. Meanwhile, high food price inflation has started to recede in a number of African countries, where agricultural shortages caused by severe drought and other weather-related shocks, compounded by distribution blockages related to conflict situations, drove food price inflation to double-digit levels in the first few months of 2017.

Figure I.7 compares the estimate for consumer price inflation in 2017 to the upper-end of central bank targets.[4] Inflation is at or below target in about 75 per cent of the countries in the sample. The countries exceeding official inflation targets are predominantly in Africa, where inflation rates remain relatively high in several countries, despite stabilizing exchange rates and some easing of food price inflation. A few countries in the CIS also continue to experience high inflation relative to their targets. Nonetheless, inflation has for the most part come down over the course of the year in these regions.

Global inflationary pressures are expected to remain relatively benign. In developed economies, inflation is expected to hover close to central bank targets in 2018–2019. Despite low unemployment in many developed economies, wage pressures generally remain weak. This may in part be a reflection of rising inequality and limited bargaining power of those on the lower end of income scales. The rise in inequality bears its own risks for the real side of the economy, as discussed below. Unless demand accelerates or there is a marked shift in wage pressures, inflation in developed economies will likely remain moderate. A re-emergence of deflationary pressures would pose a policy challenge for central banks, as they move towards the withdrawal of monetary stimulus.

In many developing regions and economies in transition, steady or declining inflation may lead to more monetary easing. Nonetheless, there is a risk that market reactions to

---

4   The sample only includes countries that have an explicit or implicit target rate for inflation, and so excludes some countries with very high inflation, such as the Bolivarian Republic of Venezuela.

Table I.2
Inflation, 2015–2019[a]

Annual percentage change	2015	2016	2017[b]	2018[c]	2019[c]	Change from WESP 2017 2017	2018
World	2.1	2.4	2.6	2.8	2.8	-0.2	-0.1
Developed economies	0.2	0.7	1.5	1.9	2.1	-0.1	-0.1
United States of America	0.1	1.3	1.7	2.1	2.1	-0.5	-0.4
Japan	0.8	-0.1	0.3	1.4	1.8	-0.3	0.0
European Union	0.0	0.3	1.6	1.8	2.1	0.2	-0.1
EU-15	0.1	0.3	1.6	1.8	2.1	0.2	-0.1
EU-13	-0.4	-0.2	1.9	2.2	2.4	0.2	0.0
Euro area	0.0	0.2	1.4	1.6	2.0	0.2	-0.1
Other developed countries	1.0	1.3	1.5	2.0	1.9	-0.3	0.1
Economies in transition	15.8	7.8	5.3	5.1	4.6	-1.7	-0.2
South-Eastern Europe	0.8	0.4	2.3	2.0	2.6	0.6	-0.4
Commonwealth of Independent States and Georgia	16.4	8.1	5.4	5.2	4.7	-1.8	-0.2
Russian Federation	15.5	7.1	3.9	4.4	3.9	-2.7	-0.3
Developing economies	4.4	5.2	4.4	4.3	4.2	-0.3	-0.2
Africa	7.0	11.3	13.0	9.5	8.1	2.9	-0.1
North Africa	7.8	11.3	17.6	8.3	7.1	9.2	0.4
East Africa	6.0	6.0	7.3	6.0	5.5	2.0	0.7
Central Africa	3.3	2.2	2.6	2.9	2.8	-0.1	-0.2
West Africa	8.3	13.2	14.3	15.4	12.8	-1.4	-0.3
Southern Africa	5.9	12.5	9.4	7.9	6.8	-0.4	-0.3
East and South Asia	2.6	2.6	2.4	3.1	3.4	-0.7	-0.3
East Asia	1.6	1.9	1.8	2.5	2.7	-0.5	-0.2
China	1.4	2.0	1.5	2.5	2.8	-0.6	-0.2
South Asia	6.9	5.5	4.9	5.8	5.9	-1.5	-0.3
India	5.9	4.9	3.5	4.5	4.8	-2.2	-0.9
Western Asia	4.9	5.4	4.8	4.5	3.9	-0.7	-0.6
Latin America and the Caribbean	7.7	9.3	5.8	4.9	4.7	-0.3	0.1
South America	9.8	11.9	6.0	5.4	5.2	-1.4	-0.2
Brazil	9.1	8.7	3.4	3.7	4.1	-2.4	-0.9
Mexico and Central America	2.5	2.8	5.4	3.8	3.4	2.4	0.8
Caribbean	3.4	6.1	4.1	3.5	3.8	0.4	0.0
Least developed countries	8.3	13.1	11.4	8.3	7.5	0.8	-0.2

Source: UN/DESA.
a Figures exclude Venezuela (Bolivarian Republic of).
b Estimated.
c Forecast, based in part on Project LINK.

Figure I.7
Forecast for inflation in 2017 relative to upper-end of central bank target

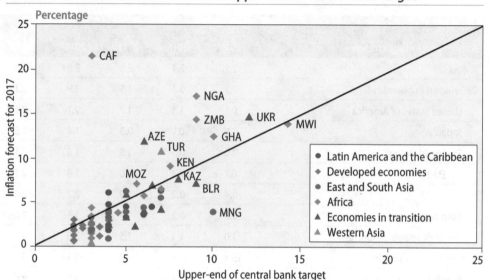

Sources: Central Bank News and
UN/DESA forecasts.

Note: See Table J in the Statistical
annex for definitions of
country codes.

monetary adjustment in developed economies could trigger greater volatility. If this were to lead to currency depreciations in developing countries — especially those with more open capital markets — inflationary pressures could rise, leaving countries exposed to capital withdrawal and higher financing costs.

Scope to reorient policy towards longer-term issues

World economy has reached a turning point in macroeconomic policy conditions

Against the backdrop of stronger economic growth and benign inflationary pressures in developed countries, the world economy has reached a turning point in macroeconomic policy conditions. Many of the world's major central banks are now able to start withdrawing the exceptional stimulus measures that have been in place for nearly a decade.

The United States Federal Reserve (Fed) has charted a path to normalize the size of its balance sheet and is inching towards interest rate normalization. The ECB has tapered the pace of asset purchases, and may stop expanding its balance sheet by the end of 2018. Meanwhile, the Bank of Canada raised interest rates by 50 basis points in the first nine months of 2017, and the Bank of England increased its policy rate by 25 basis points in November 2017, with the prospect of further interest rate hikes ahead. The monetary stance in Japan, by contrast, is expected to remain highly accommodative over the forecast horizon, as Japan continues to battle against deeply entrenched deflationary expectations.

Fiscal impulse in most large developed economies expected to be neutral or marginally expansionary in 2018

Alongside a curbing of monetary stimulus, the fiscal stance in most developed economies has become less restrictive, moving away from the tight fiscal austerity programmes in place in many countries since 2010. Public sector investment has shown a strong rebound in Canada, Germany and the United Kingdom. This marks a significant reversal from the steep investment spending cutbacks pursued by most governments in developed countries since 2010. Overall, the net fiscal impulse is expected to be neutral or slightly expansionary in 2018 in most developed countries, with stronger fiscal stimulus measures in some, including Australia, Canada and Japan. Further details on specific fiscal policy assumptions are provided in the Appendix.

The less restrictive fiscal stance comes in the wake of extended fiscal spending cuts, leaving the size of the government sector significantly reduced in North America and Europe compared to before the global financial crisis.

In developing countries and economies in transition, some of the fiscal and monetary pressures in commodity-exporting countries have eased, as commodity prices have stabilized or partially recovered losses. Nonetheless, the policy stance will remain constrained in 2018–2019, as countries continue to adjust to the lower level of commodity prices. The policy stance in energy-importing countries, including most in East and South Asia, remains broadly accommodative, with several announcing measures to stimulate investment in infrastructure.

Fiscal and monetary pressures have eased in some commodity-exporting countries

The slow withdrawal of stimulus by the Fed has thus far not led to a significant tightening of global financial conditions. Financial market volatility remains low, and capital has started flowing back towards developing economies. Many of the crisis-related legacies — such as sluggish demand, fiscal austerity and bank fragility — are easing, fostering a more conducive environment for a recovery in investment. Nonetheless, numerous cyclical and longer-term challenges persist in the world economy, including a legacy of weak investment and low productivity growth since the crisis, declining or stagnant average incomes in several regions, emerging protectionist tendencies in some arenas, and high levels of global debt.

Despite the improved short-term outlook, the global economy continues to face risks and longer-term challenges

Current high asset price valuations suggest an underpricing of risk, and developing economies — especially those with more open capital markets — remain vulnerable to spikes in risk aversion, an abrupt tightening of financing conditions, and sudden capital withdrawal. Elevated levels of policy uncertainty continue to cloud prospects for world trade, development aid, migration and climate targets, while rising geopolitical tensions could sharpen a tendency towards more unilateral and isolationist policies. These outlook risks and the policy challenges they pose are developed further in Chapter II.

Despite risks and uncertainties, current conditions include an alignment of the economic cycle among major economies, stability in financial markets and the absence of negative shocks such as commodity price dislocations.

Current macroeconomic conditions offer policymakers greater scope to spur progress on sustainable development

As conditions for wider global economic stability solidify, there is a diminishing need to focus policy efforts on stabilizing short-term growth and mitigating the effects of economic crises. Coupled with improving macroeconomic and financial conditions to support the vast investment needed to progress towards many of the SDGs, this paves the way to reorient policy towards longer-term issues, such as strengthening the environmental quality of economic growth, stimulating more inclusive growth, and tackling institutional deficiencies that are hindering development prospects.

Investment and productivity

Conditions for investment have improved

Following two years of exceptionally weak investment growth, plus a prolonged episode of overall lacklustre global investment, some signs of revival in global investment have emerged. Conditions for investment have generally improved, supported by more favourable macroeconomic conditions and reduced banking sector fragilities in developed economies. Financing costs remain low, and spreads have narrowed in many emerging markets, reflecting a decline in risk premia. This has supported rising capital flows to emerging markets amid low global financial volatility; stronger credit growth in both developed and

Spreads have narrowed in many emerging markets, reflecting a decline in risk premia

developing economies — including a rise in cross-border lending — and recovery in some commodity sectors.

Investment accounted for 60 per cent of the acceleration in global economic activity in 2017

At the global level, investment is no longer acting as a drag on growth, and, in fact, contributed roughly 60 per cent of the acceleration in global economic activity in 2017. However, the recent revival in investment is relative to a very low starting point, and thus far remains contained to a relatively narrow set of countries. A firmer and more broad-based rebound in investment activity, which is needed to support stronger productivity growth in the medium-term and accelerate progress towards the SDGs, is likely to be held back by heightened policy uncertainty, high levels of debt, and a build-up of longer-term financial fragilities in several large developing economies. The longer-term impact of the improvement in investment conditions will depend on the extent to which available financing can be channelled into productive investments, rather than financial assets.

In developed economies, private non-residential investment generally showed more resilience in the first half of 2017, as illustrated in figure I.8. In Japan, a surge in investment was spurred by a strong rebound in credit growth supported by monetary policy measures. Adjustment in mining-related sectors continued to restrain investment in Australia and Canada, although in the case of Canada this was offset by stronger residential investment, driven by the steady rise in house prices.

In developed economies, stronger investment in 2017 reflects both housing market activity and more productive investment in machinery and equipment

In the United States, following two years of steep cutbacks, investment in mining exploration, shafts and wells rebounded sharply in the first half of 2017. This may in part reflect an easing of environmental regulation, as well as technology improvements in horizontal drilling and hydraulic fracturing, which have significantly increased productivity, reducing the breakeven price of tight oil extraction. Investment in the United States was also supported by a relatively strong housing market, and investment in machinery and equipment.

Heightened uncertainty surrounding the future relationship of the United Kingdom with its trading partners after it withdraws from the European Union (EU) has depressed

Figure I.8
Average annualized percentage change in private investment, decomposed by asset type (*constant prices*)

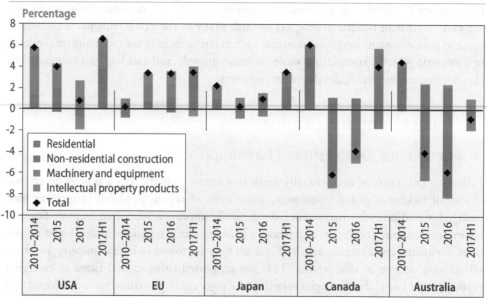

Sources: United States Bureau of Economic Analysis, Eurostat, Statistics Canada, Cabinet Office of Japan and Australia Bureau of Statistics.

Note: Figures for EU and Japan include public sector investment.

investor sentiment, deterring investment in the United Kingdom. However, investment in the EU as a whole remains steady, supported largely by both residential and non-residential construction.

It is encouraging to note that, except in the case of Australia, investment in machinery and equipment has contributed a significant share of recent investment growth in developed economies. If sustained, stronger investment in machinery and equipment could underpin stronger productivity growth over the medium-term.

In developing countries and economies in transition, investment dynamics have differed starkly across countries and regions. To a large extent these differences reflect commodity sector developments since 2014, which have driven a broad shift in income away from commodity exporters and towards commodity importers. Global investment in natural resources surged during the commodity boom of 2011–2013. The subsequent collapse in investment, as commodity prices realigned at a lower level, exemplifies the vulnerability to boom and bust cycles of countries that are overly reliant on a small number of natural resources.

Commodity exporters remain vulnerable to steep boom and bust investment cycles

Figure I.9 illustrates recent investment developments in selected large developing and transition economies. A sharp decline in investment in the commodity sector has weighed on overall investment growth in Brazil, the Russian Federation and South Africa. Several oil-exporters in Western Asia have also seen steep cuts in public investment as part of fiscal adjustment to lower oil prices. In the Russian Federation, the decline in private investment also reflects the impact of international sanctions on access to capital and business sentiment, but an investment recovery is now underway, acting as an important driver of the recovery in the CIS region. Political uncertainty and social unrest have also impacted the investment climate in Brazil and South Africa. While in East Asia investment has remained relatively strong, in South Asia it has been restrained by fragilities in India's banking sector.

Looking forward, firmer global investment may spread to a wider set of countries, in light of better investment conditions. However, investment growth will likely stay relatively modest in most countries. Investors may postpone major investment decisions, given deep uncertainties regarding tax policy and major trade policy agreements with Europe and the

A stronger rebound in investment may be muted by policy uncertainty and high debt

Figure I.9
Average year-on-year change in gross fixed capital formation in selected developing and transition economies (*constant prices*)

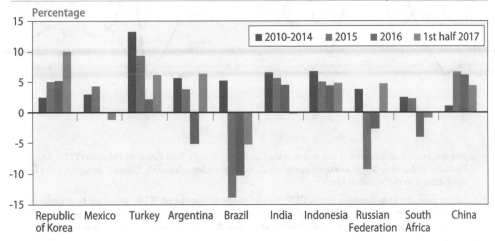

Sources: OECD Quarterly National Accounts, United Nations Statistics Division National Accounts Main Aggregates Database, CEIC, Project LINK.

United States. This could continue until it is clear how any policy shifts will impact production and transaction costs.

Considerable uncertainties regarding the impact on global markets of balance sheet adjustment in major central banks may also deter near-term investment decisions. If markets manage to weather the path of monetary policy normalization without severe disruption, the conditions for a stronger rebound in global investment over the medium-term — beyond the current forecast horizon — will start to take shape. However, high levels of debt and longer-term financial fragilities may continue to constrain investment in some large developing economies.

Productivity growth strengthening from a low level[5]

The tentative revival of global investment marks an important step towards a more broad-based recovery in global productivity and rise in the longer-term potential of the world economy, especially if it becomes more decisively geared towards productive investment in machinery and equipment. However, the overhang of the extended period of weak global investment will likely weigh on productivity growth over the medium-term forecast horizon.

Global labour productivity growth picked up in 2017

The improvement in the world economy since mid-2016 has been accompanied by a moderate pickup in productivity growth. After growing by only 1.3 per cent in both 2015 and 2016, global labour productivity is projected to increase by 1.9 per cent in 2017.[6] This rate is, however, still slightly below the 1990–2015 average of 2.1 per cent (figure I.10). The recent upturn in productivity growth has been geographically broad-based, with most developed, developing and transition economies posting gains.

Figure I.10
Labour productivity growth, developed versus emerging and developing economies

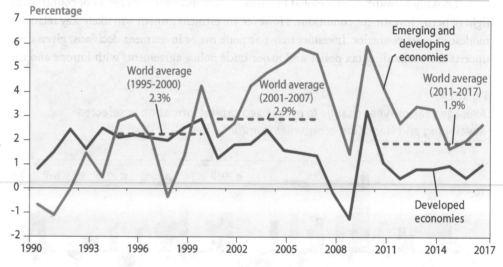

Source: UN/DESA, based on data from The Conference Board Total Economy Database™, May 2017 Update.

Note: Country groupings differ slightly from those defined in Statistical annex Table A.

---

5   The main source of data used in this section is the Conference Board's Total Economy Database (TED), May 2017 Update available from http://www.conference-board.org/data/economydatabase/. Regional aggregates differ from those defined in the Statistical annex.

6   Labour productivity is measured here as GDP (output) per person employed. While output per hour worked is generally a preferred measure, it is not available for many developing countries. Global and regional aggregates as well as cross-country comparisons of productivity growth are therefore generally based on output per person.

Among developed economies, Japan, the United States and Western Europe have all seen productivity growth strengthen over the past year, albeit from low levels. Average labour productivity growth in developed economies is estimated to have accelerated from 0.5 per cent in 2016 to 1 per cent in 2017.

It is unclear, however, whether this recent improvement in productivity growth can be sustained going forward. In order to have a better picture of the outlook, it is important to understand the factors that have been driving productivity growth developments in the past. The period since the global financial crisis has been characterized by exceptionally slow labour productivity growth in developed economies. As illustrated in figure I.11, the slowdown can be attributed to lower contributions from capital deepening (information and communications technology (ICT) and non-ICT) and total factor productivity (TFP) growth. In fact, the average contribution of TFP growth to labour productivity was negative during the period 2011–2016 in both the United States and Western Europe.

Much of the recent weakness in labour productivity is the result of sluggish private and public investment in the wake of the global financial crisis, the euro area debt crisis and the sharp fall in commodity prices. The level of capital stock in developed economies has remained stagnant since 2008 (figure I.12), as investment over this period has been barely sufficient to cover the depreciating value of existing capital stock. Weak investment has not only slowed capital deepening, but has also weighed on TFP growth by hampering the adoption of capital-embodied technologies.

A range of factors have been identified as contributing to the investment slump, including subdued aggregate demand, widespread austerity policies, fragile bank balance sheets, elevated policy uncertainty and low commodity prices. While still relevant, some of these restraining factors have eased over the past year. This suggests that the recent upturn in investment and productivity growth may prove more sustained than other temporary episodes in recent years.

However, slow productivity growth across developed economies cannot solely be attributed to the legacies of recent economic and financial crises. As documented by Dabla-

The upturn in labour productivity growth is spread across countries

Sluggish investment since the global financial crisis accounts for much of the weakness in labour productivity growth

Figure I.11
Contribution to labour productivity growth in developed economies

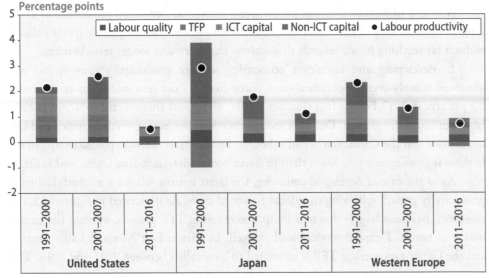

Source: UN/DESA, based on data from The Conference Board Total Economy Database™, May 2017 Update.

Figure I.12
Capital stock

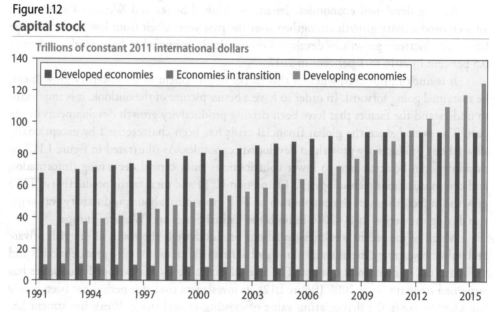

Source: UN/DESA, based on data
from IMF Investment and Capital
Stock Dataset 2017.

**Structural, long-
term forces have also
contributed to a gradual
decline in productivity
growth in developed
economies since the
1970s and 1980s**

Norris et al. (2015), productivity growth has been gradually declining since the 1970s and 1980s in virtually all developed countries. The global financial crisis and other cyclical shocks over the past decade merely exacerbated an ongoing trend. Structural, long-term forces that are contributing to the secular decline in productivity growth include demographic trends (especially aging populations), waning gains from the ICT revolution and a slowing pace of innovation and trade integration (see, for example, Adler et al., 2017). Examining productivity trends from a sector-level perspective in developed economies, Dabla-Norris et al. (ibid.) show that the long-term slowdown in productivity growth — in particular TFP growth — reflects two broad factors: a reallocation of resources to sectors where productivity levels and growth were lower, in particular service industries; and declining productivity growth within the sectors that account for an increasing share of employment, such as social and administrative services.

A return to sustained labour productivity growth in developed economies of about 2 per cent — as seen in the 1990s and early 2000s — will therefore likely remain elusive without far-reaching policy reforms that address the short- and longer-term barriers.

**All developing regions
are expected to record
labour productivity
growth in 2017, for the
first time since 2011**

In developing and transition economies, average productivity growth has also improved notably over the past two years, rising from 1.7 per cent in 2015 to an estimated 2.7 per cent in 2017. For the first time since 2011, all regions are expected to record positive labour productivity growth. Despite a modest recovery, however, growth in Africa and Latin America and the Caribbean is still subdued. Furthermore, average productivity growth in these regions remains far lower than in Asian economies, including China and India.

As in the case of developed countries, the latest upturn follows a marked decline in productivity growth following the global financial crisis. As illustrated in figure I.13, this slowdown has been largely due to a sharp downturn in TFP growth, whereas the contribution of non-ICT capital services held up well. In Africa, East Asia and Latin America and the Caribbean, average TFP is estimated to have fallen between 2011 and 2016. This

Figure I.13
Contribution to labour productivity growth in developing regions

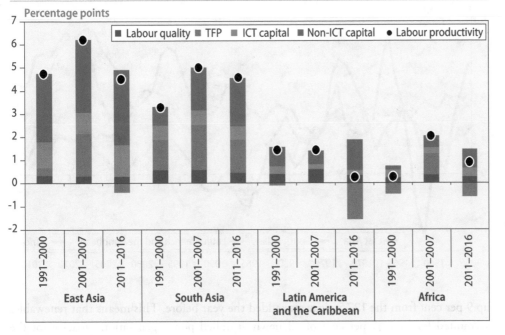

Source: UN/DESA, based on data
from The Conference Board Total
Economy Database™, May 2017
Update.

suggests that developing countries have been experiencing slower efficiency gains and technological absorption since the global financial crisis.[7]

The reasons behind the weakness in TFP growth vary from country to country and include both cyclical factors — such as weak developed market demand and low commodity prices — and structural influences, including slower trade integration and less dynamic economic transformation processes. In the cases of Africa and Latin America and the Caribbean, the recent poor productivity performance reflects more fundamental, long-term challenges. As shown in figure I.14, labour productivity growth since the 1980s has rarely exceeded 2 per cent in these regions. Rodrik (2016) attributes this weakness to a broad-based absence of industrialization or even premature deindustrialization.

For developing economies, prolonged weak productivity growth will not only adversely impact medium-term growth prospects, but could severely undermine progress on the SDGs. Therefore, policy measures to revive productivity growth, such as tackling infrastructure deficits, improving the quality of education and enhancing research and development should be prioritized.

Prolonged weak productivity growth could undermine progress on SDGs

Modest progress in renewable energy investment

Investment in renewable energy accounts for approximately 1.5 per cent of total global fixed capital formation. Approximately 138.5 gigawatts of global renewable power capacity (excluding large hydro-electric projects of more than 50 megawatts) were added in 2016,

Renewables account for more than half of all newly installed power capacity, but only for 11.3 per cent of global power generation

---

7   Measurement problems resulting from the fact that TFP is a residual may also have played a role in the observed slump in TFP growth.

Figure I.14
Labour productivity growth in major developing regions, 5-year moving average

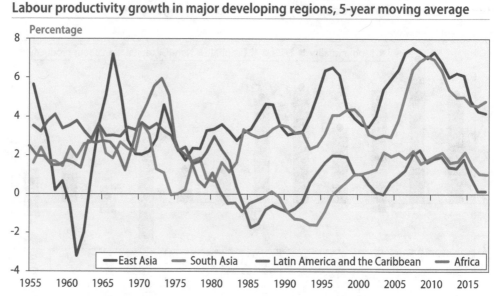

Source: UN/DESA, based on data from The Conference Board Total Economy Database™, May 2017 Update.

up 9 per cent from the 127.5 gigawatts added the year before. This means that renewables accounted for over 55 per cent of all newly installed power generation capacity for the first time. The current share of renewables in global power generation is thought to have prevented the emission of 1.7 gigatons of carbon-dioxide equivalent, or 5.3 per cent of total carbon emissions in 2016. However, renewable energy (excluding large hydro), still accounts for only 16.7 per cent of global power capacity and 11.3 per cent of global power generation. Renewable energy investment continues to be dominated by just two sectors — solar and wind, which represent 93.7 per cent of new investment.

Investment in renewable energy contracted in value terms in 2016

In value terms, total global spending in 2016 on renewable energy investment (excluding large hydro) decreased 23 per cent compared to the previous year, totalling $241.6 billion — the lowest level since 2013 (figure I.15). This was partly due to falling costs — the average investment costs per megawatt of solar photovoltaic and wind power fell by over 10 per cent (Frankfurt School-UNEP Centre/BNEF, 2017). It was also due to lower levels of investment in China, Japan and some emerging markets.

China remains world's biggest investor in renewables, despite less investment in 2016

Developed economies regained their lead over developing countries in renewables investment, mostly due to lower levels of investment in China, as weaker-than-expected electricity demand and delayed grid connections slowed energy investment in 2016–2017. However, China remains the world's biggest investor in renewables, with investment of $78.3 billion in 2016, which accounted for 32.4 per cent of global new renewables investment. In Europe, investment peaked during the 2010–2011 solar expansions in Germany and Italy, but a boom in offshore wind saw huge projects being approved by both Germany and the United Kingdom in 2015 and 2016, including the world's largest non-hydro renewable energy investment — the 1.2 gigawatt Hornsea offshore wind project, located off the coast of England. Africa and the Middle East have also started to account for a greater number of large projects. In Asian and Pacific countries, a long upswing in investment came to an end in 2016 with slowdowns in the financing of photovoltaic projects, including in Japan.

Figure I.15
Global new investment in renewable energy

Billions of US dollars

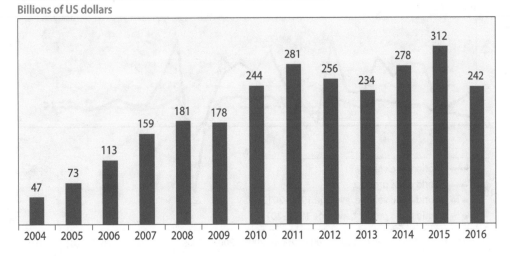

Source: Frankfurt School-UNEP Centre/BNEF (2017).

Despite the drop in 2016, preliminary data indicate slightly higher levels of renewables investment in 2017. In the first three quarters of 2017, new renewables investment in clean energy increased by 2 per cent year-over-year (Louw, 2017).[8] Seven massive wind projects, each costing between $600 million and $4.5 billion, in Australia, China, Germany, Mexico, the United Kingdom and the United States, were part of this boost.

Preliminary data point to stronger renewable investment in 2017

International trade and commodities

Emerging Asia drives rebound in international trade flows

Buoyed by the cyclical upturn in global growth, world trade rebounded in 2017, expanding at an estimated pace of 3.7 per cent during the year (figure I.16). This follows exceptionally weak trade flows in 2016, with global trade volume expanding at a post-crisis low growth rate of 2.2 per cent.

World trade growth rebounded in 2017

The recovery in international trade was accompanied by a pickup in world industrial output and a rise in the Global Manufacturing Purchasing Managers' Index to a six-year high. Demand for international air freight and container shipping also gained momentum in 2017, amid stronger export orders and relatively higher prices of key commodities, in particular crude oil and metals. The modest investment revival in several developed and developing economies — which has contributed to increased trade of capital and intermediate goods — is seen as spurring the global trade rebound.

Nevertheless, while trade elasticity (calculated as the ratio of global trade growth to WGP growth) rose from 0.9 in 2016 to 1.2 in 2017, it remains low compared to the ratios seen in the 1990s and early 2000s. This suggests that structural factors are continuing to weigh on the growth momentum of global trade, as elaborated below.

Trade elasticity remains low

---

8   Clean energy investment differs from renewable energy investment, as the former also includes low carbon services (e.g., carbon markets) and energy smart technologies (e.g., battery storage and electric vehicles). Renewable energy investment accounted for around 82 per cent of global clean energy investment in 2015.

Figure I.16
Growth of world trade and world gross product

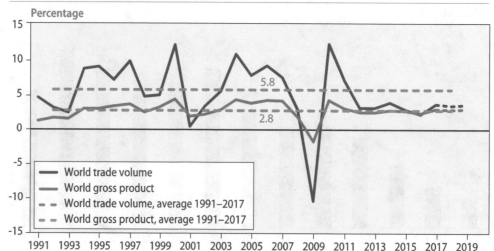

Source: UN/DESA.

In the first eight months of 2017, world merchandise trade[9] grew at its fastest pace in the post-crisis period. The strong growth, however, was in part due to a low base effect, given the exceptional weakness in trade flows observed in the first half of 2016. From the imports perspective, there was a marked variation in the strength of import demand between regions (figure I.17).

Emerging Asia has driven the rebound in global merchandise imports

In the first eight months of 2017, emerging Asia contributed 60 per cent of growth in global merchandise imports. This was triggered by stronger domestic demand across the region and supported by policy stimulus measures in many economies, including China. In several major developed economies, including the EU, Japan and the United States, imports of capital goods rebounded during the first half of 2017, as firms responded to improving conditions for investment, as discussed in the previous section.

Import demand from Africa and the Middle East continued to decline

Among the other developing regions, Latin America saw a modest recovery in import demand as large economies, including Argentina and Brazil, emerged from recession. In contrast, however, import demand from Africa and the Middle East continued to decline, reflecting the continued weakness in commodity-related revenue, depreciated domestic currencies and dampened investment activity. Notably, investment prospects remain subdued in many Organization of the Petroleum Exporting Countries (OPEC) member countries, weighed down by cuts to oil production on top of fiscal consolidation efforts. Investment activity in many economies in the region has also been affected by political uncertainty.

From the exports perspective, the recovery in global merchandise exports was broad-based across developed, developing and transition economies (figure I.18). A pickup in investment activity in developed economies as well as in a few developing economies, including China, provided an impetus to export growth of the developing regions. In the emerging Asia region, exports were also buoyed by an upturn in trade in electrical and electronic products (see further details in the section on East Asia in Chapter III), reflecting the region's close integration with global value chains in the industry. Meanwhile, exports from the United States benefited to a certain extent from a weaker dollar.

---

9   Merchandise trade volume data comes from the CPB Netherlands Bureau for Economic Policy Analysis. Regional groupings differ from those defined in the Statistical annex.

Figure I.17
Contribution to global merchandise import volume growth by region

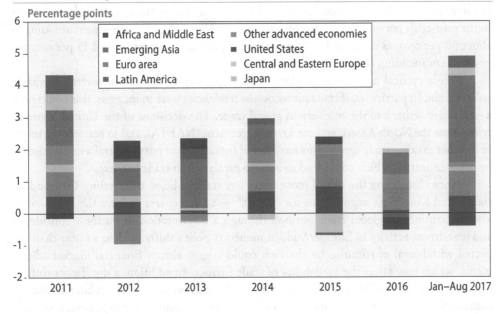

Source: UN/DESA based on data from CPB Netherlands Bureau for Economic Policy Analysis.

Figure I.18
Contribution to global merchandise export volume growth by region

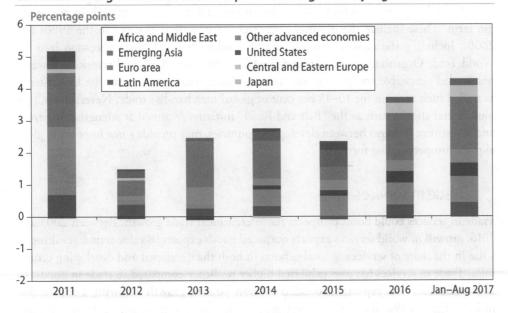

Sources: UN/DESA based on data from CPB Netherlands Bureau for Economic Policy Analysis.

Looking ahead, world trade is expected to remain on a moderate growth trajectory, expanding by 3.5 per cent in 2018 and 3.6 per cent in 2019. These projections, however, are contingent on continued benign growth and investment conditions in the global economy. For the commodity exporting economies, the projected modest rise in global commodity prices will support import demand, amid easing pressures on revenue and domestic currencies.

Trends in global capital expenditure have important implications for international trade flows, given the high import intensity of fixed investment relative to other compo-

World trade to continue growing at a moderate pace

nents of aggregate demand (Bussière et al., 2013). Auboin and Borino (2017) found that the sharp slowdown and subsequent subdued recovery in the most trade-intensive components of GDP, particularly investment, accounted for 80 per cent of the global trade slowdown in the post-crisis period. On average globally, the import content of investment amounts to about 30 per cent, as compared to 23 per cent for private consumption and 15 per cent for government spending (IMF, 2016).

While cyclical headwinds to global trade have largely dissipated, several downside risks remain. In particular, if trade protectionist tendencies were to increase, this could pose a significant setback to the recovery in global trade. The decisions of the United States to renegotiate the North American Free Trade Agreement (NAFTA), and to reassess the terms of its other existing trade agreements have raised concerns over possible retaliatory measures by other countries, which could lead to a sharp escalation in trade barriers.

Notwithstanding the risk of more restrictive trade policies, uncertainty surrounding the United Kingdom's negotiations for "Brexit" — as it prepares to leave the EU — may also undermine the global trade outlook through a deterioration in business confidence and investment activity in Europe. Sudden monetary policy shifts, such as a faster-than-expected withdrawal of stimulus by the Fed, could trigger abrupt financial market adjustments, which may affect the availability of trade finance. In addition, a significant shift in import demand from China would alter the global trade outlook. In particular, a decline in demand for commodities in China could adversely affect commodity exporters, especially exporters of metals. In 2016, China accounted for over 70 per cent of global demand for iron ore, and over 40 per cent of demand for nickel and copper.

Several ongoing structural shifts remain constraints to trade growth in the medium term. These include the diminishing effects of structural changes in the 1990s and 2000s, including the rapid expansion of global value chains, China's accession into the World Trade Organization (WTO) and the ICT revolution. A gradual transition towards non-traded renewable energy may also impact global trade growth over the longer-term, as traded fuels account for 10–15 per cent of global merchandise trade. Nevertheless, new multilateral efforts, such as the "Belt and Road" initiative,[10] aimed at strengthening trade and investment linkages between developing countries, may provide some impetus to global trade prospects going forward.

Trade in services

Trade in services could boost prospects for international trade growth. Between 2005 and 2016, growth in world services exports outpaced goods exports in value terms, resulting in a rise in the share of services in total exports in both the developed and developing economies. Trade in services has also exhibited higher resilience compared to trade in goods. In 2016, global services exports rebounded to show positive growth following a contraction in 2015 (figure I.19). In contrast, goods exports continued to experience a decline in value terms. Major economies continue to dominate global exports and imports of services. The top 10 exporters accounted for over 50 per cent of global services exports in 2016, reflecting the uneven participation in global services trade.

---

10   The initiative of jointly building the Silk Road Economic Belt and the 21st Century Maritime Silk Road was launched in 2013 by China.

Figure I.19
Goods and services exports *(values)* **by country groupings**

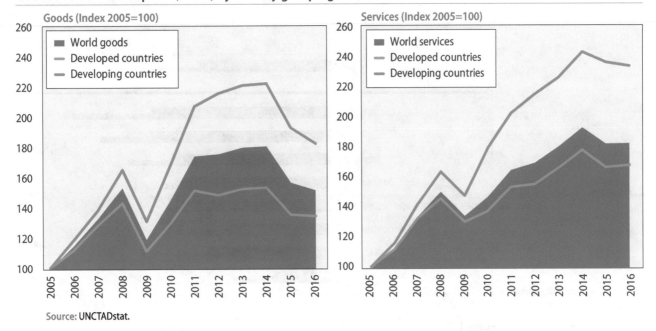

Source: UNCTADstat.

Increased trade in services could potentially boost the growth and development prospects of developing economies. Services exports of developing economies have risen rapidly over the past decade, as reflected by the increase in developing economies' share of global services exports from 23 per cent in 2005 to 29 per cent in 2016. By category, the main shares of global services exports of developing economies comprise construction, travel and transport services, in contrast with the trade profile of developed economies, which are more focused on higher value-added services (figure I.20). Nevertheless, the stronger growth of exports in telecommunication and ICT, financial and other business services — all growing at an annual pace of over 6 per cent between 2008 and 2016 (figure I.21) — is in line with the aspirations of developing economies to diversify their economic structures.

Services exports of developing economies have risen rapidly over the past decade

Conventional balance of payments statistics do not fully reflect the importance of services trade to an economy. Services can provide intermediate inputs in the production process and are often bundled into the final value of goods produced. This implies that there is a services element included in the value-added of output in all sectors. Exporting this element is referred to as mode 5 of services trade (Cernat and Kutlina-Dimitrova, 2014). In 2011, the value-added of services accounted for 44 per cent of total exports in developed economies and 32 per cent in developing economies. These figures are significantly higher than the direct exports of services reported in balance of payments data in the same year, of 25 per cent of total exports in developed and 14 per cent in developing economies (figure I.22). In recent years, close to two-thirds of the growth in the value added of direct exports has been attributed to an increase in services embodied in exports.

Services value-added is an enabler of trade in all economic sectors

Furthermore, neither cross-border services trade data nor analyses of value-added in gross exports capture the increasing importance of services within manufacturing companies. In 2015, by adding services activities within manufacturing firms, the contribution of services to overall exports was close to two-thirds (Miroudot and Cadestin, 2017).

Figure I.20
Developing economies: Share in global services exports by category

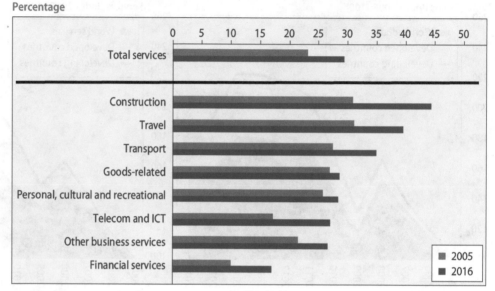

Percentage

Figure I.21
Average annual growth rate of services exports by category, 2008–2016

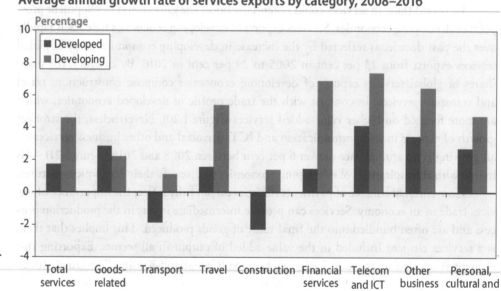

Source: UNCTADstat.

Moreover, both the analyses of value-added in gross exports and of in-house services in manufacturing firms revealed that the importance of services for trade is on par with their relevance for output, investment and employment. For example, in developing economies, services accounted for 55 per cent of output and 53 per cent of investment inflows in 2015, and 44 per cent of employment in 2016. These analyses also confirm the increased tradability of services, particularly when they are associated with inherently tradable goods and services.

Figure I.22
Participation of services in total direct exports and in total forward linkages in exports, 2011

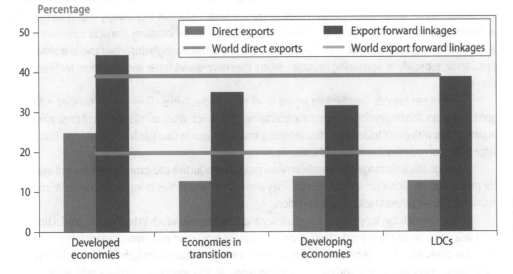

Percentage

Legend:
- Direct exports
- World direct exports
- Export forward linkages
- World export forward linkages

Categories: Developed economies, Economies in transition, Developing economies, LDCs

Source: UNCTAD, based on the World Bank's Export Value Added Database.

Other modes of services trade have been growing

The importance of services trade has also been underestimated given that under the General Agreement on Trade in Services (GATS), the definition of services trade is significantly broader than that defined by balance of payments statistics.[11] Based on GATS, cross-border trade represents only one out of four different modes of services trade. Other modes of services trade such as commercial presence (mode 3) and the movement of natural persons (mode 4) are increasingly important (UNCTAD, 2016a). In 2013, 69 per cent of services exports in the EU were through mode 3. In addition, given the sizeable value of remittances channelled to developing countries, mode 4 of supplying services is of substantial importance for developing countries. In 2016, worldwide remittance flows were estimated to be $575 billion, with $429 billion flowing to developing countries (World Bank, 2017a). The relevance of migration for the services sector is also highlighted by the fact that around 71 per cent of migrant workers (150 million of the 232 million migrants in 2013, according to ILO, 2015) are concentrated in the services sector.[12]

The services sector is important for achieving the 2030 Agenda

Services can boost an economy by providing inputs that increase the efficiency and capacity of all sectors, and by inducing a structural transformation which may favour higher-yielding sectors (see Box I.2). Services are, therefore, a valuable component in a country's efforts to achieve the 2030 Agenda for Sustainable Development.

For a country's economy to efficiently integrate GVCs, it needs to possess a well-developed ecosystem of business, professional and infrastructure services. Such an ecosystem helps micro, small and medium size enterprises (MSMEs) to also participate in global and regional value chains, leading to more developmental gains. Infrastructure services, such as financial services and telecom and ICT services, are especially important in this regard. Financial services are mentioned in both targets of SDGs that refer to MSMEs (8.3 and 9.3), and telecom and ICT services promote MSMEs' inclusion through digital financial services and e-commerce.

---

11   For more information, please see https://www.wto.org/english/tratop_e/serv_e/cbt_course_e/c1s3p1_e.htm

12   The cited number of migrant workers in services does not include those working in the construction sector.

Box I.2
Services and structural transformation

The services sector, which encompasses a wide range of activities, plays an increasingly important role in determining the direction of structural transformation in the global economy. Services constitute a major share of output, employment and investment, and play an increasingly important role in international trade, especially in developing countries, where they have grown faster and with more resilience than goods.

Services can provide intermediate inputs to all economic activities. They can be bundled with goods. They can also be developed within manufacturing companies. When considering all of these roles in conjunction with direct trade in services, services account for close to two-thirds of overall exports in a large sample of countries (Miroudot and Cadestin, 2017).

Through this wide range of channels, services facilitate productive and export processes and enable participation in global value chains (GVCs). They allow different activities to interact. Knowledge and technology-based services facilitate specialization.

These channels can support gains in efficiency and effectiveness, which in turn reduce production and trade costs, contribute to productivity gains and increase productive and export capacity. The shifts in relative prices from these gains are an important force driving structural transformation in production, employment, investment, trade and consumption decisions. Sectors supported via these services channels can outperform other sectors and develop a more prominent role in the economy's structure.

Structural changes driven by these services roles may favour sectors with higher productivity, technological intensiveness or upgrading potential, leading to services-led growth. This implies significant development opportunities, as called for in target 8.2 of the SDGs, especially given the large productivity gaps between sectors in low-income countries (Mashayekhi and Antunes, eds., 2017).

The scope for productivity gains through these channels is particularly high in developing countries, where the value-added of services remains lower than in developed countries in many sectors (figure I.2.1). In fact, according to some estimates, the services sector is responsible for two-thirds of total productivity growth in developing countries (te Velde, forthcoming).

Figure I.2.1
Shares of services in total backward linkages in exports of selected sectors, 2011

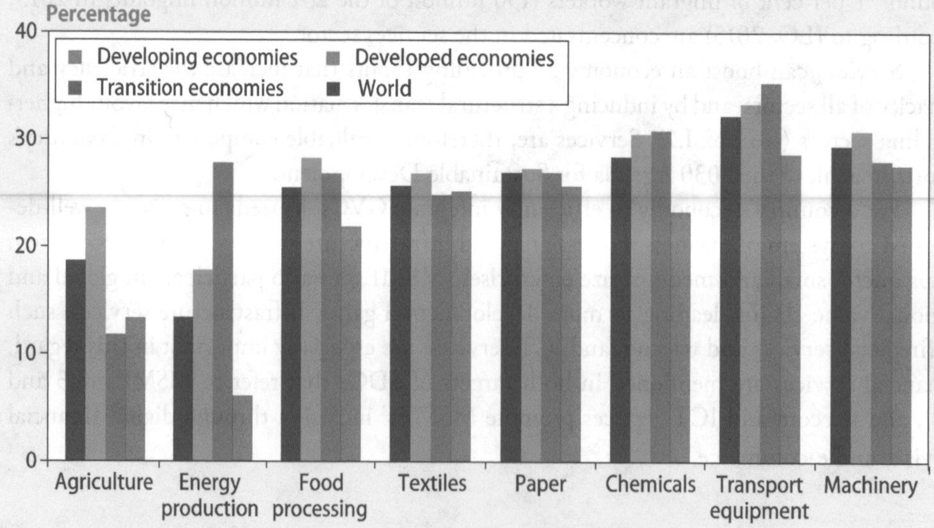

Source: UNCTAD, based on World Bank's Export Value Added Database.

Percentage

- Developing economies
- Transition economies
- Developed economies
- World

Agriculture | Energy production | Food processing | Textiles | Paper | Chemicals | Transport equipment | Machinery

Box I.2 (*continued*)

Development linkages between services and structural changes are demonstrated by shifts from low to high-productivity sectors that have stimulated growth in Asia since 1990. In Viet Nam, services have contributed to transforming the economy and promoting industrialization. As a result, manufacturing has grown rapidly and no less than one-third of aggregate productivity growth can be linked to services (Hoekman and te Velde, eds., 2017).

Still, services-led changes do not automatically spur growth. In Africa and in Latin America and the Caribbean, structural changes involved worker displacements to lower-productivity activities, including services and the informal sector. This led to reduced growth. In Latin America, the contraction in the manufacturing sector contributed to this outcome by forcing a resource reallocation across sectors, (McMillan, Rodrik and Verduzco-Gallo, 2014).

Services are more likely to support a positive structural transformation in countries that exhibit strong productivity growth in manufacturing. Most successful countries have seen simultaneous productivity changes in services and other sectors, in a balanced growth strategy, but in many countries services have assumed the role of the main growth driver. For example, in India, Hansda (2006) found that services are more growth inducing than agriculture or industry.

Effective policies and regulations are required to ensure that services-led economic transformation favours sectors with higher productivity, particularly because the development potential of the service economy and trade is yet to be fully explored in many developing countries (Mashayekhi, Olarreaga and Porto, 2011).

Having sound regulatory frameworks as a precondition to trade liberalization, and linkages to international markets — by allowing access to foreign services and to inputs and factors that strengthen domestic services — can strengthen the transformative role of services. The importance of trade for supporting productivity growth in services is confirmed by the higher productivity of exporting services firms in low income countries compared to non-exporting services firms, as well as the higher productivity of exporting services firms compared to some exporting firms in other sectors, notably agriculture (te Velde, forthcoming).

Favouring trade openness requires a multidimensional trade policy with bilateral, regional and multilateral trade agreements, trade promotion, market intelligence and trade facilitation. Preferential treatment, flexibilities and capacity building for developing countries are key components of this trade policy mix (Mashayekhi, 2017).

Authors: Bruno Antunes, Taisuke Ito and Mina Mashayekhi (UNCTAD/DITC)

International transport and the environment

In line with stronger world trade growth, the volume of international transport is expected to grow significantly in the coming years. While on the one hand this is a welcome sign of a healthier economy, it also comes at an environmental cost from the associated rise in carbon dioxide (CO_2) emissions. Two key sectors linking world trade and emission levels are international shipping, which moves over 80 per cent of global traded volume (UNCTAD, 2017b) (see figure I.23), and international aviation, which is closely related to the expansion of tourism, 55 per cent of which is done by air (UNWTO, 2017) (see Box I.3 and figure I.24). In 2015, total emissions from these two industries amounted to 4 per cent of global emissions. Longer-term projections suggest that over the next 25 years, approximately 30 per cent of the global rise in oil demand will emanate from the aviation and shipping sectors (IEA, 2017).

International shipping and aviation emissions do not fall under the purview of the Paris Agreement on climate change. Since the agreement targets domestic emissions, international emissions are not explicitly covered within the framework of nationally determined contributions, which reflect national targets and actions. In other words, though the emissions are calculated as part of the national greenhouse gas inventories of the United Nations Framework Convention on Climate Change Parties, they are excluded from national totals

Stronger world trade, while a welcome sign of a healthier world economy, also bears an environmental cost

International shipping and aviation emissions do not fall under the purview of the Paris Agreement

Box I.3

Trends in international tourism

International tourist arrivals in the first half of 2017 grew at its strongest pace since 2010

International tourist arrivals (overnight visitors) increased by 4 per cent to reach 1,235 million in 2016, up by 46 million visitors compared to 2015. It was the seventh consecutive year of growth above the long-term average. A comparable sequence of uninterrupted solid growth has not been recorded since the 1960s. The strong expansion in international tourism activity has been broad-based across destinations, supported by higher travel demand, increased connectivity and more affordable air transport—partly linked to the lower cost of oil.

　　Growth in international tourist arrivals accelerated in the first six months of 2017, with an expansion of 6 per cent compared to the same period last year, the strongest half-year increase since 2010. The performance was underpinned by sustained growth across many destinations, combined with a recovery in regions that suffered declines in previous years due to security incidents. By World Tourism Organization (UNWTO) regions, growth was strongest in the Middle East (+9 per cent), Africa and Europe (both +8 per cent), followed by Asia and the Pacific (+6 per cent) and the Americas (+3 per cent).

Figure I.3.1

International tourist arrivals, evolution by half year

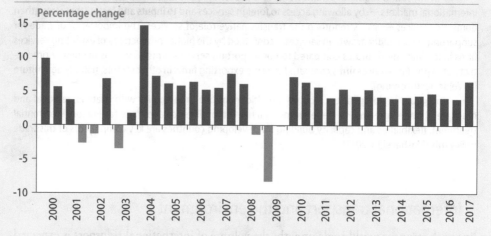

Source: UNWTO.

The Mediterranean, in particular, enjoyed strong demand in the first half of 2017, with major destinations such as Croatia (+25 per cent), Portugal (+13 per cent) and Spain (+11 per cent) reporting remarkable growth in international arrivals, while Egypt (+51 per cent), Tunisia (+27 per cent) and Turkey (+24 per cent) rebounded strongly from declines in previous years.

International travel was fuelled by strong outbound demand from major markets, including Canada, China, France, the Republic of Korea, Spain, the United Kingdom, and the United States. Furthermore, growth in spending rebounded markedly in Brazil and the Russian Federation, following a few years of decline.[a]

International tourism receipts reached US$1.2 trillion in 2016

International tourism receipts increased by 2.6 per cent in real terms (adjusted for exchange rate fluctuations and inflation) to reach $1,220 billion in 2016, based on visitor expenditure data reported by destinations worldwide. International tourism receipts comprised of earnings generated from expenditure by international visitors (both overnight and same-day) on goods and services, including accommodation, food and drink, local transport and entertainment. In the past decade, growth in tourism receipts has largely mirrored the trend of international tourist arrivals, though at a slightly slower pace.

[a] For the latest tourism data and trends, please refer to UNWTO (2017) or the UNWTO World Tourism Barometer at mkt.unwto.org/barometer.

(continued)

Box I.3 *(continued)*

Figure I.3.2
Inbound tourism

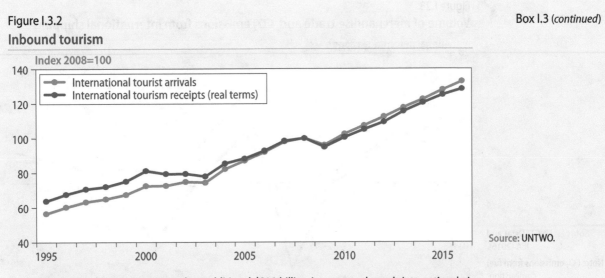

Index 2008=100

- International tourist arrivals
- International tourism receipts (real terms)

Source: UNTWO.

International tourism generated an additional $216 billion in exports through international air passenger transport services (rendered to non-residents), bringing the total value of tourism exports to $1.4 trillion, or $4 billion a day on average. This represents 7 per cent of the world's exports of goods and services, and 30 per cent of services exports alone.

As an export category, tourism ranks third globally, behind fuels and chemicals, and ahead of food and automotive products. In many developing economies, tourism is the top export category and the main source of foreign currency revenue. For both advanced and emerging economies, the sector generates much needed employment opportunities, contributing to inclusive and sustainable growth and development.

Manila conference sets roadmap to measure sustainable tourism

The United Nations has designated 2017 as the International Year of Sustainable Tourism for Development (IY2017),[b] reiterating the potential for tourism to advance the 17 Sustainable Development Goals (SDGs) and the 2030 Agenda for Sustainable Development. The IY2017 aims to support a change in policies, business practices and consumer behaviour that contribute to a more sustainable tourism sector, in line with the SDGs. It aims to promote the role of tourism in five key areas:

1. Inclusive and sustainable economic growth;
2. Social inclusiveness, employment and poverty reduction;
3. Resource efficiency, environmental protection and climate change;
4. Cultural values, diversity and heritage; and
5. Mutual understanding, peace and security.

A significant number of events have taken place around the world in the context of the IY2017. In June 2017, over 1,000 stakeholders from 88 countries, including ministers, chief statisticians and the private sector, gathered in Manila, the Philippines for the 6th International Conference on Tourism Statistics: Measuring Sustainable Tourism.[c] Organized by UNWTO and the Government of the Philippines, the conference aimed to build international consensus on ways to measure sustainable tourism. This is led by the conviction that effective sustainable tourism policies require an integrated, coherent and robust information base. The conference agreed to expand current tourism statistics beyond their economic focus to also include the social and environmental aspects of tourism.

The Manila Conference represents a global commitment towards sustainable tourism and the need to measure it through a consistent statistical approach. The resulting 'Manila Call for Action on Measuring Sustainable Tourism' reflects the collective vision and commitment of all participants to develop and implement a statistical framework for Measuring Sustainable Tourism (MST)[d] in its economic, environmental and social dimensions, as well as across relevant spatial levels (global, national and subnational).

MST is supported by the United Nations Statistical Commission and builds upon established United Nations statistical standards, notably the Tourism Satellite Account: Recommended Methodological Framework and the System of Environmental-Economic Accounting.

b See information about the International Year of Sustainable Tourism for Development at www.tourism4development2017.org.

c More information about the 6th International Conference on Tourism Statistics at www.mstconference.org.

d More about the Measuring Sustainable Tourism (MST) initiative at http://statistics.unwto.org/mst.

Authors: Michel Julian, John Kester and Javier Ruescas (UNWTO)

Figure I.23
Volume of merchandise trade and CO$_2$ emissions from international shipping

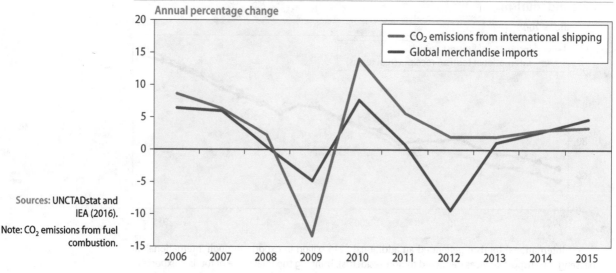

Sources: UNCTADstat and IEA (2016).

Note: CO$_2$ emissions from fuel combustion.

Figure I.24
International tourism and international aviation CO$_2$ emissions

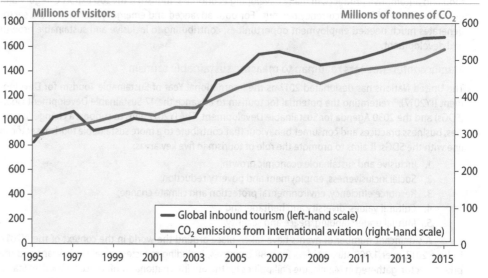

Sources: UNWTO (2017) and IEA (2016).

Note: CO$_2$ emissions from fuel combustion. Inbound tourism measured as arrivals of non-resident visitors (overnight visitors, tourists and same-day visitors, excursionists) at national borders.

and reported separately. However, if added to national totals, emissions would be as large as the fifth largest CO$_2$ emitter in the world (Japan). Considered independently, each industry would rank as a top 10 emitter.

The environmental regulation of international shipping and aviation has been entrusted to the International Maritime Organization (IMO) and the International Civil Aviation Organization (ICAO), respectively. It is up to these organizations to set emissions targets for the two industries. Both agencies, under current policies, may not be delivering sufficient measures to reduce emissions to levels consistent with the objectives of the Paris Agreement (UNCTAD, 2016b). In 2016, the United Nations Secretary-General reminded both agencies of the urgent need to address the growth of emissions under their mandates

(United Nations, 2016a; UN News Centre, 2016). Both industries also enjoy tax-exempt fuel, unlike domestic transportation fuel.

Emissions from these modes of transport have been on the rise and will continue to rise if left unchecked. CO_2 emissions from fuel combustion from international marine and aviation bunkers in 2015 were, respectively, 77 per cent and 105 per cent higher than in 1990, growing faster than road transport (IEA, 2017). Global CO_2 emissions from fuel combustion increased 58 per cent in the same period (ibid). In business-as-usual scenarios, emissions from both sectors are projected to triple or even quadruple by 2050, despite improvements in fleet efficiency (ICAO, 2016; IMO, 2015).

These rises highlight the urgent need to improve energy efficiency and restrict CO_2 emissions in these sectors (Sims et al., 2014). In 2016, ICAO adopted the Carbon Offsetting Scheme for International Aviation (CORSIA), which mandates that, starting in 2021, aircraft operators will be required to purchase qualifying carbon offset credits from greenhouse gas reduction and limitation projects in other industries to offset growth in CO_2 emissions above a 2019–2020 baseline level.[13]

However, despite this historical progress, the new scheme still needs more precision (for example, regarding the penalties for non-compliance and enforcement criteria to be utilized) and may not sufficiently address aviation greenhouse gas (GHG) emissions (Olmer and Rutherford, 2017). Importantly, the scheme does not aim to reduce aviation emissions beyond baseline levels. Instead it focuses on offsetting surplus emissions. In the shipping sector, by contrast, GHG reduction policy options are currently only under consideration. The IMO will have a first GHG emissions reduction strategy in April 2018. An operational strategy will not be ready before 2023. Emissions from ships could be included in the Emission Trading System of the EU from 2023 if the IMO does not deliver a global measure to reduce GHG emissions for international shipping (IMO, 2017).

Beyond emissions reduction, it is also important to focus on non-CO_2 impacts to protect the environment and human health. For instance, the Arctic's ecosystems are under increasing pressure as global warming melts sea ice across the region and new shipping routes gradually open up in the Arctic regions, and as both the Arctic and Antarctic become increasingly popular tourist destinations. The IMO International Code for Ships Operating in Polar Waters (Polar Code), which entered into force on 1 January 2017, establishes mandatory measures and recommended provisions to manage shipping in Arctic and Antarctic polar waters for the safety of those on board as well as pollution prevention. Some aspects are still under discussion, such as the use of heavy fuel oil in the Arctic.

Air pollution measures have recently been strengthened in both industries. In October 2016, the ICAO issued new recommendations regarding local air quality. In the same month, the IMO decided to reduce the maximum sulphur content of ship fuel oils from 3.5 per cent to 0.5 per cent, effective from 1 January 2020, with more stringent caps in certain regions (designated emissions control areas). Ship owners will either have to switch to more expensive and higher quality marine fuel or use alternative fuels such as liquefied natural gas. Alternatively, ships can fit emissions-cleaning systems (often referred to as "scrubbers") or use any other technological method to limit sulphur emissions to 6 grams per kilowatt hour or less. Knock-on effects of this change in rule could ripple out to the oil industry by increasing the price of oil products (diesel, jet fuel and petrol) and to commodities trading through higher freight rates.

Emissions from international marine and aviation bunkers have grown faster than road transport emissions over the last 25 years

Air pollution measures have been strengthened in both shipping and aviation industries

13 As of 23 August 2017, 72 States, representing 87.7 per cent of international aviation activity, had expressed their intent to participate in CORSIA from its outset.

Nevertheless, reducing air pollution remains vitally important. The sulphur cap limit is expected to save thousands to millions of lives in the coming decades, mainly in coastal communities in the developing world (Corbett et al., 2007; Corbett and Winebrake, 2016; Winebrake et al., 2009). Airborne particulate matter pollution from ships has also been shown to enhance lightning density directly over shipping lanes, with consequences for human life and the global economy through wind and hail damage, as well as from direct lightning strikes (Thornton et al., 2017).

Commodity prices

Commodity prices act as a link between the real and financial sectors, and play a key role in the economic dynamics of the majority of countries in Africa, South America and Western Asia (see figure I.4). Some developed economies, such as Australia and Canada, as well as many economies in transition, are also very sensitive to developments in commodity prices.

Commodity price movements are heavily correlated, driven by a common trend (see Diebold, Liu and Yilmaz, 2017). In late 2014 and in 2015, most commodity prices dropped sharply from the high levels reached in the boom period of 2011 to 2013. Most sectors saw an upward trend during 2016. However, since early 2017, these cross-asset price linkages have played a much smaller role, and price dynamics have been driven primarily by sector-specific developments rather than a common trend. The recent evolution and prospects for major commodity sectors are discussed below with additional detail in the Appendix.

Oil market is rebalancing

The oil market is in the process of rebalancing, as demand growth surpasses supply growth. The level of commercial crude oil stock has already been in decline despite rapid crude production growth in the United States. The market is likely to rebalance by the first quarter of 2018, eroding the excess crude oil inventory built up since 2014.

OPEC and non-OPEC oil exporters, including Azerbaijan, Kazakhstan and the Russian Federation, agreed to implement a coordinated reduction in production from January 2017 to March 2018, amounting to 1.8 million barrels per day (bpd) in total, although considering compliance performance, actual cuts may be considerably less. Meanwhile, supply restraint related to production cuts will be offset by increased supply from non-OPEC countries. Crude oil supply from non-OPEC countries in 2017 is forecast to increase, driven by the United States. In total, world crude oil supply for 2017 is expected to record a modest rise from 2016 levels.

Strong demand for oil expected

Strong demand is expected from China, India and the United States — the world's three largest energy consumers. A recovering demand from Europe is another supporting factor for the solid growth projection coupled with the recent rise in refining margins in Asia, Europe and the Americas throughout 2017.

Speculative activity continues to remain influential, creating short-term price fluctuations. Oil prices weakened in June 2017 over the market's concern vis-à-vis the slow decline of commercial crude oil stock. However, the Brent spot price recovered to reach $59 per barrel in mid-September as the market confirmed a consistent demand growth for crude oil (figure I.25). While prices may continue to fluctuate in response to the short-term news, the Brent spot price is expected to average $52.5 per barrel in 2017 and $55.4 per barrel in 2018. Compared to average levels in 2011–2014, price levels have roughly halved.

Non-oil commodities: Upward trend fizzled out

The upward trend in commodity prices that started at the beginning of 2016 came to a halt in 2017. Individual commodity markets have shown a mixed pattern in the first half of 2017, but all sub-indices of the UNCTAD Non-oil Nominal Commodity Price Index

Figure I.25
Major commodity prices

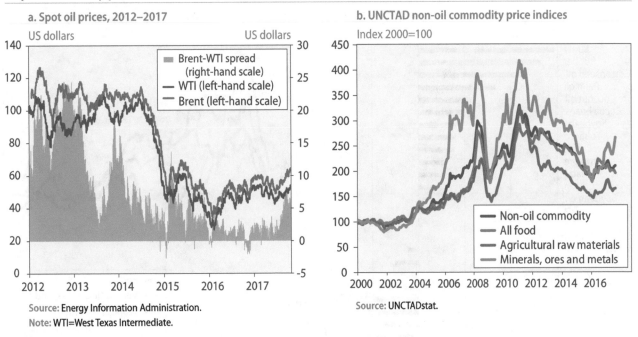

a. Spot oil prices, 2012–2017

US dollars

US dollars

- Brent-WTI spread (right-hand scale)
- WTI (left-hand scale)
- Brent (left-hand scale)

Source: Energy Information Administration.
Note: WTI=West Texas Intermediate.

b. UNCTAD non-oil commodity price indices

Index 2000=100

- Non-oil commodity
- All food
- Agricultural raw materials
- Minerals, ores and metals

Source: UNCTADstat.

decreased between January and June 2017. The third quarter of 2017 has seen rising prices for minerals, metals and ores, but overall, commodity prices are still significantly lower than at the peak of the last commodity boom (figure I.25). It seems unlikely that commodity prices will return to their peak levels of 2011 in the near future.

Among the subcategories of the UNCTAD Non-oil Nominal Commodity Price Index, agricultural raw materials showed the steepest price drop from January to August 2017, at 8.8 per cent, followed by food at 7.7 per cent. The price index of minerals, ores and metals rose by 7.7 per in August 2017 compared to January 2017, mainly based on a price rally in July and August 2017.

In the period between January and August 2017, the prices of major commodities showed a diverse pattern (figure I.26). Sugar declined the most, by close to 30 per cent. Rubber, cottonseed oil, palm oil, and coconut oil also saw prices drop by double digits. However, aluminium, copper and tropical logs increased by more than 10 per cent, with aluminium showing the largest increase at 13.4 per cent.

All sub-indices of the UNCTAD food price index saw marked losses between January and August 2017, with vegetable oilseeds and oils experiencing the sharpest drop (figure I.26). Cocoa bean prices are close to their lowest level in almost a decade. This sharp price drop had dramatic consequences for cocoa producers, particularly in Côte d'Ivoire (see Box I.4). Looking ahead, growing demand is unlikely to outpace strong production and cocoa beans prices are expected to remain low.

The price of minerals, ores and metals rallied in 2016, mainly driven by supply cuts and uncertainties. This upward trend came to a halt at the end of the first quarter of 2017. The UNCTAD minerals, ores and metals price index was down 8.5 per cent from 254 points in February 2017 to 232 points in June 2017, but rallied to 265 points in August

Commodity prices show a diverse pattern

Figure I.26
Movements in selected commodity prices

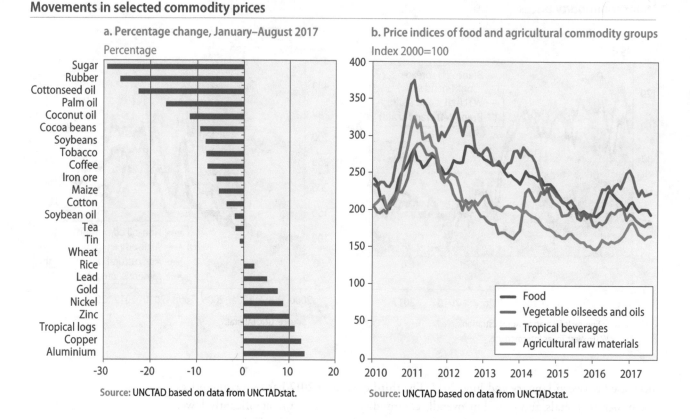

a. Percentage change, January–August 2017

b. Price indices of food and agricultural commodity groups

Source: UNCTAD based on data from UNCTADstat.

Source: UNCTAD based on data from UNCTADstat.

2017. The main driver of this downward movement was a sharp decline in iron ore prices, due to expectations of lower iron ore demand from China.

Global financial flows

Revival in capital flows to emerging economies

Global financial conditions improved in 2017, but significant risks and uncertainties remain

Global financial conditions improved in 2017, supported by the improving outlook in the world economy and expectations for a smooth and gradual monetary policy transition in the United States. In addition, financial volatility has visibly declined across major asset classes, reaching record-lows in recent months. Furthermore, international bank lending has also shown signs of recovery, while stock markets have registered large gains, not only in developed countries — climbing to record highs in some cases — but also in several emerging economies (figure I.27). This points to a rising appetite for risk among investors, although it should also be viewed with some caution, as an underpricing of risk could lead to sudden corrections in stock markets.

The improving global financial and liquidity environment, coupled with the ongoing pickup in global trade, is aiding the recovery of investment and supporting global growth. Yet, there remain significant risks and uncertainties, which could rapidly alter the current financial environment and even hamper a more robust and sustained trajectory for the world economy.

Box I.4
Commodity markets and the Sustainable Development Goals: Some policy lessons

There are several direct and indirect linkages between developments in the international commodity markets and the Sustainable Development Goals (SDGs). For instance, a direct relationship exists between food prices and SDG 2, which is aimed at ending hunger and achieving food security. For poor net food-buying households, an increase in food prices constitutes a loss of purchasing power and poses a threat to food security. For net food-selling households, however, an increase in food prices entails higher revenue and thus higher food security. Over the medium term, market adjustments might mitigate such first-round effects on poverty, but in the short term, hikes in food prices pose a serious challenge to meeting the SDGs in developing countries.

The extent to which international commodity markets impact development indicators also depends on existing policy frameworks. Policies such as social safety nets can mitigate the negative impact of commodity price shocks on the poor segments of the population. At the same time, redistributive policies are needed to ensure windfall revenues are more widely shared.

Zambia's experience during the last commodity boom is a useful example. Between 2004 and 2010, Zambia, a major exporter of copper, experienced annual average GDP per capita growth of above 5 per cent, driven by the sharp increase in global copper prices. During the same period, however, the poverty head count ratio increased from 56.7 per cent to 64.1 per cent of the population and the prevalence of undernourishment from 48.5 per cent to 51.7 per cent (figure I.4.1). This suggests that the commodity windfall revenue from the copper price boom was not effectively redistributed to benefit the poor. In addition, the doubling of retail prices of maize between 2004 and 2009 exacerbated poverty and undernourishment in Zambia, given that it is the population's main food staple.

This example demonstrates that there is no automatic process linking commodity price booms with improvements in the living conditions of the poor in commodity-dependent developing countries

Figure I.4.1
GDP growth and poverty indicators in Zambia, 2000–2015

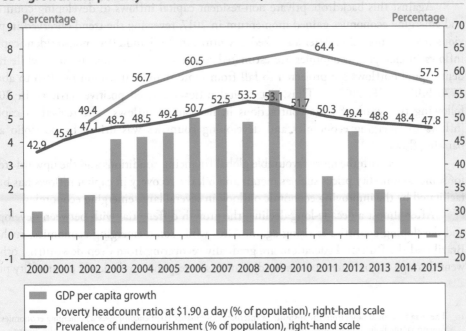

Sources: Author's own elaboration based on data from the World Development Indicators online database and World Bank (2017b) and UN/DESA estimates for the poverty headcount ratio in 2015.

(continued)

Box I.4 (*continued*)

(CDDCs). Rather, policies must be adopted to ensure that upward commodity price movements contribute to meeting the SDGs in the CDDCs.

When designing national commodity sector policies, the links between international commodity markets and local conditions need to be considered. Managing risks due to unanticipated commodity price movements is also important for the sustainability of the commodity sector in CDDCs. In this regard, recent developments in the cocoa sector in Côte d'Ivoire provide important lessons.

The cocoa sector in Côte d'Ivoire has undergone several reforms since 2012, which include the introduction of a mechanism of forward selling anticipated crop and guaranteed minimum producer prices. In October 2016, the Government also raised producer prices to CFA1,100 per kg — equivalent to about US¢ 85 per pound — at the beginning of the 2016/17 season, when the international market price for cocoa stood at US¢ 123 per pound. However, in January 2017, the price of cocoa plummeted to US¢ 100 per pound and to US¢ 90 per pound in July 2017. Many traders who had bought cocoa in advance defaulted on their contracts since the margin between producer prices and international market prices was not sufficient to make a profit. Consequently, the livelihoods of many of the estimated six million Ivorians who depend on cocoa as their main source of income were threatened. In other words, the most vulnerable group within the cocoa value chain bore the brunt of unfavourable international commodity price developments.

More equitable risk sharing along the cocoa value chain and better overall risk management could have mitigated this financial stress on cocoa farmers and their families. Thus, risk management tools could include insurance against contract default and other risks or quick access to the existing cocoa stabilization fund to protect farmers' incomes.

In summary, policymakers need to consider the deep linkages between international commodity markets and the SDGs in the CDDCs. Importantly, more coherent and effective strategies must ensure that commodity price movements do not harm the most vulnerable segments of the population, and that poor households benefit from positive commodity price developments. Given the integration of small producers into international commodity markets, managing risks emanating from commodity price volatility is a key element of such policies.

Authors: Stefan Csordas and
Janvier D. Nkurunziza
(UNCTAD)

**Capital inflows to
emerging economies
gain momentum, driven
by portfolio and
banking flows**

Against this backdrop, private non-resident capital inflows to developing countries and emerging economies gained momentum in 2017, reversing the trend observed in previous years (figure I.28). After a marked downturn in 2015 and 2016, non-resident capital inflows in emerging economies are estimated to exceed $1.1 trillion in 2017, while resident capital outflows are projected to fall from more than $1.0 trillion in 2016 to about $770 billion (IIF, 2017).[14] Thus, net capital inflows entered positive territory in 2017, following two years of large contractions in net capital inflows. The revival of capital inflows to emerging economies and developing countries was driven by portfolio and banking flows.

Together with the more favourable global financing conditions and the upward trend for some commodity prices such as metals and oil, the recovery in capital inflows has been facilitated by the improving economic outlook in several large emerging economies.

After almost a decade-long decline, the growth differential with between developed and developing countries is rising again. Also, while some emerging economies, such as Brazil and the Russian Federation, are gradually recovering from deep downturns, others went through major macroeconomic adjustments in response to the lower commodity pric-

---

14   The data for capital flows from the Institute of International Finance (IIF) encompasses 25 emerging economies: Argentina, the Bolivarian Republic of Venezuela, Brazil, Chile, China, Colombia, the Czech Republic, Egypt, Hungary, India, Indonesia, Lebanon, Malaysia, Mexico, Nigeria, the Philippines, Poland, the Republic of Korea, the Russian Federation, Saudi Arabia, South Africa, Thailand, Turkey, Ukraine and the United Arab Emirates.

Figure I.27
Stock market indices

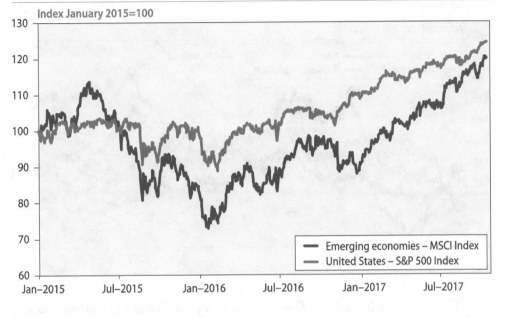

Index January 2015=100

Legend:
— Emerging economies – MSCI Index
— United States – S&P 500 Index

Source: UN/DESA, based on JP Morgan.

Figure I.28
Capital inflows to emerging economies

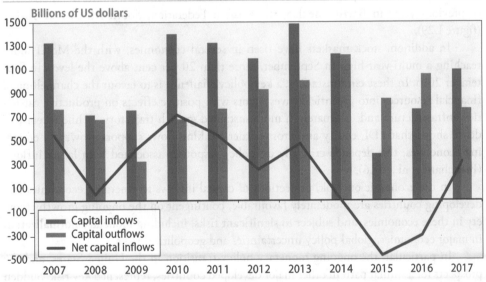

Billions of US dollars

Legend:
■ Capital inflows
■ Capital outflows
— Net capital inflows

Source: IIF (2017).

Note: The sample of countries include 25 large emerging economies. Net capital inflows exclude errors and omissions. Data for 2017 are projections.

es and capital flows observed between 2014 and 2016. For instance, current accounts deficits have narrowed visibly in India and South Africa, and inflation has declined in several countries. Importantly, greater exchange rate flexibility, high levels of reserves and in many cases improved policy frameworks, including the use of countercyclical policies, have not only facilitated macroeconomic adjustments but have also improved emerging economies' resilience to external shocks.

Figure I.29
Exchange rates of selected emerging-market currencies vis-à-vis the United States dollar

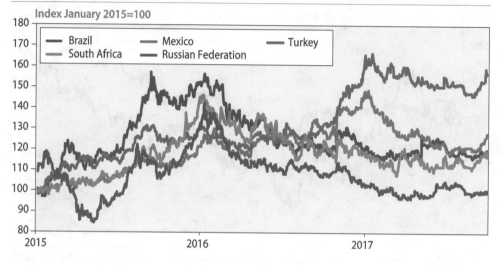

Index January 2015=100

Brazil · Mexico · Turkey
South Africa · Russian Federation

Source: UN/DESA, based on IMF representative rates.

Note: A rise indicates a depreciation.

A key challenge is to translate higher liquidity into more productive investments

The resurgence in capital inflows has led to a reduction of financial spreads and the appreciation of domestic currencies in emerging economies. For instance, sovereign and corporate bond spreads reached historically low levels in developing countries in Asia and Europe, while exchange rates have also recovered from the downward trend observed in previous years in Brazil, Mexico, the Russian Federation, South Africa and Turkey (figure I.29).

In addition, stock markets have risen in several economies, with the MSCI index reaching a multi-year high in September, more than 20 per cent above the levels in September 2016. In these circumstances, a key policy challenge is to favour the channelling of financial resources into greenfield investments with positive effects on productive capacities, infrastructure and, ultimately, a more sustained growth trajectory. While recent evidence shows that FDI, equity and cross-border banking flows support growth in emerging economies, this depends critically on policy responses associated with larger inflows (Blanchard et al., 2016).

In the economic outlook, projections of capital inflows to emerging economies and developing countries are moderately favourable, contingent on the ongoing growth recovery in these economies, and subject to significant risks, including monetary normalization in major economies, global policy uncertainties and geopolitical risks.

The normalization of monetary policies in major economies represents a key risk in the medium term

In particular, the ongoing monetary policy transition in the United States, and the prospects for a similar path in other major developed countries, represent a key risk. Sudden changes in investors' expectations, large stock market corrections or monetary policy missteps by major central banks could trigger significant financial turmoil, leading to spikes in volatility, rising financing costs and disruptive capital outflows. However, emerging economies are in a relatively stronger position to navigate turbulent global financial conditions. Recent evidence confirms that macroeconomic fundamentals do not provide full insulation, for example, to sudden spikes in risk aversion and large capital flows reversals, including episodes of "sudden stops" (Eichengreen and Gupta, 2016).

In containing the build-up of excessive financial risks while at the same time supporting growth, emerging economies should consider the use of a wide range of policy instruments. Macroeconomic and foreign exchange policies can be supported by macroprudential policies, such as targeted and selective capital controls. This is a challenging task for economies that are well integrated into financial markets, as recent evidence suggest that global financial conditions tend to generate large spillovers into local financial markets. For example, Rey (2015) highlights a global financial cycle in capital flows, asset prices and credit growth, which is not aligned with a country's idiosyncratic macroeconomic conditions. This can severely limit the independence and effectiveness of emerging markets' monetary policies.

Portfolio flows

The recovery in capital inflows in emerging economies throughout 2017 has been driven by portfolio flows, particularly debt flows. The "search for yield" boosted portfolio flows, which are estimated to reach about $350 billion in 2017, after posting only $163 billion in 2016 (figure I.30). For instance, sizeable inflows into emerging markets have led to strong gains in the Emerging Market Bond Index (EMBI) in 2017. Bonds issuances also gained momentum in China, Colombia, India, Indonesia, Mexico and Turkey, while issuance of sovereign bonds in oil-exporting and low-income countries also visibly increased in 2017 (BIS, 2017a; IMF, 2017a).

In fact, the relatively high and in some cases rising interest rate differentials, coupled with improved inflation prospects, have encouraged the demand for domestic currency bonds in Brazil, India and the Russian Federation (IIF, 2017). Meanwhile, equity flows increased in Asia and Latin America in countries such as Brazil, India, the Republic of Korea and Thailand, leading in some cases to significant gains in stock markets.

Portfolio capital outflows from China have also tempered, after a significant upsurge in previous years, encouraging authorities to relax some monetary rules supporting the renminbi.

Figure I.30
Portfolio inflows to emerging economies

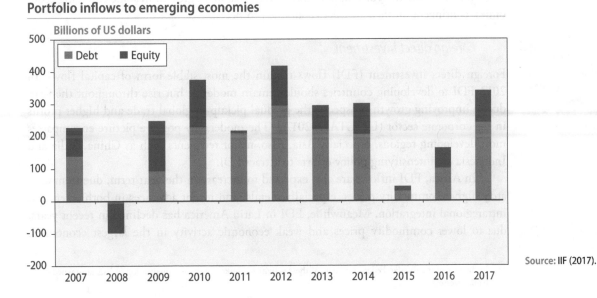

Source: IIF (2017).

Moderately positive expectations regarding portfolio flows to emerging economies are on the horizon, contingent on the growth rate differential with developed economies and a smooth monetary transition by the Fed. In fact, stock market valuations also appear attractive in several emerging economies vis-à-vis developed countries, as illustrated by cyclically adjusted price-earnings ratios (BIS, 2017a; IIF, 2017). Yet, unexpected turbulences in global financial markets could impact portfolio flows, generating major challenges to emerging economies, especially those with a more highly indebted corporate sector.

Bank flows

Banking flows are gaining momentum, in line with the pickup in global trade

Cross-border bank lending to developing countries has remained volatile and largely subdued in recent years, as large international banks, particularly in Europe, have continued to face deleveraging pressures.

The collapse in cross-border bank finance was the main contributor to the slump in overall private financial flows following the global financial crisis. From January 2007 to December 2016, banks divested assets worth at least $2 trillion in the world economy, of which more than half was divestment by European banks (Lund et al., 2017). Interestingly, this encouraged lending activities by several banks from large emerging economies, illustrating the higher relevance of South-South lending. For example, China's four largest banks have quadrupled their share of foreign assets on their balance sheets in the last decade. Banks from Brazil, India and the Russian Federation[15] are also expanding international activities (ibid.).

More recently, the financial position of the banking sector in developed countries has continued to improve. For instance, global systemically important banks (G-SIBs) have strengthened their balance sheets with additional capital injections, while liquidity has also risen due to declining loan-to-deposit ratios and less reliance on short-term funding (IMF, 2017a). Against this backdrop, cross-border banking flows are showing gradual signs of recovery. Data until the first quarter of 2017 shows that year-on-year growth in international bank claims turned positive for the first time since 2015 (BIS, 2017a). For instance, larger banking flows to emerging economies have been visible in China, Mexico and Nigeria. A further increase in banking flows is expected in the near term in tandem with the pickup in global trade, which could support credit and investment growth in some emerging economies, contingent on their broader economic prospects.

Foreign direct investment

FDI remains the most stable source of capital, but LDCs face difficulties in attracting larger inflows

Foreign direct investment (FDI) flows remain the most stable form of capital flows. In 2017, FDI to developing countries should remain moderate but rise throughout the year, due to improving growth prospects, the gradual pickup in global trade and higher profits in the corporate sector (UNCTAD, 2017c). The moderately positive picture encompasses most developing regions, especially Asia. Also, major recipients such as China, India and Indonesia are intensifying policy efforts to attract FDI.

In Africa, FDI inflows are also expected to increase in the near term, due to moderately higher commodity prices, especially metals, and recent advances in both inter- and intraregional integration. Meanwhile, FDI in Latin America has declined in recent years, due to lower commodity prices and weak economic activity in the largest economies.

---

15 In the case of the Russian Federation, part of these activities is linked to the recapitalization of Russian-owned banks overseas.

FDI is expected to remain subdued in the near term (ECLAC, 2017). For example, foreign investments in some parts of the region, especially in Mexico and Central America, are likely to be restrained by lingering policy uncertainties in the United States and the ongoing renegotiation of NAFTA. Likewise, Africa also experienced a decline in FDI in 2016, as growth slowed, amid challenging political and security situations in several economies.

In addition, some countries continue to grapple with severe structural impediments in attracting stronger FDI flows, particularly LDCs and small island developing States (SIDS). The limited amount of FDI in these countries not only reduces access to external financial resources but also constrains expansion of their productive capacities. FDI flows to structurally weak and vulnerable economies remain concentrated in extractive industries, where their development impact is limited. In 2016, FDI to LDCs and SIDS fell by 13 per cent and 6 per cent, respectively (UNCTAD, 2017b).

From a longer-term perspective, developing economies are emerging as an increasingly important source of investment to LDCs, landlocked developing countries, SIDS and some other countries in Africa. While a large share of these investments has been channelled into natural resource sectors, there have been signs of diversification recently.

Policy uncertainties can significantly affect the scale and contours of FDI flows

More generally, the scope for beneficial linkages and technology absorption arising from South-South FDI is supported by the fact that the technology and skills of multinational firms from developing countries is often closer to those in firms in host countries. In this regard, South-South FDI may help develop and diffuse clean technologies. It stands to reason that policymakers promote FDI within South-South cooperation and collaboration frameworks.

Despite the favourable outlook for FDI, flows could be muted by renewed geopolitical risks or a surge in policy uncertainties. Global financial turbulence triggered by a sudden adjustment in expectations over the Fed's monetary policy normalization could also have an impact in the near term. Finally, tax reform in the United States could affect FDI flows, if the reform encourages multinational firms to reduce retained earnings held by overseas affiliates.

Trends in net resource transfers and international reserves

Net transfer of resources

Net financial transfers to developing countries remained negative in 2017, albeit less so than in previous years, thanks to a recovery of capital inflows (figure I.31). In total, the net transfer of financial resources from developing and transition countries to developed economies is estimated at $405 billion, corresponding to 1.3 per cent of their aggregate GDP. This measures the total receipts of net capital inflows from abroad minus total income payments (or outflows), including increases in foreign reserves and foreign investment income payments. The recent trends in net financial transfers continue to be driven by large capital outflows from China.

Net financial transfers to developing countries were negative in 2017, but less so than in previous years

In relative terms, the economies in transition have seen the largest net outflow of resources in 2017, equivalent to 4.2 per cent of GDP (figure I.31). East and South Asia also recorded significant net outflows, estimated at 2.4 per cent of GDP. In absolute terms, this constitutes by far the largest regional outflows, totalling $493 billion, driven mostly by China. By contrast, Africa and the LDCs have continued to experience positive net transfers of resources. While these inflows account for more than 5 per cent of GDP, they

Figure I.31
Net transfer of resources to developing economies and economies in transition

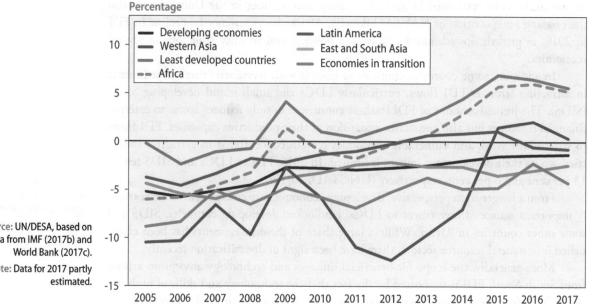

Source: UN/DESA, based on
data from IMF (2017b) and
World Bank (2017c).

Note: Data for 2017 partly
estimated.

are relatively low in absolute levels ($103 billion in the case of Africa and $56 billion in the LDCs).

International reserves

Since 2013, international
reserves as a share of
world gross product have
been declining

By definition, a combined surplus (or deficit) in the current, financial and capital account is reflected in an increase (or decrease) in the level of international reserves. As capital outflows increased in recent years, many developing countries, particularly China, used international reserves to help stabilize exchange rates.

As shown in figure I.32, total international reserves as a share of world gross product fell to 15.5 per cent, or $12.23 trillion in 2017. Foreign exchange reserves as a percentage of GDP of developing countries and economies in transition stood at 10.6 per cent in 2017, down from a peak of 12.3 per cent in 2013. This suggests that countries were spending reserves to moderate the impact of capital outflows on exchange rates. As noted above, China experienced large capital outflows in 2015 and 2016, and as a result, holdings of foreign exchange reserves also declined.

Central banks typically invest reserves in safe liquid assets. The share of global reserves held in dollar-denominated assets was 63.8 per cent in the second quarter of 2017, down slightly from 65.8 per cent at the end of 2015. The holdings of Chinese renminbi as foreign reserves, which make up 1 per cent of reserves globally, were reported by the IMF for the first time in 2016.

Trends in public resources

International public finance complements efforts by developing countries to mobilize domestic resources for development. In addition, international public finance plays an impor-

Figure I.32
Foreign exchange reserves as a percentage of world gross product

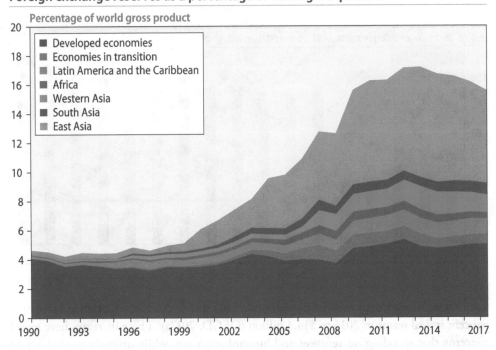

Percentage of world gross product

Legend:
- Developed economies
- Economies in transition
- Latin America and the Caribbean
- Africa
- Western Asia
- South Asia
- East Asia

Source: UN/DESA, based on data from IMF (2017c).

Note: Excludes the value of gold held as official reserves. Data for 2017 partly estimated.

tant role in financing global public goods. The provision of international public finance, including ODA from members of the OECD Development Assistance Committee and lending by multilateral development banks, increased between 2015 and 2016, continuing a rising trend since the turn of the millennium. While the provision of international public finance from developing countries, in the form of South-South cooperation, has also tended to increase in recent years, it remains volatile.

Official development assistance

As displayed in figure I.33, global ODA flows increased to $142.6 billion in 2016, representing an 8.9 per cent rise in real terms from 2015. As a share of gross national income of donors, ODA averaged 0.32 per cent, still significantly below the United Nations target of 0.7 per cent. Only six countries reached this target. In real terms, i.e. correcting for inflation and currency fluctuations, ODA has doubled since 2000 (OECD, 2017a). However, although donors agreed to halt the recent decline in ODA to LDCs in the Addis Ababa Action Agenda (AAAA), preliminary figures indicate that bilateral aid to LDCs fell by 3.9 per cent in real terms in 2016 to $26 billion. ODA makes up more than two thirds of external finance for LDCs (OECD, 2017b).

The increase in total ODA in 2016 was partly due to higher expenditures on in-donor refugees. Excluding these expenditures, ODA still grew by 7.1 per cent in real terms. ODA expenditure to host refugees inside donor countries increased by 27.5 per cent in real terms from 2015 to reach $15.4 billion. This equates to 10.8 per cent of total net ODA, up from 9.2 per cent in 2015 and 4.8 per cent in 2014, in line with the higher number of refugees over the past two years. Meanwhile, ODA reporting rules for hosting refugees were updated and clarified in the 2017 high-level meeting of the OECD Development Assistance

Global ODA flows increased significantly in 2016, but assistance to LDCs declined

Figure I.33
Net disbursements of official development assistance by all donors

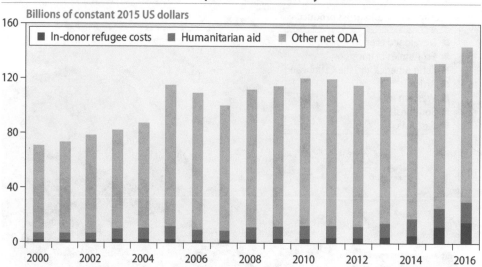

Source: OECD (2017a).
Note: Preliminary data for 2016.

Committee, as standards used by providers were not uniform. Humanitarian aid rose by 8 per cent in real terms in 2016 to $14.4 billion (OECD, 2017a). These increases have raised concerns that spending on refugees and humanitarian aid, while urgently needed, could negatively impact funding for long-term development projects.

Estimates of South-South cooperation expenditure suggest it surpassed $20 billion in 2014 (United Nations, 2016b), while the OECD, which also estimates concessional development finance from developing countries, arrived at comparable figures of $24.6 billion in 2015 (OECD, 2017b).

Multilateral development banks

Lending by multilateral development banks has grown rapidly

While public financial flows from multilateral development banks (MDBs) are much smaller than their private counterparts, they are generally less volatile and play a key role in financing sectors and long-term projects critical to sustainable development. MDBs have responded to the high expectations in terms of SDG financing set out in the AAAA, and proposed an action plan to optimize balance sheets at the 2015 November meeting in Antalya, Turkey, which was subsequently endorsed by the Group of Twenty (G20) leaders. The first results of the steps taken by the MDBs to improve their balance sheets and expand lending are visible. Annual commitments of non-grant subsidized finance from the seven MDBs reached $84.9 billion in 2016, an increase of 14.3 per cent, with disbursements totalling $65.8 billion, an increase of 14.8 per cent (see figure I.34). The growth of commitments suggests a possible further increase in disbursements in 2017.

Figure I.35 illustrates the trends in disbursements of the major MDBs. The disbursements of the World Bank's International Bank for Reconstruction and Development rose sharply by 18.5 per cent to $22.5 billion in fiscal year 2016 over 2015 (World Bank, 2016a). The International Finance Corporation, the private sector arm of the World Bank Group, saw an increase of 7.4 per cent in lending disbursements to $10 billion. Meanwhile, the European Investment Bank decreased its disbursements, yet remains, by a wide margin, the largest bank in terms of disbursements.

Figure I.34
Multilateral development bank financing

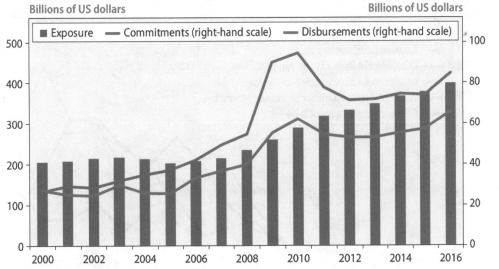

Billions of US dollars   Billions of US dollars

■ Exposure — Commitments (right-hand scale) — Disbursements (right-hand scale)

Source: UN/DESA, based on data from annual reports of multilateral development banks.

Note: Includes non-grant subsidized finance from Asian Development Bank, African Development Bank, European Bank for Reconstruction and Development, Inter-American Development Bank, Inter-American Investment Corporation, International Bank for Reconstruction and Development, and International Finance Corporation. Concessional lending classified as ODA is excluded.

Figure I.35
Annual disbursement of the multilateral development banks

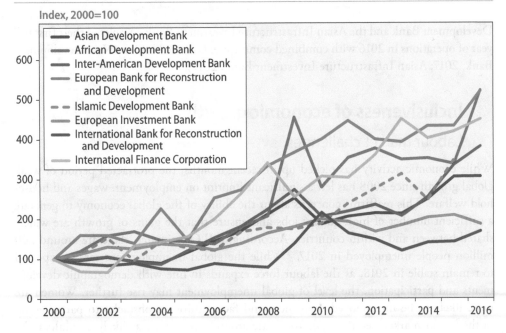

Index, 2000=100

- Asian Development Bank
- African Development Bank
- Inter-American Development Bank
- European Bank for Reconstruction and Development
- Islamic Development Bank
- European Investment Bank
- International Bank for Reconstruction and Development
- International Finance Corporation

Source: UN/DESA, based on data from annual reports from relevant organizations.

Recent trends vary significantly among the multilateral development banks that are based in developing countries. These differences in part reflect strong variations in local economic conditions over the past few years. For instance, the disbursements of the Development Bank of South Africa fell sharply by 27.5 per cent in 2016. The scaling back of its lending activities follows weak economic growth in the country and a change of government. In the case of the Brazilian Development Bank, disbursements declined for a third consecutive years, falling by 35 per cent. By contrast, disbursements by the Corporacion Andina de Fomento grew by over 40 per cent to almost $8.5 billion in 2016. The New

Some multilateral development banks based in developing countries have scaled back lending amid weakness in the local economy

Figure I.36
Annual disbursement of selected regional and national development banks from developing countries

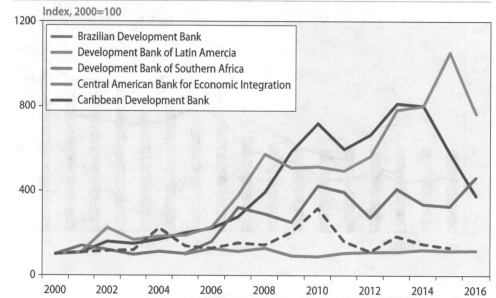

Index, 2000=100

- Brazilian Development Bank
- Development Bank of Latin Amercia
- Development Bank of Southern Africa
- Central American Bank for Economic Integration
- Caribbean Development Bank

Source: UN/DESA, based on data from annual reports from relevant organizations.

Development Bank and the Asian Infrastructure Investment Bank completed their first full year of operations in 2016 with combined commitments of $3.3 billion (New Development Bank, 2017; Asian Infrastructure Investment Bank, 2017).

Inclusiveness of economic growth

Labour market challenges

While economic activity has picked up in recent months, the protracted period of weak global growth since 2008 has left a significant imprint on employment, wages and household welfare. This reaffirms concerns about the ability of the global economy to generate a sufficient number of high-quality jobs and ensure that the gains of growth are widely shared between and within countries. According to ILO estimates, there are around 200 million people unemployed in 2017.[16] While the global unemployment rate is expected to remain stable in 2018, as the labour force expands in line with demographic developments and participation, the level of global unemployment may rise further. Women are more likely to be unemployed than men, and face significant obstacles to participation in the labour market (see Box I.5). Youth are around three times as likely as adults to be unemployed (United Nations, Economic and Social Council, 2017). Moreover, more than one-third of the population in low income countries that are in work are living in poverty, and more than 40 per cent of the world's workers are in vulnerable forms of employment, with little or no access to social protection, low and volatile income, and high levels of job

---

16   ILOSTAT, ILO modelled estimates, November 2016.

Box I.5
What is holding women back in the labour force?
Multi-dimensional challenges to labour market attainment

The *World Employment and Social Outlook: Trends for Women 2017* (ILO, 2017a) shows that women around the globe continue to fare worse than men across most labour market dimensions. Their participation rate — at just over 49 per cent — is nearly 27 percentage points lower than the rate of men. When participating in the labour market, they face higher unemployment rates, and are often subject to significantly different employment conditions. For instance, 14.9 per cent of women are contributing family workers, as opposed to 5.5 per cent of men. The combination of differences in employment conditions, sectoral and occupational segregation, and outright discrimination results in a significant gender pay gap.

Indeed, women face multiple labour market barriers. The decision to participate or not in the labour market depends on the interplay of three fundamental factors, which are shaped by social norms and life-cycle circumstances. First, a woman's personal preference to pursue paid work is a very important determinant. Surveys indicate that some 70 per cent of women — regardless of their employment status — prefer to work at paid jobs.

In reality, however, more than half of all women globally are out of the labour force. This implies that a preference for paid work is not sufficient in itself to ensure the participation of women in the labour force. It also suggests that significant challenges restrict the capacity and freedom of women to participate in the workforce. Second, women are often pressured to conform to gender roles prescribed by the family, community, class, religion or society to avoid the risk of social exclusion. Indeed, gender roles embodied in some religions can have a strong negative influence on a woman's probability to participate in the labour market. Third, socio-economic constraints, such as having to care for dependents or the need for transportation, especially in developing countries, compete with the potential returns from the labour market. However, the ultimate decision to participate in the workforce depends on the relative strength of these factors. The personal preference to pursue paid work is an important driver of participation, but its importance is often outweighed by socio-economic and gender role constraints.

Estimates reported by the ILO (ibid.) suggest that reducing the gap in participation rates between men and women by 25 per cent by the year 2025 (as G20 leaders committed to in 2014) would yield significant economic gains, raising global GDP in 2025 by an additional 3.9 per cent (equivalent to raising global GDP growth over the next eight years by almost half a percentage point per annum). The regions with the largest gender gaps, namely the Arab States, North Africa and South Asia, would see the greatest benefits.

The achievement of such a goal would also unlock large potential tax revenues of about $1.5 trillion (in 2010 US dollars, using PPP exchange rates). Using a fraction of this additional revenue to address gender inequalities in the labour market, such as the socio-economic constraints discussed above, would result in positive multiplier effects in the economy. Reducing and redistributing unpaid care work through improved public care services and social infrastructure would allow women to have better access to the labour market. This includes the provision of adequate maternity protection and parental leave and benefits for both men and women. Women's labour market participation should also be supported by flexible working arrangements and reintegration measures that allow women to reconcile work and care responsibilities and transition more easily from maternal leave back to work. For instance, in its most recent budget, Canada made an historic commitment to an inclusive, high-quality, and accessible care framework. This will help to make sure that even vulnerable communities have equal access to care and, hence, further enable women to take part in the labour market. Moving forward, the ILO proposes a comprehensive policy framework that rests on three pillars: reshaping gender role conformity and personal preferences, addressing socio-economic constraints and raising equality in labour market conditions.

Authors: Stefan Kühn, Steven Tobin and Sheena Yoon (ILO)

insecurity (ILO, 2017b). South Asia and sub-Saharan Africa are the regions most affected by vulnerable employment.

Notwithstanding these deeper challenges, headline labour market indicators in a broad spectrum of developed economies, economies in transition and developing economies continue to exhibit some improvements. Figures I.37 and I.38 compare current and long-term unemployment rates to levels prevailing in 2010. In the sample of countries shown, unemployment rates have come down since 2010 in the vast majority of countries. Exceptions include Greece, Italy, Spain and South Africa, which have suffered exceptional challenges post-2010. Several commodity exporting countries that suffered a sharp drop in revenue in 2015–2016 have also seen a deterioration in labour market conditions.

The share of long-term unemployment remains high in a number of countries, although a few countries, such as Israel, the Republic of Moldova, the United Kingdom and the United States have seen significant outflows from long-term unemployment into jobs since 2010.

The relatively large pools of long-term unemployed in some countries have been one factor behind weak wage growth and rising wage inequality in recent years (OECD, 2011). Growth in real wages has not kept up with productivity, partly as a result of the prevalence of low quality, low paid jobs, and more part-time and temporary contracts. This has compounded a deterioration in workers' bargaining power.

Figure I.39 shows real wage growth in 2016 and average annual wage growth since 2007 in selected countries. Most countries in the sample exhibited some real wage gains in 2016, although wages deteriorated significantly in Norway, reflecting income losses related to the decline in oil prices.

Despite Greece's strong wage growth in 2016, over the past decade real wages have sharply deteriorated. The level of average real wages in Greece remains nearly 20 per cent below its level in 2007. Average real wages in Italy, Mexico, Portugal and the United Kingdom also remain below 2007 levels. For the most part, real wage growth has averaged less than 1 per cent per annum in the sample of countries. Stronger wage growth in Canada and Norway reflects income gains during the commodity boom of 2011–2013, while Germany and Sweden both recovered from the global financial crisis more rapidly than many other countries.

The relatively modest wage growth in recent years has restrained a more rapid rebound in household demand, which has in turn held back investment, compounding the slow growth in aggregated demand.

National average wages may not fully reflect developments in household welfare if wage gains have not been shared evenly across income groups. Since 2007, in a number of countries, including Denmark, Germany, Ireland, the Netherlands, Norway and the United States, real wage growth for those on lower incomes has lagged behind wage growth for the highest 10 per cent of earners. Minimum wage growth has failed to keep pace with average wages in several countries as well.

The recent rise in wage inequality in some developed economies prolongs the general trend of rising wage inequality over the last two decades. Over the same period, a number of developing economies, predominantly in Latin America, have seen wage inequality decline (ILO, 2017c).

Rising wage inequality amplifies the macroeconomic impacts of weak average wage growth, as households with lower incomes tend to consume a greater share of current

Figure I.37
Unemployment and long-term unemployment in selected developed economies

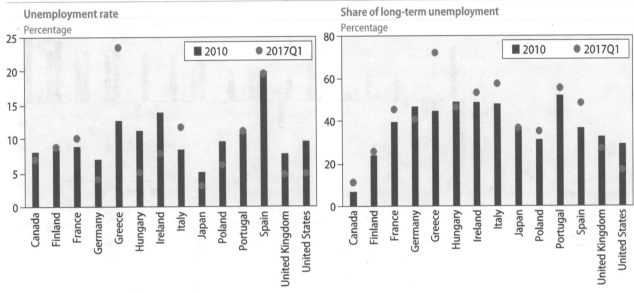

Source: ILOSTAT, Unemployment and labour underutilization.

Figure I.38
Unemployment and long-term unemployment in selected developing and transition economies

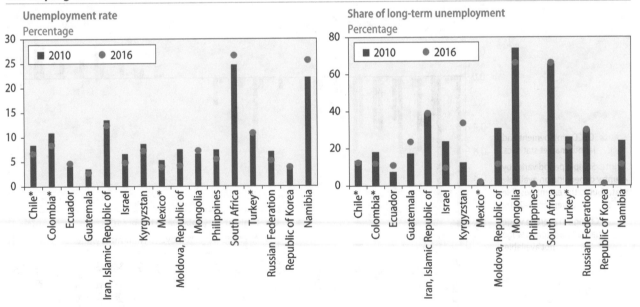

Source: ILOSTAT, Unemployment and labour underutilization.

* Data for 2017Q1 rather than 2016.

Figure I.39
Average annual real wage growth

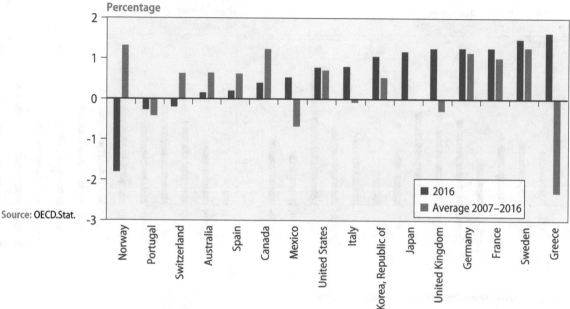

Source: OECD.Stat.

Figure I.40
Change in wage inequality measures since 2008

Source: OECD employment and
labour market statistics.

Note: Sample period varies by
country depending on available
data, but to the extent possible
covers 2008–2016.

* Change in average wage
relative to minimum wage
not available.

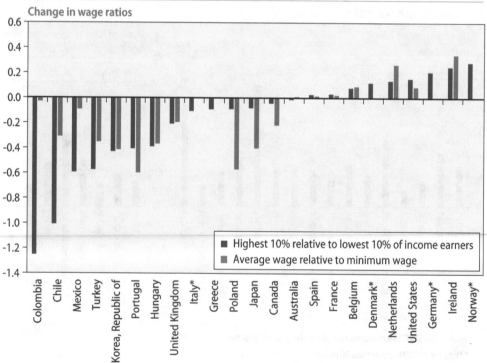

income than wealthier households, who tend to channel more into savings. Further rises in wage inequality in developed economies risk reigniting deflationary pressures, complicating the conduct of monetary policy and increasing the probability of spikes in financial market volatility.

The challenge of eradicating poverty

At least 750 million people live below the extreme poverty line in 2017, with almost no change from last year. At the same time, the Food and Agriculture Organization of the United Nations estimates that 815 million people were undernourished in 2016, compared to 777 million in 2015 (FAO, 2017). Put simply, this means that raising people above the extreme poverty line of $1.90 per day may only be sufficient to provide them with adequate food. Reaching the target of eradicating extreme poverty, therefore, should be viewed as a small, but crucial, step towards the ultimate goal of eradicating poverty in all its forms. To provide some perspective: supporting around 750 million people in 2017 with $1.90 a day would cost around 0.7 per cent of global GDP, or 1.1 per cent of GDP of the richest 1 billion people — a goal that should be within reach.

There is no doubt that extreme poverty has declined over the past two decades. In the 1980s and in the beginning of 1990s almost 2 billion people lived on less than $1.90 a day, which was 30 to 40 per cent of the global population. In 2000, about a quarter of the world remained in extreme poverty. In 2017, 13 years before the 2030 Agenda aims to end extreme poverty and hunger, around 10 per cent of the population live below the $1.90 threshold.

Despite enormous progress, especially in the last 20 years, the evidence shows that not enough has been done to ensure the SDG target of eradicating extreme poverty is met by 2030. Current estimates based on projections for consumption growth[17] and population growth estimates from the United Nations Population Division, suggest that there may be around 650 million people living in extreme poverty in 2030.

Reducing poverty is likely to be uneven. Progress in poverty reduction over the last 20 years has been achieved mainly through enormous progress in large Asian economies, such as China (figure I.41). The number of people living in extreme poverty in Asia dropped from around 1.5 billion in the beginning of 1980s to around 300 million people currently. Model-based projections suggest these numbers may further halve by 2030, leaving only about 3 per cent of people in Asia in extreme poverty.

The situation looks different on the African continent (figure I.42), especially in the sub-Saharan region. In the beginning of the 1980s, around 45 per cent of Africans lived in extreme poverty, reaching almost half of the population in the 1990s. Since then, this share has declined to around 30 per cent. Nevertheless, the projections suggest that over 25 per cent of people in Africa may remain in extreme poverty by 2030. Moreover, despite the improvement in poverty rates, expressed as a share of the population in figure I.42, unless more effort and action is taken, the level of extreme poverty in Africa may rise by almost 60 million by 2030 (figure I.43).

Eradicating extreme poverty should be within reach

Despite progress, not enough has been done to ensure the SDG target of eradicating extreme poverty is met by 2030

A quarter of the people in Africa may remain in extreme poverty by 2030

---

17 Projections carried out as an extension of the current short-term forecast baseline, using the World Economic Forecasting Model (https://www.un.org/development/desa/dpad/wp-content/uploads/sites/45/publication/2016 _Apr_ WorldEconomicForecastingModel.pdf). Inequality, as captured by the standard deviation of the log of income, is assumed to remain constant over the projection period. The reported projections represent a single scenario, based on a relatively neutral set of assumptions regarding trend productivity growth and other key parameters.

Figure I.41
Population below $1.90/day poverty line

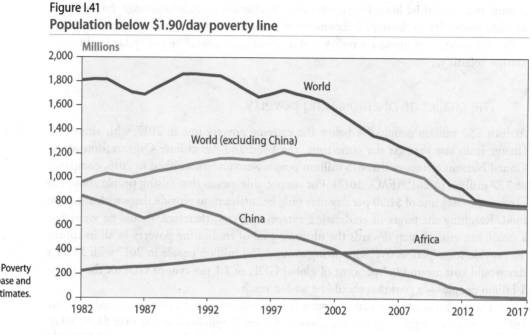

Sources: World Bank Poverty
and Equity Database and
UN/DESA estimates.

Figure I.42
Share of population below $1.90/day poverty line in Africa

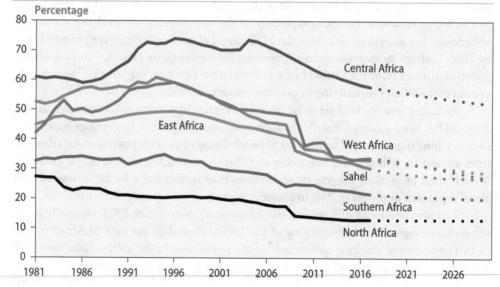

Sources: World Bank Poverty
and Equity Database and
UN/DESA projections to 2030.

Because of its geographical, historic, economic, and climate complexity the changes among African regions and countries are far from even. The scenario suggests that all countries on the continent will reduce the share of people living below the poverty line. In the region of Sahel, progress is likely to be minimal as a result of challenging climatic conditions as well as multiple conflict situations. The fastest growing economies in East and West Africa are expected to see the steepest falls in poverty rates, raising more than 10 percent of their populations out of extreme poverty by 2030, although given the strong population growth, the number of people in extreme poverty may nonetheless rise.

Figure I.43
Population below $1.90/day poverty line in Africa

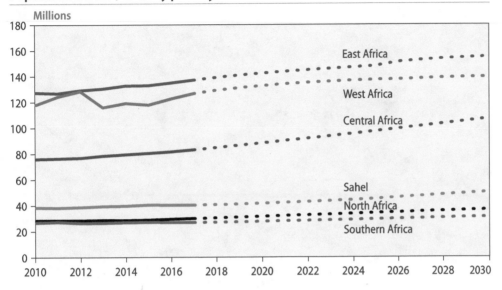

Millions

East Africa
West Africa
Central Africa
Sahel
North Africa
Southern Africa

Sources: World Bank Poverty and Equity Database and UN/DESA projections to 2030.

The scenario presented illustrates the urgent need to foster an environment that will both accelerate medium-term growth prospects and tackle poverty through policies that address inequalities in income and opportunity. Policies that have been largely successful at reducing income inequality include short-term transfers and income support to smooth consumption among the most deprived, and longer-term policies that address inequalities in opportunity, such as investment in early childhood development, access to healthcare and education, and investment in rural roads and electrification (World Bank, 2016b).

Appendix
Global assumptions

Baseline forecast assumptions

This appendix summarizes the key assumptions underlying the baseline forecast, including recent and expected developments in major commodity prices, monetary and fiscal policies assumptions, and exchange rates for major currencies.

Commodity prices

Food and agricultural commodities

Between January and October 2016, the price of sugar (*average ISA daily prices*) climbed from 14.05 cents per pound to 22.22 cents per pound due to a widening supply-demand gap (figure I.A.1). The price hike triggered a supply expansion, which brought the price of sugar down to 14.37 cents per pound in August 2017. Going forward, forecasts of rising global supply suggest that price increases are unlikely for the upcoming season.

The price of rice (*Thailand, white milled, 5 per cent broken*) has dropped from $414 per ton in August 2016 to $382 per ton in August 2017. Looking forward, rice stocks are expected to slightly increase during the 2017–2018 season so that further significant price increases seem unlikely.

The 2016–2017 season marked a record production of wheat and maize. As a consequence, the wheat price (*Hard Red Winter No.2*) at $191 per ton in April 2017 was down 4.5 per cent year-on-year. After a brief price rally from May to July 2017, the wheat price settled at $203 per ton in August 2017. The maize price (*Yellow Maize No. 3*) reached its lowest level in more than seven years at $158 per ton in April 2017 and remained low at $159 per ton in August 2017. Strong demand is projected to lead to a reduction of grain stocks, which could generate a mild increase in prices.

Projections of a record production for soybeans for the 2016–2017 season led to a price decline among vegetable oilseeds and oils during the first half of 2017. In August 2017, the UNCTAD Vegetable Oilseeds and Oils Price Index averaged 223 points, 12.2 per cent down from January 2017. Forecasts for 2017–2018 show increasing demand but also rising oilseed production so that prices are expected to remain stable.

The International Coffee Organization composite indicator price for coffee followed a downward trend in the first half of 2017, based on favorable supply and a weakening Brazilian real. In August 2017, the coffee price averaged 128 cents per pound, down 2.1 per cent year-on-year. Forecasts of healthy production during the 2017–2018 season suggest that price increases are unlikely in the absence of unfavourable weather conditions.

The markets for tea were characterized by high variability over the past two years. Between July 2015 and April 2016, the tea price (*Kenya, BPF 1, Mombasa auction prices*) plummeted from 403 to 238 cents per kilogram, mainly driven by surplus supply. After a trend reversal in mid-2016, the tea price averaged 362 cents per kilogram in August 2017. The tea price is expected to remain volatile as weather-related risks in main growing regions complicate supply forecasts.

Prices of cocoa beans started to trend downwards in July 2016 amidst predictions of a supply surplus for the 2016–2017 season. In April 2017, the price of cocoa beans averaged 89 cents per pound, its lowest level in almost a decade. This price trend was fueled by expectations of significant production increases in Côte d'Ivoire and Ghana and a record supply surplus. The sharp price drop had dramatic consequences for cocoa producers, particularly in Côte d'Ivoire (see Box I.4). Looking ahead, growing demand is unlikely to outpace strong production and cocoa beans prices are expected to remain low.

The price of rubber (*RSS 3, Singapore*) surged 21.8 per cent from 223 cents per kilogram in December 2016 to 271 cents per kilogram in February 2017 after floods in Malaysia and Thailand constricted supply. Rubber prices receded to 188 cents per kilogram in August 2017 after supply conditions eased. Going forward, demand growth is expected to outpace production increases so that mild price increases seem likely.

The price of cotton (*Cotlook Index A*) is considerably higher in 2017 than in 2016. The average monthly cotton price during the first half of 2017 was 86 cents per pound, 24.2 per cent higher than during the same period of 2016. The market outlook for cotton tentatively predicts an increase in production as well as a continuation of Chinese government auctions of stockpiles, which could cause downward pressure on prices.

Figure I.A.1
Selected commodity prices, January 2011–August 2017

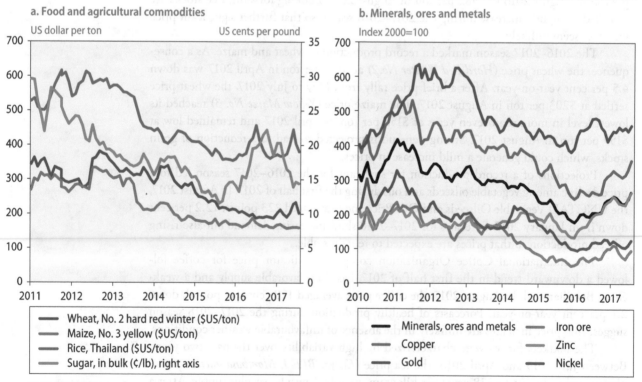

Source: UNCTADstat.

Minerals, ores and metals

The price of nickel (*London Metal Exchange*) followed a downward trend during the first half of 2017 (figure I.A.1). After mine shutdowns in the Philippines due to environmental concerns had driven the nickel price up to $11,010 per ton in December 2016, the nickel price receded to $8,928 per ton in June 2017. The price of nickel increased thereafter to $10,849 in August 2017 amidst strong demand and uncertainty about supply conditions in major exporters, namely the Philippines and Indonesia.

The price of iron ore (*China import, fines 62% Fe, spot, CFR Tianjin port*) is strongly driven by Chinese demand, as the country imports more than two-thirds of the world's total seaborne iron ore. The price almost doubled between January and December 2016 based on recuperating demand from China and lower output from high-cost mines. In the second quarter of 2017, weakening demand for steel in China and concerns over oversupply caused a drop in the iron ore price, which stood at $76 per dry ton in August 2017. Favourable supply conditions make substantial price increases unlikely in the near future.

The price of copper (*London Metal Exchange*) was fluctuating around an upward trend in the first half of 2017. In August 2017, the copper price stood at $6,477 per ton, which was 36.2 per cent higher than in August 2016. According to latest projections, the copper market will be in deficit in 2017 and 2018 so that further increases seem likely.

Zinc markets have been characterized by high volatility over the past two years. Mine closures and production cutbacks led to a supply deficit that triggered a rally of the zinc price (*London Metal Exchange*) of 88.4 per cent between January 2016 and February 2017, when it reached $2,848 per ton. During the second quarter of 2017, the zinc price was volatile and stood at $2,981 per ton in August 2017. The high zinc prices will likely induce supply to increase, restraining further price rises in future.

The gold price increased by 7.5 per cent from $1,193 per troy ounce in January 2017 to $1,282 per troy ounce in August 2017. This is 4.4 per cent below the level of August 2016, when the gold price was at the peak of a price rally driven by geopolitical and macroeconomic uncertainty. Going forward, increases in the United States policy rates remain a downside risk to the gold price, while upside risks include geopolitical conditions.

Oil price

Amid a rebalancing of demand and supply, the price of Brent crude oil is assumed to average $52.5 per barrel in 2017, $55.4 per barrel in 2018 and $59.7 per barrel in 2019 (figure I.A.2).

Monetary policy

Many of the central banks in developed economies will begin to ease or withdraw monetary stimulus measures in 2018–2019, although monetary conditions will remain broadly accommodative. Interest rates will continue to diverge between the euro area, Japan and the United States (figure I.A.3), reflecting differences in the timing and pace of withdrawal.

North America: The Fed is expected to raise its key policy rate by 25 basis points by the end of 2017. The target for the federal funds rate will then increase gradually, by 50 basis points in 2018 and 75 basis points in 2019. The Fed initiated its balance sheet normalization program in October 2017, and will gradually reduce its holdings by approximately $10 billion per month over the forecast horizon (figure I.A.4). Meanwhile, the Bank

Figure I.A.2
Price of Brent crude: recent trends and assumptions

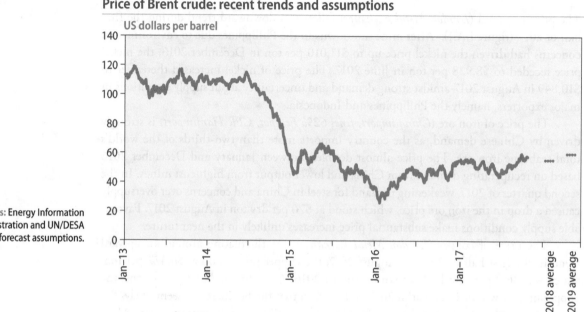

Sources: Energy Information
Administration and UN/DESA
forecast assumptions.

Figure I.A.3
Key central bank policy rates: recent trends and assumptions

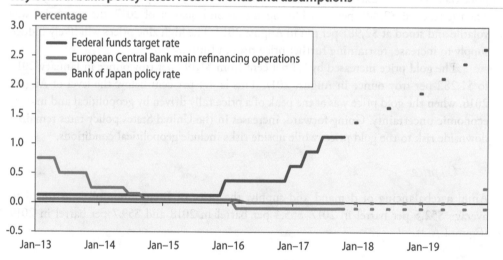

Sources: National central
banks and UN/DESA forecast
assumptions.

of Canada raised interest rates by 50 basis points in the first nine months of 2017, and is expected to roughly track the interest rate rises in the United States over 2018–2019.

Japan: To pursue the inflation target of 2 per cent, the Bank of Japan (BoJ) is expected to maintain a set of unconventional monetary easing measures, known as Quantitative and Qualitative Monetary Easing (QQE). The measures include a negative interest rate on commercial banks' excess reserves of -0.1 per cent, while the BoJ also guides the yield on 10-year Japanese Government Bonds between 0 per cent and 0.1 per cent. The BoJ is expected to maintain the pace of the monetary base expansion by actively purchasing financial assets. Consequently, the total assets of the BoJ are projected to surpass Japan's nominal annual GDP by early 2018.

Figure I.A.4
Total assets of major central banks, December 2006–December 2019

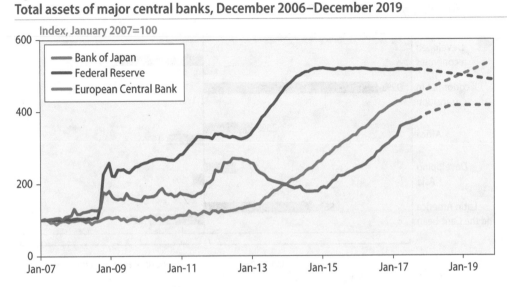

Index, January 2007=100

- Bank of Japan
- Federal Reserve
- European Central Bank

Sources: National central banks and UN/DESA forecast assumptions.

European Union: In 2017, the ECB reduced the amount of its monthly asset purchases, albeit with an extension of the purchase program, and dropped the reference to possibly lower interest rates in its policy guidance. The ECB is expected to initiate further steps to remove some of its stimulus in 2018, gradually tapering asset purchases, which will continue until at least September 2018. At the same time, the ECB is expected to continue the reinvestment of maturing asset holdings for an extended period of time, maintaining a significant element of support for financial markets. Interest rate normalization will begin only well past the end of the asset purchase program, with a first 25 basis point rise expected by the end of 2019. In response to higher inflationary pressures, the Bank of England is expected to further tighten its policy stance in 2018.

Monetary policy stances vary among developing countries and economies in transition. Figure I.A.5 illustrates the share of each major global region that has increased and reduced interest rates over the course of 2017. There has been a clear tendency towards monetary loosening in the economies in transition and in Latin America and the Caribbean — partially reversing the interest rate hikes in 2015 or 2016.

Commonwealth of Independent States (CIS): As inflationary pressures caused by the sharp exchange rate adjustments in 2015–2016 are abating and currencies rebound, most central banks in the CIS continued to relax monetary policy in 2017, with several policy rate cuts in the Russian Federation. In certain cases, high levels of dollarization and weak financial intermediation are hampering control over the lending rates and money supply. Concurrently, some countries (for example, Kyrgyzstan) are taking measures to restrict dollar-denominated lending and to convert outstanding foreign exchange loans to domestic currency loans. Compared with other emerging markets, real interest rates remain high in many CIS economies.

South-Eastern Europe: In South-Eastern Europe, formal or informal currency pegs or unilateral euroization constrain the conduct of monetary policy, but the overall monetary conditions are accommodative. In countries with flexible currencies, policy rates remain at a record low, such as in Albania, thanks to the earlier disinflationary trend and the continuing ECB monetary loosening. Interest rates were also gradually reduced in Serbia. Looking

Figure I.A.5
Shifts in policy rates in 2017, GDP weighted

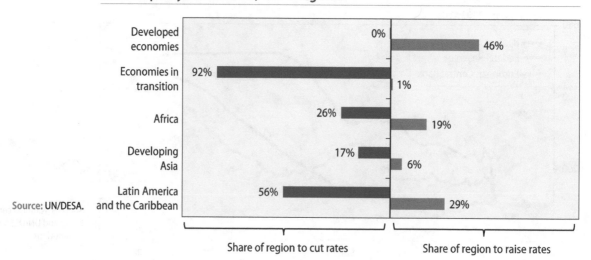

Source: UN/DESA.

forward, gradual monetary tightening by the Fed and the reversal of the ECB stance may put some pressure on monetary policy in the region.

Africa: While inflation remains elevated in many countries, disinflationary pressures are creating space for several central banks to ease monetary policy. However, monetary policy is expected to remain tight in the Democratic Republic of the Congo, Egypt, Sierra Leone and Tunisia, to stabilize currencies and inflation. In terms of exchange rates, most currencies stabilized in 2017, following the high volatility witnessed by many African currencies in 2016.

East Asia: Against a backdrop of subdued inflationary pressures and high external uncertainty, monetary policy in the East Asia region is likely to remain accommodative over the forecast period. In 2017, Indonesia and Viet Nam reduced their key policy rates, in efforts to stimulate bank lending and boost growth. For many countries, however, there is fairly limited room for further rate cuts. Policy rates are at historic lows in several countries, with rates in the Republic of Korea, Taiwan Province of China and Thailand at below 2 per cent. Furthermore, as developed economies normalize monetary policy, central banks in East Asia are faced with the risk of managing potential large capital outflows. In China, the People's Bank of China (PBoC) is expected to maintain a neutral and prudent monetary policy stance. Amid concerns over growing financial risks, the PBoC is expected to use a range of monetary and macro-prudential tools to curb financial vulnerabilities while preserving growth.

South Asia: Monetary policies continue to be moderately accommodative amid subdued inflationary pressures and lingering output gaps in some economies. Yet, credit growth remains subdued in most economies. Accommodative monetary stances are expected to continue in the outlook period, with further easing in some countries. However, sudden changes in global financial conditions could significantly affect the monetary stances and trajectories in the region.

Western Asia: Central banks in Bahrain, Jordan, Kuwait, Qatar, Saudi Arabia and the United Arab Emirates are expected to raise policy interest rates in line with the Fed. The Central Bank of the Republic of Turkey is expected to ease its policy stance moderately as the inflation rate has started declining in the second half of 2017. The Central Bank of Israel is projected to maintain its policy rate at 0.1 per cent.

Latin America and the Caribbean: Against the backdrop of rapidly declining inflation, weak economic activity and improved financial stability, several South American central banks (including those in Brazil, Chile, Colombia and Peru) eased monetary policy during 2017. The Central Bank of Brazil has cut its main policy rate aggressively from 14.25 per cent in October 2016 to 8.25 per cent, the lowest level since 2013. As South America's recovery gains momentum and economic slack diminishes, the monetary easing cycle is expected to come to an end. In the absence of negative shocks, policy rates are projected to remain largely unchanged over the next year. A moderate tightening of monetary policy is possible in the latter part of the forecast period.

In Mexico, the lengthy tightening cycle that started in late 2015 and lifted the main policy rate from 3 per cent to 7 per cent has likely come to an end. With inflation starting to come down, but remaining well above the 3 per cent target, the central bank is expected to pursue a neutral stance in the short term.

In countries that are fully dollarized (Ecuador, El Salvador and Panama) or operate a peg to the dollar (Antigua and Barbuda, Dominica, Bahamas and Barbados), monetary policy is essentially imported from the United States. Local interest rates are projected to rise in line with those of the Fed.

Fiscal policy

Fiscal policy in most developed economies is expected to be broadly neutral in 2018–2019. A few countries have announced more expansionary measures, including Australia, Canada, Japan and New Zealand.

United States: While the budget for 2018 remains unclear, policy changes are expected to contribute marginally to growth in 2018 (roughly 0.1 percentage points), and remain neutral in 2019. Additional government spending, largely in the areas of defence, will be partly offset by cuts in spending on education, healthcare, environmental protection and development aid. Some degree of corporate tax cuts is expected, which will have a small, but positive, impact on growth in both years.

Japan: Fiscal policy will remain accommodative over the 2017 and 2018 fiscal years. In 2017, general expenditures increased by 0.9 per cent, and the same margin of increase is expected in the 2018 fiscal year. While health care and social welfare expenditures will rise to cope with the rapidly aging society, the Government will commit to fiscal consolidation after 2018, and targets a primary balance surplus in 2020.

European Union: Fiscal policy will have a broadly neutral impact on growth in the forecast period. The implemented fiscal adjustments have led to measurable improvements in fiscal positions. In 2016, only Spain and France exceeded the EU limit for budget deficits of 3.0 per cent of GDP by registering deficits of 4.5 per cent and 3.4 per cent, respectively. In the outlook period, several countries, including Austria and Germany, will increase fiscal spending to integrate a large number of migrants. However, fiscal policy space will remain limited in the EU as a whole, with the aggregate debt-to-GDP ratio standing at 86 per cent, and Belgium, Cyprus, France, Greece, Italy, Portugal and Spain exhibiting debt-to-GDP ratios of close to or in excess of 100 per cent. In the United Kingdom, fiscal policy will remain under pressure from the effects created by the decision to leave the EU.

Among developing countries and economies in transition, the fiscal policy stance in many commodity exporters will remain relatively tight.

CIS: Despite some uptick in commodity prices in 2016–2017, energy-exporters in the CIS continue to face tight budget constraints, even though privatization proceeds partially mitigated the revenue shortfall. Stronger than anticipated growth and the higher oil price allowed for some additional fiscal spending in the Russian Federation in 2017, but in 2018–2019 fiscal expenditure should decline in nominal terms according to budget plans. In Kazakhstan, additional funds were allocated to the budget in 2017, largely for supporting the banking sector through purchases of non-performing assets. In both countries, new fiscal frameworks, lowering the dependency on oil revenues, have been introduced. In Turkmenistan, numerous state subsidies were removed in 2017. The budget will be consolidated following recent spending on large infrastructure projects. A more supportive fiscal stance is expected in Uzbekistan, utilizing the accumulated wealth fund. Among the energy importers, IMF programmes place restrictions on fiscal policy in Ukraine and in a number of other countries. In Belarus, fiscal space is constrained by external debt repayments, although the recent aid from the Russian Federation alleviates some pressure. In Tajikistan, the need to bail out the banking sector places additional burden on the budget. A number of CIS countries were able to place Eurobonds in 2017, including Ukraine, which returned to international capital markets.

South-Eastern Europe: In South-Eastern Europe, fiscal consolidation remains a priority to address public debt levels; Albania and Serbia have undergone tangible fiscal adjustment. In the former Yugoslav Republic of Macedonia and Montenegro, by contrast, significant public spending on infrastructure projects is expected to continue in the near-term.

Africa: Firming commodity prices have eased fiscal pressures in economies throughout the continent. However, in the outlook period, fiscal policy stances are expected to remain tight in most countries, as fiscal consolidation efforts continue. Under the IMF's Extended Fund Facility (EFF) arrangement, Côte d'Ivoire, Egypt, Gabon and Tunisia are projected to implement measures to reduce their budget deficits. Importantly, fiscal revenues could come under stress should the upward trend in commodity prices come to a halt or reverse, as observed during the first half of 2017.

East Asia: Given limited room for further monetary easing and elevated risks in the external outlook, fiscal policy in the East Asian economies is likely to play a more active role in supporting domestic economic activity. In 2017, several countries including China, the Philippines, the Republic of Korea, Taiwan Province of China and Thailand announced a range of fiscal and pro-growth measures, including accelerating infrastructure investment, improving access to finance for small and medium enterprises, and enhancing corporate tax incentives. China is expected to continue pursuing a proactive fiscal policy stance, as ongoing structural reform measures to reduce overcapacity in the heavy industries and to rein in financial risks dampen growth.

South Asia: Fiscal policies are officially in a moderately tight stance in most economies. However, as in previous years, the actual fiscal stances are expected to be more expansionary in most economies, especially in relation to key social areas and public investments. Thus, budget deficits will likely remain high, but manageable, in the outlook period. Some economies, notably India, are implementing tax reforms to strengthen their tax revenues, but further efforts are needed to significantly improve the capacity to implement countercyclical policies across the region.

Western Asia: Despite the recent recovery in oil prices, fiscal authorities in Cooperation Council for the Arab States of the Gulf (GCC) economies are expected to remain cautious against loosening the policy stances. Some GCC economies are expected to introduce the value-added tax by the end of 2018. Fiscal consolidation efforts are projected to continue in Iraq, Jordan, Lebanon and Turkey. The fiscal policy stance is likely to be accommodative in Israel given its strong fiscal position.

Latin America and the Caribbean: The fiscal accounts of many Latin American and Caribbean countries deteriorated significantly over the past few years. South America's commodity exporters, in particular, have seen sharp increases in fiscal deficits that have resulted in higher public debt-to-GDP ratios. In response, many of the region's governments have implemented fiscal adjustment measures. The pace and pattern of these consolidation programmes have differed notably across countries. In general, governments have pursued a gradual approach to minimize the negative impact on economic activity. In some cases, such as in Colombia, Ecuador, Mexico and Peru, capital expenditures were reduced, contributing to a decline in potential output. Despite these adjustment measures, primary balances have remained below debt-stabilizing levels. The ongoing consolidation needs imply that fiscal policy will likely remain relatively tight in the outlook period. However, higher commodity prices and improved growth prospects could boost government revenues and help ease the fiscal pressures.

Exchange rates

The dollar/euro exchange rate is assumed to average 1.129 in 2017, 1.154 in 2018 and 1.151 in 2019 (figure I.A.6).

The yen/dollar exchange rate is assumed to average 111.28 in 2017, 113.37 in 2018 and 114.79 in 2019.

The renminbi/dollar exchange rate is assumed to average 6.74 CNY/dollar in 2017, 6.59 in 2018 and 6.65 in 2018.

Figure I.A.6
Major currency exchange rates: recent trends and assumptions

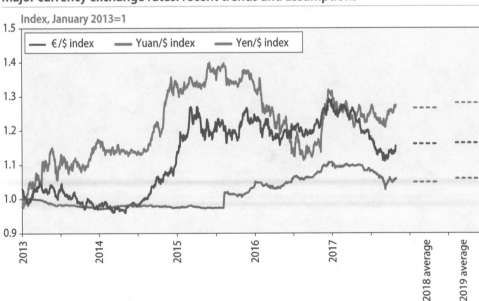

Index, January 2013=1

Sources: IMF Exchange Rate Query Tool and UN/DESA forecast assumptions.

Chapter II
Uncertainties, risks and policy challenges

Uncertainties and risks

While many of the fragilities from the global financial crisis have eased, a number of uncertainties still loom on the horizon, with the potential to derail the recent upturn in global economic growth. Despite the recent uptick, the pace of global growth remains imbalanced and insufficient to make rapid progress towards achieving the ambitious targets set out in the 2030 Agenda for Sustainable Development. If downside risks to the outlook were to materialize, global growth rates could slow, with more setbacks towards achieving the Sustainable Development Goals (SDGs), particularly those of eradicating extreme poverty and creating decent jobs.

Rising trade protectionism and prolonged policy uncertainty

Amid growing discontent with globalization, a rise in trade protectionism could pose a risk to the global trade outlook, with potentially large spillovers to global growth. In the aftermath of the global financial crisis, the use of trade-restrictive measures rose considerably across both developed and developing regions. These measures include new or higher tariffs, quantitative restrictions, and a range of custom procedures. As of October 2016, only 740 of the 2,978 trade-restrictive measures introduced following the global financial crisis by World Trade Organization (WTO) members had been removed (WTO, 2016).

Trade protectionism remains an important risk for global growth

More recently, however, the introduction of trade restrictive measures has slowed. Between October 2016 and May 2017, WTO members introduced an average of 11 new trade-restrictive measures a month, which is the lowest monthly average in almost a decade (WTO, 2017). While this is a positive development, the high existing stock of trade restrictions and the prospects of trade policy adjustments in several major countries could hamper progress towards deeper global trade integration.

In 2017, the United States of America began to renegotiate the terms of the North American Free Trade Agreement (NAFTA) which has governed trade relations between Canada, Mexico and the United States since 1994. It also initiated an investigation into China's policies and practices that may impact exports from the United States. While the review of existing trade agreements could potentially benefit all parties, for example by improving regulatory transparency, and addressing labour and environmental issues, there is a risk that a strong focus on bilateral trade balances may result in rising trade barriers.

Prolonged uncertainty over trade policy could weigh on investor sentiment

Meanwhile in Europe, considerable uncertainty remains over policy frameworks that will govern trade, financial and migration arrangements between the United Kingdom of Great Britain and Northern Ireland and its European Union (EU) and non-EU partners post-March 2019. This prolonged period of high policy uncertainty itself may significantly dampen investor sentiments and real economic activity.

A move towards a more restrictive and fragmented international trade landscape will hinder a stronger and more sustained revival in the global economy, given the deep and mutually reinforcing linkages between trade, investment and productivity growth. A recent study by the Organisation for Economic Co-operation and Development (OECD, 2017c) found that for the OECD countries, a more rapid increase in trade openness was associated with higher total factor productivity (TFP) growth in the medium and long run.

In addition, Didier and Pinat (2017) showed that insertion into the middle of global value chains is associated with stronger growth. A significant rise in trade barriers by a major economy would disrupt intricate cross-border production networks, adversely affecting trade and growth prospects of all countries involved. This could be further exacerbated by retaliatory measures, leading to a prolonged period of weak global trade with spillovers to investment activity and productivity.

A more restrictive global trade environment could disproportionately affect the most vulnerable countries

Importantly, a sharply more restrictive global trade environment could disproportionately damage the most vulnerable countries. Nicita and Seiermann (2016) cautioned that large and increasing non-tariff measures pose specific challenges for the least developing countries (LDCs), including through trade distortions that affect their export competitiveness. The study estimated that eliminating these trade-distorting effects of non-tariff measures would increase LDC exports to G20 countries by about 10 per cent. An alternative measure by Evenett and Fritz (2015) estimates that foreign trade distortions reduced exports of the LDCs by 31 per cent between 2009 and 2013, thus hurting their development prospects.

Renewed stress in global financial markets

Global financial markets have been remarkably buoyant in 2017, as reflected by the increase in stock prices to historical highs, low volatility in both the equity and bond markets, and a rebound in portfolio flows into emerging economies.

Benign financial market conditions mask several lingering risks and vulnerabilities

The increase in investor risk appetite, however, masks several lingering risks and vulnerabilities in the global financial system. Notably, the prolonged period of abundant global liquidity and low borrowing costs has contributed to a further rise in global debt levels and a buildup of financial imbalances. Near-zero interest rates have also eroded the profitability of financial institutions in a few developed countries. Meanwhile, in commodity-exporting countries, persistently subdued global commodity prices continue to weigh on private and public balance sheets.

The decline in global financial market volatility is taking place against a backdrop of elevated policy uncertainty (figure II.1). This disconnect between economic policy risks and investor behaviour suggests a certain degree of underpricing of risk and market complacency.

Moreover, the rise in cyclically-adjusted price-earnings ratios to multi-year highs (figure II.2) raises concerns that stock market valuations may be overstretched. In this current environment, financial markets are susceptible to sudden shifts in investors' perception of market risk, which could in turn trigger a sharp correction in asset prices and an abrupt tightening of global liquidity conditions.

Monetary policy normalization could trigger a sudden adjustment in global financial conditions

The monetary policy normalization process in developed economies has the potential to trigger a sudden adjustment in global financial conditions. Amid improving growth and labour market conditions, the United States Federal Reserve (Fed) announced in September 2017 that alongside the gradual normalization of policy rates, it will begin to reduce the

Figure II.1
Policy uncertainty index vs Cboe volatility index (*VIX*)

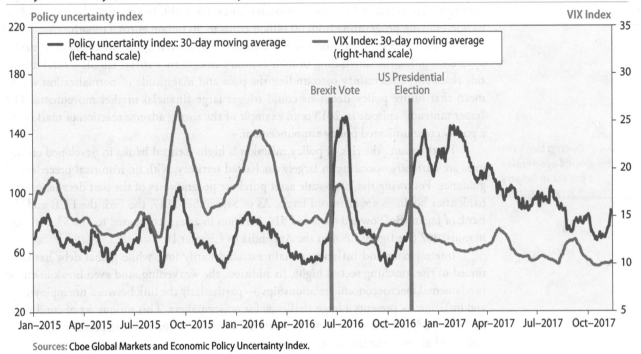

Sources: Cboe Global Markets and Economic Policy Uncertainty Index.

Note: The Cboe Volatility Index (VIX Index) is a measure of market expectations of near-term volatility conveyed by S&P 500 stock index option prices.

Figure II.2
Price-earnings ratio of S&P 500 index vs long-term interest rates

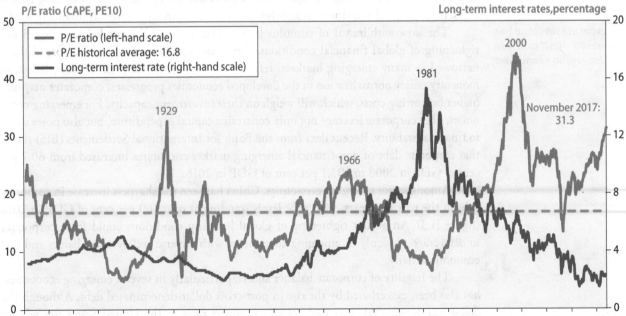

Source: Robert J. Shiller.

Note: CAPE, PE10 refers to the cyclically-adjusted price-earnings ratio applied to the S&P 500 Index. It uses 10 years of real earnings to smooth income fluctuations arising from business cycles. Long-term interest rates refer to 10-year US Treasury rates.

size of its balance sheet. This will be conducted through the introduction of monthly caps on the rolling off of its mortgage-backed and United States Treasury securities holdings. Meanwhile, in October 2017, the European Central Bank (ECB) announced a scale-back of its bond buying programme from 60 billion euros to 30 billion euros a month.

While the rest of the world will benefit from improved aggregate demand in developed economies, the unwinding of their central bank balance sheets entails several downside risks. Any uncertainty surrounding the pace and magnitude of normalization would mean that future policy decisions could trigger large financial market movements. The "taper tantrum" episode in 2013 is an example of the strong adverse reaction of markets to a poorly communicated policy announcement.

Central banks in developed economies operate in largely uncharted territory

Furthermore, the risk of policy mistakes is high. Central banks in developed economies are currently operating in largely uncharted territory, with no historical precedent as guidance. Following the large-scale asset purchase programmes of the past decade, central bank asset holdings are at record levels. As of September 2017, the Fed, the ECB and the Bank of Japan (BoJ) owned a total of $14.2 trillion in assets, compared to just $3.2 trillion in mid-2007 (see figure I.A.4 in the Appendix to Chapter I).

Interest rates and inflation remain extraordinarily low, while global debt has continued to rise, reaching record highs. In addition, the weakening, and even breakdown, of fundamental macroeconomic relationships — particularly the link between unemployment and inflation — presents a huge challenge for policymakers. This unique set of conditions makes any adjustment of financial markets less predictable than during previous recoveries and could amplify the impact of policy errors.

A key area of uncertainty is the extent to which the unwinding of central bank balance sheets in developed countries will induce portfolio rebalancing in the private sector, thus pushing up term and risk premia. A sudden increase in risk premia would cause significant adjustments to the value of risky assets, which could, in turn, lead to a sharp reversal of portfolio flows to emerging economies. This could disrupt domestic financing conditions, increasing risks to financial stability in countries with large external financing needs.

Corporate leverage has increased significantly in emerging economies

The slow withdrawal of stimulus by the Fed has thus far not led to a significant tightening of global financial conditions. Financing costs remain low, and spreads have narrowed in many emerging markets, reflecting a decline in risk premia. Nonetheless, as monetary policy normalization in the developed economies progresses, corporates may face higher borrowing costs, which will weigh on their investment capacity. For emerging economies, high corporate leverage not only constrains capital expenditure, but also poses a risk to financial stability. Recent data from the Bank for International Settlements (BIS) shows that corporate debt of non-financial emerging market corporates increased from 60.7 per cent of GDP in 2008 to 102.1 per cent of GDP in 2016.

Among major emerging economies, China has seen the sharpest increase in corporate debt in the past few years, with debt levels standing at over 160 per cent of GDP in 2016 (figure II.3). An abrupt tightening of global liquidity conditions could force corporates to deleverage suddenly in emerging economies, with adverse spillovers on banks and real economic activity.

The fragility of corporate balance sheets, particularly in several emerging economies, has also been exacerbated by the rise in post-crisis dollar-denominated debt. Although the dollar has depreciated since early 2017, as interest rates in the United States rise relative to those in other major developed economies, the dollar is likely to gain in strength. This would raise debt servicing costs and currency mismatch risks for both corporates and governments that have a high dollar-denominated debt burden. For many emerging econo-

Figure II.3
Outstanding credit to non-financial corporates in selected emerging economies

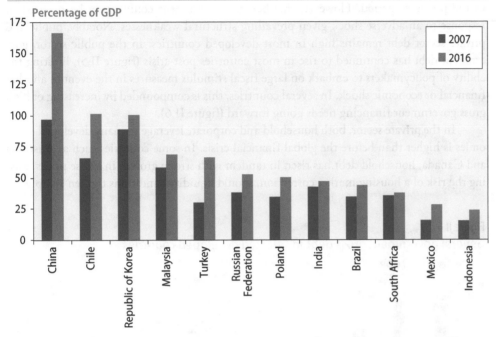

Source: Bank for International
Settlements, Total Credit
Statistics.

mies, the broad-based strengthening of the dollar from 2014 to 2016 contributed to a rise in gross external debt as a share of GDP (figure II.4). A further strengthening of the dollar may increase the risk of corporate distress and raise fiscal sustainability concerns.

International commodity price movements also pose a risk to global financial stability. A renewed downturn in commodity prices would exacerbate fiscal and corporate sector vulnerabilities in many commodity-dependent economies, particularly in Africa, Latin America and Western Asia.

Figure II.4
Gross external debt in selected emerging economies

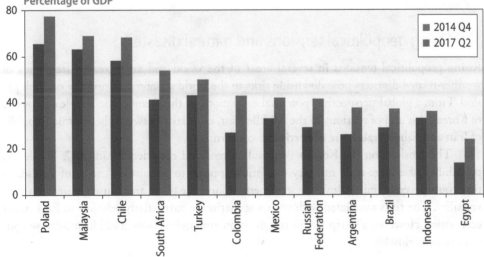

Sources: UN/DESA, based on
data from World Bank Quarterly
External Debt Statistics Database
and IMF (2017b).

Public and private debt levels remain elevated in many developed economies

Among developed economies, many financial vulnerability indicators, including credit-to-GDP gaps, debt service ratios and non-performing loans have declined compared to the pre-crisis period. However, this benign environment could easily be reversed in response to an adverse shock given prevailing structural weaknesses. Notably, public and private sector debt remains high in most developed countries. In the public sector, government debt has continued to rise in most countries post-crisis (figure II.5), limiting the ability of policymakers to embark on large fiscal stimulus measures in the event of another financial or economic shock. In several countries, this is compounded by increasing or high gross government financing needs going forward (figure II.6).

In the private sector, both household and corporate leverage in many developed economies is higher than before the global financial crisis. In some countries such as Australia and Canada, household debt has risen in tandem with strong growth in house prices, raising the risk of a housing market correction, should liquidity conditions tighten sharply.

Figure II.5
General government gross debt in selected developed countries

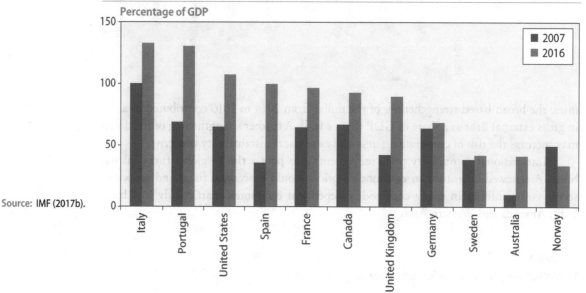

Source: IMF (2017b).

Rising geopolitical tensions and natural disasters

Increased tensions on the Korean Peninsula and in the Middle East pose risks to global growth

Rising geopolitical tensions in several areas of the world and an increased frequency of weather-related disasters pose downside risks to the world economy during the outlook period. From a global perspective, potential escalations of the Democratic People's Republic of Korea crisis and of tensions in the Middle East, especially between the Islamic Republic of Iran and Saudi Arabia, are of particular concern.

The tensions on the Korean Peninsula intensified considerably in 2017. While the probability of a large-scale military escalation appears to remain low, fears of an escalation could severely impact investor sentiment around the globe and cause greater financial volatility. The risks associated with such a scenario are particularly relevant to East Asian economies. However, a sharp rise in risk aversion among investors could have adverse consequences worldwide.

Figure II.6
Gross government financing needs of selected developed economies

Percentage of GDP

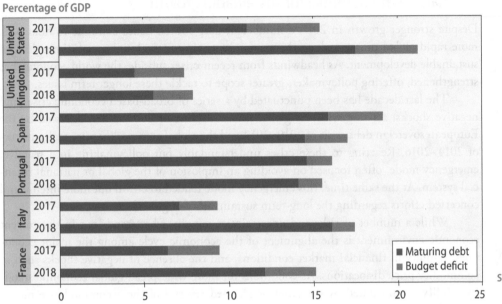

Source: IMF (2017d).

An escalation of tensions in the Middle East could disrupt the region's energy exports, potentially triggering a spike in the oil price. While the relationship between oil prices and economic growth in oil-importing countries has weakened significantly over the past few decades, a sharp increase in the oil price would likely be associated with lower-than-projected global growth in 2018 and 2019.

In many other parts of the world, the continuation of violent conflict or political instability prevents meaningful progress towards sustainable development. The needed humanitarian assistance associated with violent conflict has more than doubled in the past five years, with conflict situations in many countries and regions either worsening or unchanged in 2017. In cases such as the Democratic Republic of the Congo, Nigeria, Somalia, South Sudan and Yemen, armed conflict — often in combination with famine — has resulted in the most severe humanitarian crises in decades, including large-scale displacement. Similarly, the extended crises in parts of North Africa and Western Asia continue to prevent any meaningful prospects for growth or long-term development in impacted areas, with significant spillovers to neighbouring countries. Without significant progress toward conflict prevention and resolution, prospects for economic development remain limited.

In many countries, violent conflict or political instability impede progress towards sustainable development

Meanwhile, weather-related shocks continue to intensify, as shown by the frequency of statistically unlikely events in the last few years alone, highlighting the urgent need to build resilience against climate change and contain the pace of environmental degradation. The number, frequency, scale, and geographic span of weather extremes continue to increase, and these factors are shaping and driving macroeconomic prospects in many countries. Climate change impacts are projected to worsen in coming decades, with most of the losses and damage falling on developing countries, in particular small island developing States (SIDS) and LDCs. Addition policy challenges faced by SIDS are discussed in Box II.1.

Higher frequency of weather-related disasters poses risks, especially for many developing countries

Policy challenges

Raising the potential for sustainable growth

Despite stronger growth in 2017, a number of deep-rooted issues continue to hold back more rapid global progress along the economic, environmental and social dimensions of sustainable development. As headwinds from recent crises subside, the world economy has strengthened, offering policymakers greater scope to tackle these longer-term issues.

The last decade has been punctuated by a series of broad-based economic crises and negative shocks, starting with the global financial crisis of 2008–2009, followed by the European sovereign debt crisis of 2010–2012 and the global commodity price realignments of 2014–2016. Reacting to these crises understandably put policymaking in a reactive, emergency mode, often focused on avoiding an implosion of the global or national financial system. At the same time, this emergency mode tended to crowd out more intense and concerted efforts regarding the long-term sustainability of growth.

While a number of risks and uncertainties remain, what stands out in the current economic environment is the alignment of the economic cycle among the major economies, stability in financial market conditions, and the absence of negative shocks such as commodity price dislocations. As conditions for more widespread global economic stability solidify, as illustrated by the onset or planned reversal of the accommodative monetary policy stances in major developed economies, there is less need to focus policy efforts on stabilizing short-term growth and mitigating the effects of economic crises. Coupled with improving investment conditions, this creates greater scope to reorient policy towards longer-term issues, such as strengthening the environmental quality of economic growth, making economic growth more inclusive, and tackling institutional deficiencies that hold back development.

Numerous longer-term challenges persist across the world that continue to hold back more rapid progress towards sustainable development. Weak governance structures, inadequate basic infrastructure, high levels of exposure to weather-related shocks and natural disasters, as well as challenges related to security and political uncertainty are prevalent. Declining or stagnant wage growth, and high levels of unemployment, vulnerable employment and working poor afflict numerous economies across the globe.

The quality of economic growth continues to be undermined by rising inequality, unremittent environmental degradation, and persistently high levels of poverty in some regions. As a consequence, policymakers should use the current macroeconomic backdrop in order to address four key areas: (1) increasing economic diversification; (2) creating a supportive environment for long-term investment in key areas; (3) reducing inequality; and (4) improving the quality of institutions.

Among these endemic issues, economic diversification must be developed in countries that remain heavily dependent on a few basic commodities. Commodity exporters remain vulnerable to steep boom and bust investment cycles, as volatile prices pass through to macroeconomic conditions. This is clearly evidenced by the heavy economic costs faced by many commodity exporters as a result of recent commodity price realignments.

Without diversification, countries are much more vulnerable to external shocks, seriously complicating macroeconomic policy management and impacting their capacity for stable growth. Expanding less volatile sectors of the economy should be accompanied by fiscal reforms to restructure and broaden the revenue base in order to reduce fiscal dependency on short-term commodity revenue. The planned introduction of a value-added tax in

Cooperation Council for the Arab States of the Gulf (GCC) countries is a recent example of such fiscal reforms (see Box III.4).

Investments in human capital, creating more transparent governance and institutions, closing infrastructure gaps and investing in environmental resilience can also help support economic diversification, while spurring the creation and diffusion of technology and support social progress.

Better investment conditions have led to a modest revival in productive investment in some large economies. However, this revival is relative to a very low starting point, following a prolonged episode of lacklustre global investment, that has allowed the capital stock in developed economies to stagnate. This legacy of weak investment and low productivity growth since the global financial crisis continues to weigh on medium-term growth prospects. Reinvigorating global productivity and raising the longer-term capacity for sustainable growth remain key global policy challenges, in order to accelerate progress towards the SDGs.

Targeted investments are needed for higher productivity and potential growth

Investment patterns play a crucial role in stimulating productivity growth through a myriad of channels. Investing in research and development spurs innovation activities and the creation of knowledge, which drives advancements along the technology frontier.

Meanwhile, investment in machinery and equipment plays a crucial role in improving firms' capacity to adopt existing technology and processes, promoting growth through knowledge diffusion. Investment in infrastructure not only provides the basic enabling conditions for economic growth and development, but also for the creation and strengthening of competitive advantages and promotion of product specialization. Crucially, investment in human capital and expanding healthcare access support the productive capacities of the labour force, including their capacity to exploit new and existing technologies.

In this regard, concrete policy measures include investment in the quality of education, broadening access to education and upskilling or reskilling of the workforce. Policies can also be designed to create financial incentives, via tax breaks and subsidies, to encourage private sector firms to invest in innovation and infrastructure.

Promoting private sector involvement in areas that raise the long-term sustainable growth path is an essential element of garnering the financial resources to support sustainable development. A range of measures can support this process, including public investments that crowd-in private investments and public-private partnerships, better institutional capacities in the public sector, regulatory changes and structural reforms.

It is also important, as a prerequisite for achieving the 2030 Agenda for Sustainable Development, to ensure that investment is channeled towards longer-term sustainable and resilient infrastructure. With recent economic growth comes greater risks to environmental sustainability. At a time when many developing countries continue to suffer from severe shortages of energy supply, there is enormous potential to lay the basis of environmentally sustainable growth in the future through smart policies and investments today. The same can be said for investment in other basic infrastructure, especially where developing countries can benefit from the chance to leapfrog technologies.

Investing in resilient and sustainable infrastructure is crucial to adapt to climate change

High impact weather-related shocks and climate extremes are rising. Disruption to water, electricity, transportation and communication networks in the wake of disaster events severely impacts communities' well-being, security, social welfare and health. Diffusion of best-practice network design, predictive tools, outage identification and crisis response must be ramped up for disaster preparedness. South-South cooperation in the transmission of clean and resilient technologies should be fully explored, as the technology and skills of

Box II.1
**Foreign direct investment in the small island developing States:
Trends and policies**

Growth in the small island developing States (SIDS) is projected to rise modestly from an estimated 2.6 per cent in 2017 to 2.7 per cent in 2018 and 2.8 per cent in 2019. These growth projections reflect a relatively subdued outlook for the SIDS, particularly when compared to the LDCs, which as a group are expected to grow by 5.4 per cent in 2018 and 5.5 per cent in 2019.

For commodity exporting SIDS, revenues will be supported by the gradual recovery in global commodity prices. In the aftermath of devastating natural disasters, reconstruction efforts will provide a temporary boost to growth in a few Caribbean and Pacific SIDS. In addition, many SIDS are expected to benefit from an improvement in remittance inflows and tourism earnings,[a] amid the continued expansion in global income. The short-term growth outlook for the SIDS, however, remains highly susceptible to natural catastrophes and weather-related shocks. For the SIDS with poorly diversified economic structures, growth remains vulnerable to large swings in commodity prices.

From a medium-term perspective, the SIDS continue to face significant challenges in their access to development finance. A worrying trend for the SIDS is the recent decline in foreign direct investment (FDI). In 2016, aggregate FDI flows into the SIDS fell for the second consecutive year, declining by 6.2 per cent to $3.5 billion (UNCTAD, 2017c). For many SIDS, FDI represents an important external source of development finance, accounting for more than 10 per cent of GDP annually.

Given rich marine biodiversity, FDI flows into the SIDS over the years have been largely concentrated in the tourism and fishing sectors. Several countries have also experienced strong FDI in the mining sector, thanks to large endowments of commodities such as oil and gas, gold and bauxite. The provision of various incentives for foreign companies to establish financial and trading operations have also boosted FDI in business process and offshore financial services (UNCTAD, 2014). More recently, FDI flows into many Caribbean and Pacific SIDS have increasingly been channeled into the telecommunications sector.

The SIDS face considerable structural headwinds in attracting stronger FDI flows. The small market size of these economies prevents gains from economies of scale, leading to higher production costs. This is compounded by remoteness from international markets, inadequate infrastructure and high transport costs.

Foreign investors also face risks arising from the high exposure of SIDS to global environmental challenges, including to a large range of effects of climate change and potentially more frequent and intense natural disasters.[b] Hurley (2015) highlights that climate adaptation costs are among the highest in the world for the SIDS.

These long-term factors have been exacerbated by the generally weak economic performance of SIDS since the global financial crisis. Slow GDP growth and large fiscal imbalances have created a macroeconomic environment that is not conducive to FDI (De Groot and Ludeña, 2014).

(continued)

a See http://media.unwto.org/
press-release/2017-09-07/
international-tourism-
strongest-half-year-results-2010

b For more information,
please see https://
sustainabledevelopment.
un.org/topics/sids

multinational firms from other developing countries are often a closer match. Developed and developing countries alike must accelerate the transition to sustainable energy.

Closing crucial infrastructure gaps will not only bring wider macroeconomic productivity gains, it will also advance the social dimensions of sustainable development and poverty alleviation. In order to eradicate extreme poverty by 2030, an environment must be fostered that will both accelerate medium-term growth prospects and tackle poverty through policies that address inequalities in income and opportunity. Stemming and redressing the rise in inequality in both developed and developing countries is crucial for ensuring balanced and sustainable growth going forward. This requires a combination of short-term policies to raise living standards among the most deprived, and longer-term policies that address inequalities in opportunity.

In the short term, introducing a more progressive system of taxation and benefits to strengthen the redistributive role of fiscal policy and social safety nets will not only spur

**Stemming and
redressing the rise in
inequality is crucial for
ensuring balanced and
sustainable growth**

Box II.1 (*continued*)

In several Caribbean SIDS, public debt levels exceed 100 per cent of GDP, implying a need for fiscal consolidation and raising financial distress risks. In fact, over the past decade, many SIDS had to restructure their debt in an effort to reach more manageable levels. Persistently weak fiscal positions have also limited governments' ability to provide much-needed infrastructure. These conditions have resulted in a low level of profitability of FDI in SIDS, compared to other regions.

In efforts to attract more FDI flows, several SIDS have introduced a range of policy strategies, including:

Policies to improve the overall business climate	• Reducing bureaucratic hurdles • Guaranteeing property rights
Policies to reduce challenges specific to foreign investors	• Liberalizing migration policies for foreign workers • Guaranteeing non-discrimination in (government) procurement between domestic and foreign suppliers • Concluding Double Taxation Agreements (DTAs) with other countries
Setting up investment promotion agencies	• Opening foreign trade offices aimed at providing information to potential investors
Financial incentives	• Tax holidays or exemptions from import and export duties • Grants or subsidies for the initiation or continuation of certain investments (costly option)

Policymakers need to bear in mind that what matters for sustainable development is not only the quantity of FDI inflows, but also the quality. Some FDI activities create very limited positive spillovers in national economies. Hence, strategies should be tailored towards attracting quality FDI in line with long-term national development plans. This includes FDI that promotes greater economic diversification, supports domestic industries through backward linkages and promotes the adoption and diffusion of technology. Importantly, policymakers need to ensure that FDI activities do not cause environmental damage, which would further exacerbate the structural weaknesses of the SIDS.

While important, FDI represents only one area of financing for development. In fact, the past decade has seen changes in the financing landscape, with new actors and financing sources gaining importance, including donors that are not members of the Development Assistance Committee of the OECD.

These include non-government organizations, climate funds, innovative financing mechanisms and South-South cooperation initiatives. Private portfolio capital has also become a more important source of financing, as well as workers' remittances and voluntary private contributions. These changes have broadened the options for financing activities in the context of the 2030 Agenda. Nevertheless, a major challenge is to coordinate these new sources of financing and mechanisms within a coherent financing for a development framework at the national level.

Authors: Anya Thomas (UN/DESA/DSD), Poh Lynn Ng (UN/DESA/DPAD) and Ingo Pitterle (UN/DESA/DPAD)

domestic demand, but also contribute to more sustainable and inclusive growth. Active labour market policies can broaden access to the labour market, especially for women. Addressing urgent cases of need to protect the most vulnerable, especially in conflict-affected areas, remains a global priority.

Over the longer term, investment in tackling inequalities in opportunity will not only improve the quality of growth but increase its longer-term potential. This includes, for example, investment in early childhood development, building and ensuring universal access to functioning healthcare systems, broadening access to education, and investment in rural roads and electrification. Creating opportunities to retrain and acquire new skills, as well as programmes to help match available jobs to available skills, are crucial complements to social safety nets, aiding displaced workers and young people to integrate into the job market. These programmes can help tackle the widespread global challenge of youth unemployment. In addition, they can provide security against job displacement related to ongoing and future structural change in production that may be associated with deeper trade integration or technological change.

Strengthening governance and improving the quality of institutions must move to the forefront of policy objectives

Weak governance and political instability remain fundamental obstacles to achieving the 2030 Agenda for Sustainable Development. Strengthening legal institutions and administrative capacities, coupled with progressive reform in the regulatory environment and the business environment, can increase transparency in administrative processes, support effective protection of property rights and improve capacities for redistributive fiscal policy.

Addressing some of these barriers is essential to ensure that available finance is channeled towards productive investment. It may also strengthen business confidence, help reduce country risk perceptions, and support inflows of capital in some countries. Tackling the institutional deficiencies that underpin many of these obstacles must move to the forefront of policy objectives.

Reorienting policy to deal with these challenges and maximizing co-benefits between development will bring both short-term and long-term benefits. Current investment in education, expanding access to healthcare, building resilience to climate change, improving the quality of institutions, and building financial and digital inclusion will support economic growth and job creation in the short-term, accelerate progress along the social and environmental sustainable development dimensions, and raise the longer-term potential for sustainable growth.

Making the international financial system work for sustainable development

A new framework for sustainable finance is needed to channel available finance towards socially beneficial investment

A well-designed global financial architecture is at the heart of a dynamic global economy promoting sustainable development. A sound financial system is essential to ensure smooth international financial flows from the developed to the developing economies, and to channel available financial resources towards socially beneficial investment. Despite the current buoyant financial market sentiment, there are lingering risks and vulnerabilities that could derail global growth and hamper progress towards the SDGs. In addition, more resources should be mobilized to finance the large investment needs required to achieve the SDGs.

In this context, policymakers face three interconnected sets of challenges. *First*, they must tackle the short-term financial risks outlined above. Most importantly, this means steering the world economy through monetary policy normalization in developed economies and a potential tightening of liquidity conditions.

Second, policymakers must accelerate efforts to make the international financial system more stable and resilient to crisis. Much has been done in this regard since the global financial crisis, but as significant flaws in regulatory and supervisory frameworks persist, the international financial system is still prone to boom and bust cycles, which can entail large economic and social costs in the short- and medium-term. *Third*, they must redouble their efforts to realign the global financial architecture with the 2030 Agenda for Sustainable Development and the Addis Ababa Action Agenda (AAAA), in order to support investment in areas that will enhance productivity gains and progress towards social and environmental goals. This requires creating a renewed framework for sustainable finance and shifting away from short-term profit towards long-term value creation (Schoenmaker, 2017).

Developing countries are better prepared to navigate sudden changes in global financial conditions than in previous decades

Managing the ongoing monetary policy normalization in the United States — and then in Europe — encompasses significant challenges not only for the authorities that decide on the pace and timing of decisions, but also for policymakers in developing countries that could face abrupt shifts in financing conditions.

In particular, the Fed, the ECB and the Bank of England will need to strike a delicate balance in raising policy rates and unwinding their massive balance sheets. On the one hand, they must support real economic activity and maintain price stability. On the other hand, they need to prevent financial market turbulence and avoid a further buildup of the financial vulnerabilities that have accumulated over the prolonged period of ultra-loose monetary conditions. Finding the adequate balance will require accurate assessments of underlying economic and financial conditions and trajectories, appropriate decisions on the timing and pace of monetary normalization, and well-communicated plans that anchor market expectations.

Meanwhile, developing countries, especially emerging economies with large external financing needs, should prepare themselves for a period with potentially lower and more volatile capital flows, tighter liquidity conditions and a more constrained monetary policy space. The majority of large emerging economies appear to be in a better position to navigate turbulent global financial conditions than in previous decades. This is due to greater exchange rate flexibility, relatively high levels of international reserves and, in some cases, improved macroeconomic management. While appropriate measures depend on country-specific conditions, policymakers should generally try to contain corporate leverage, which will help enhance resilience to external shocks.

The past decade witnessed far-reaching reforms to tackle legacies from the global financial crisis and to make the international financial system more stable. Efforts have been centred on regulatory and supervisory measures to strengthen the banking sector, particularly the global systemically important banks (G-SIBs), which are located in China, Europe, Japan and the United States. The main objectives were to strengthen the balance sheets of large banks by improving their capital, liquidity and risk management positions, and to address the "too-big-to-fail" problem by establishing viable resolution frameworks for internationally operating banks.

The issue of "too-big-to-fail" remains largely unresolved

Economists largely agree that balance sheets of large, internationally operating banks have strengthened since the global financial crisis. For instance, capital ratios and liquidity indicators in G-SIBs have risen considerably (figure II.7), while capital shortfall has almost disappeared (BIS, 2017b). In addition, banks have made progress in addressing overhanging issues of the crisis, especially in writing off bad loans. Despite visible improvements, it is unclear how vulnerable balance sheets of large globally operating banks are to a combination of higher interest rates and significantly lower asset prices. Progress has also been uneven, with several European banks still struggling to reduce the amount of non-performing loans. With respect to the "too-big-to-fail" problem, the progress has been slow, underscoring the need to further strengthen national resolution mechanisms, while also developing cross-border resolution plans.

Financial risks seem to have risen in non-banking institutions, which are usually subject to less restrictive regulations

Against this backdrop, financial stability risks appear to have shifted from the banking sector to non-banking institutions, which often do not face the same regulatory restrictions as banks. For instance, in developed economies some concerns have been raised regarding the financial strength of life insurers (IMF, 2017a). At the same time, the non-bank financial sector has grown rapidly in several emerging economies in recent years. According to some estimates, shadow banking represents up to 35–40 per cent of the financial sector in some countries of East Asia (Ghosh et al., 2012). A vital role in promoting financial stability and containing these risks is played by macroprudential policies. Macroprudential policy measures can reduce excessive credit growth and curb leverage, as well as limit

Figure II.7
Global systemically important banks: capitalization and liquidity indicators

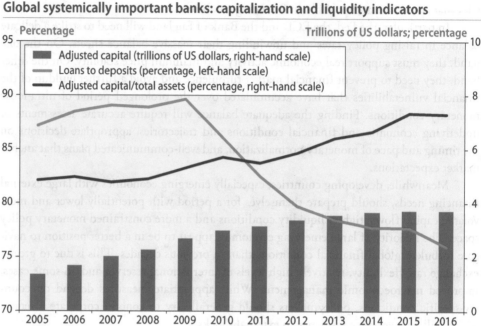

Source: UN/DESA, based on data
from IMF (2017a).

liquidity risks and address structural vulnerabilities in the financial sector. This is especially important in countries with greater financial openness, larger financial markets and more complex financial instruments. Looking ahead, it is important to coordinate macroprudential policies with monetary policies, so that the objectives of price and financial stability reinforce each other, strengthening a more sustainable growth trajectory (Box II.2).

Financial sector incentives need to shift from the current focus on short-term profit towards a target of long-term value creation

Aligning the international financial sector's framework and incentives towards long-term investments and sustainable development is a key issue moving forward. The financing needs for SDGs are enormous. The current international financial system does not allocate enough financial resources towards long-term sustainable development, including significant gaps in areas such as infrastructure, healthcare, education and renewable energies. Therefore, achieving the SDGs requires an increase in the mobilization of long-term public and private resources and a new set of policies and regulatory frameworks that incentivize investment patterns that are consistent with sustainable development. Crucially, this includes a shift from the current focus on short-term profits towards a target of long-term value creation.

Currently, there are several practices that reinforce a short-term approach, including quarterly financial reporting by firms, monthly or quarterly benchmarks for performance, fee structures with asymmetric returns, and mark-to-market accounting. Institutional investors have been widely identified as a potential source of financing for sustainable development, because of the size of assets under their management and their long-term liability structure. For example, infrastructure investment could be particularly attractive to these investors because of its low-risk and stable real return profile.

Yet, a shift of even a minor fraction of these vast resources towards sustainable development is enormously challenging. Promoting this requires designing and enacting a new set of policies and capital market regulations along the investment chain that are aligned with long-term performance indicators.

Box II.2
The initial and learning stages of macroprudential policies in emerging economies

A clear lesson for policymakers that arose from the global financial crisis is that price stability does not ensure macroeconomic stability, contrary to the neoliberal views that have been advocated in previous decades. Thus, in the wake of the crisis, there have been stronger calls for the use of stricter financial regulations to contain macro-financial risks. It also became apparent that credit and asset price boom-and-bust cycles can entail large economic and social costs in the short and medium-term.

Given the high degree of interconnectedness between financial institutions, a shock could spread rapidly across the entire system. Hence, there has been a growing consensus that financial regulation should move from a "micro" approach based on individual institutions towards a "macro" framework, with an emphasis on systemic risks of the financial system as a whole. In fact, the tendency of financial markets to be highly procyclical and to go through recurring cycles of *"manias, panics and crashes,"* as described by Kindleberger (1978), coupled with macro-financial feedback mechanisms, increases its exposure and vulnerability. In this regard, the implementation of macroprudential policies has visibly risen in emerging economies in recent years, with the objectives of strengthening financial sector resilience and curbing the build-up of imbalances. While some policy tools in this area are certainly not new, the macroprudential framework is clearly a recent phenomenon.

Figure II.2.1 provides an overview of the various financial risks that policymakers face, the macroprudential instruments that are available and their objectives. Importantly, evaluating financial vulnerabilities and imbalances requires consideration of the time dimension (credit growth, risks in corporate

Figure II.2.1
A panorama of macroprudential policies in emerging economies

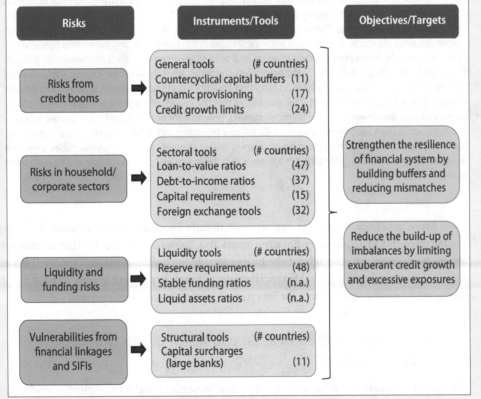

Source: UN/DESA based on Arregui (2016) and Vazquez (2016).

Note: SIFIs: systemically important financial institutions.

(continued)

Box II.2 (*continued*)

and household sectors) as well as structural characteristics (interlinkages between financial institutions). In brief, operationalizing macroprudential policies requires translating systemic risk assessments into policy measures. This entails the design, implementation, calibration and activation/deactivation mechanisms, evaluation of potential leakages, and evaluation of impact (IMF/FSB/BIS, 2016). Recent examples of macroprudential measures in emerging economies are the introduction of loan-to-value ratio targets in Hong Kong SAR, sectoral capital requirements in Brazil and Poland, dynamic provisioning in Colombia and Peru, caps to foreign exchange loans in the Republic of Korea, liquidity ratio and countercyclical reserve requirements in Colombia, and reserve requirements in Brazil, Peru and Turkey, among others.

Assessing the recent experiences of the emerging economies in their usage of macroprudential tools is complex. However, it is possible to derive a few stylized facts. *First*, a "one-size-fits-all" approach is not suitable in the case of macroprudential policies. Country-specific circumstances, including diverse institutional frameworks, affect not only the capacity to implement certain policy measures, but also their effectiveness. *Second*, emerging economies are currently undergoing a learning path, characterized by experimentation and trial and error processes, regarding not only the policy tools but their institutional frameworks. In fact, there is a wide range of macroprudential instruments, and in many cases the optimal arrangements entail the use of several tools. In addition, macroprudential measures need to be calibrated through activation and deactivation rules that should be refined over time. *Third*, a better understanding needs to be developed regarding the interaction and the complementarities of macroprudential policies with other policies. This is particularly the case with monetary policy, as the feedback mechanisms between the objectives of price stability and financial stability encompass several challenges. It is also the case with capital controls, where the objectives of managing the size and composition of capital flows sometimes overlap with macroprudential policies. Interestingly, capital controls have re-emerged as a policy tool since the global financial crisis, as emerging economies have gained more independence to implement them, while new and less dogmatic views regarding their effectiveness have arisen in academia and international organizations.

Against this backdrop, the evidence concerning the effectiveness of macroprudential policies is still in its infancy, and remains largely aggregate and preliminary. Thus, it is not possible to derive strong policy conclusions nor to extrapolate successful policy measures. Yet, incipient evidence suggests that macroprudential measures do play a role in containing procyclical pressures and promoting financial stability. For example, restrictions on loan-to-value and debt-to-income ratios are associated with a reduction in credit growth, most notably in the emerging economies' household sector (Cerruti, Claessens and Laeven, 2015). Also, macroprudential tools targeting liquidity risks tend to restrain leverage and growth in house prices. In addition, some studies emphasize that the impact of these measures is contingent on aspects such as the development of financial markets, potential for domestic and cross-border leakages and the coordination with monetary policy (Galati and Moessner, 2017). New questions are also arising. For example, a crucial issue for emerging economies is how to assess financial vulnerabilities when the financial sector is deepening. Overall, it is apparent that this is a crucial policy area and will be even more so in the decades to come.

Author: Sebastian Vergara
(UN/DESA/DPAD)

More generally, long-term investments require investors' time horizons to be protracted enough to finance long-duration assets and, importantly, require that investors are able to hold a position throughout the business cycle, including downside events. This was a critical issue during the global financial crisis, as many firms were unable to hold illiquid assets, with severe consequences for investment in sustainable development.

Using trade integration as an engine for global growth and development

Concerted international efforts are needed to advance a global SDG-oriented trade agenda that increases the development impact of trade. The trade integration process of the last decades has created vast opportunities for countries to enhance and implement their economic and social development strategies. Still, the uneven distribution of the benefits of trade integration — both between and within countries — threatens to undermine the development potential of trade, to further increase inequalities and to hamper the achievement of the SDGs.

These challenges call for a proactive, holistic and coherent policy mix that recognizes the evolving nature of trade in response to technology, connectivity and new business models, promotes positive structural transformation, and facilitates competitiveness, diversification and upgrading of production structures.

Mainstreaming trade policies into development frameworks can help promote poverty reduction, industrialization, job creation, food security, gender equality and environmental sustainability. In addition, the risks, costs and trade-offs associated with trade liberalization measures, including constraints on national regulatory autonomy and policy space, must be addressed. This requires adjusting the content, pace and sequencing of liberalization so that regulatory and institutional frameworks retain the possibility to respond to new challenges.

The challenges associated with trade integration also call for promoting skills development, expanding social safety nets and introducing adjustment mechanisms, including by allowing countries to adequately revise commitments (UNCTAD, 2017d). In this context, support to developing countries, and in particular the LDCs, remains critical, for example through inclusive rules of origin, preferential treatment, capacity building initiatives and aid for trade.[1]

A universal, rules-based, open, transparent, non-discriminatory and equitable multilateral trading system is a key element of a global partnership for sustainable development. United Nations Member States have repeatedly committed to promoting the multilateral trading system, in line with the internationally-agreed development goals, as provided by target 17.10 of the SDGs[2] (Box II.3).

Rising uncertainty over the direction of trade policies has reinforced the importance of revitalizing the multilateral trading system as a global public good and a cornerstone of the global governance framework. Multilateral rules and disciplines are the best guarantee against protectionism, and fundamental to transparency, predictability and stability of international trade. These rules and disciplines are underpinned by the WTO's dispute settlement mechanism, which ensures the smooth flow of panel proceedings and remedial actions in case of non-compliance. The importance of the multilateral trading system is also supported by the fact that membership has become almost universal. Since 1995, 36 countries — including 9 LDCs — have acceded to the WTO, bringing the total number of members to 164. Against this backdrop, a positive outcome at the Eleventh WTO Ministerial Conference in December 2017 in Buenos Aires, Argentina (MC11) is critically important as it would enhance the relevance and effectiveness of the multilateral trading system.

Fully delivering on existing mandates is critical, including those emerging from the Tenth WTO Ministerial Conference in December 2015, Nairobi, Kenya (MC10) to redress existing imbalances and uphold the development dimension. This is, however, complicated by the fact that the outcome of MC10 revealed a lack of consensus on the mandate. While many WTO members reaffirmed the Doha Development Agenda, others did not,

Linking trade to development requires a coherent policy mix, adequate liberalization and support to developing countries

The multilateral trading system is a global public good and needs to remain a cornerstone of the global governance framework

The upcoming Eleventh WTO Ministerial Conference aims to address a range of key issues

---

1   UNCTAD's toolkit on trade and services policy supports developing countries' engagement in the trading system, including in preparation for the Eleventh WTO Ministerial Conference and its follow-up.

2   For instance, see General Assembly resolution 70/187 of 22 December 2015 and 71/214 of 21 December 2016. See also United Nations, General Assembly (2015; 2016).

saying that new approaches are necessary to achieve meaningful outcomes in multilateral negotiations.

Several countries held the view that the lack of consensus opened the door to unbundle a single undertaking and to address new issues. Many others argued that, without a consensus decision to the contrary, the Doha Round remained in force. This disagreement is also reflected in the implementation of some MC10 decisions, which remain issues in the run-up to MC11.

Priority issues of MC11 include the following: (a) elements of domestic support in agriculture, based on updated notifications; (b) a mandated permanent solution for public stockholding for food security purposes; (c) the multilateral process on fishery subsidies; (d) domestic regulations in services including trade facilitation; (e) special and differential treatment and issues of particular relevance for the LDCs, including cotton, and; (f) a set of new issues such as e-commerce, micro, small and medium enterprises and investment facilitation. Market access in agriculture and services, non-agricultural market access (NAMA), rules other than fishery subsidies, and other key issues to the Doha Round are put on hold in the absence of major progress.

The domestic support pillar is central for MC11 in the face of persistent agricultural subsidization by major economies

Important subsidization in agriculture by major economies persists, especially in the EU and the United States, but also in China and India. Major economies have shifted most of their support to the so-called green box, which is meant to be minimally or non-trade-distorting. However, given the scale of the support, there are de facto major trade-distorting effects.

The absence of meaningful agricultural policy reform since the beginning of the Doha Round and the persistence of distorted markets, largely seen as penalizing most developing countries, makes the domestic support pillar a central issue for MC11. This includes proposals to give greater scrutiny to, and possibly capping, the amount of trade-distorting support.

Of particular relevance is the case of cotton. The so-called Cotton-4 countries (Benin, Burkina Faso, Chad and Mali) have proposed a progressive phasing out of all forms of trade-distorting domestic support for cotton and its by-products. The MC11 will also aim for a package of commitments prohibiting subsidies that contribute to overfishing and over-capacity, and addressing illegal, unregulated and unreported fishing as a means to support the implementation of target 14.6 of the SDGs. Developing countries relying on fish for food security, livelihood and export earnings have emphasized the need to retain flexibility.

Food security is also at the centre of the MC11 agenda

There is also growing attention among major developed and several developing countries given to obtaining a permanent solution for trade-related measures that are taken for food security purposes, particularly for public stockholding programmes. An interim peace clause was agreed at the Ninth WTO Ministerial Conference and reaffirmed at MC10, protecting developing countries that buy stocks of food from their farmers from legal challenges. The Special Safeguard Mechanism (SSM) is also relevant for food security measures subject to negotiations, as it is considered an important tool to counteract against sudden import surges or price falls to protect the local production of staple food.

Domestic regulation of services remains a controversial issue

Multilateral discussions on services are focused on domestic regulation disciplines, which emerge from the General Agreement on Trade in Services (GATS) to ensure that licensing, technical standards, qualification requirements and procedures do not constitute unnecessary barriers to trade. The debate has shifted to a set of specific elements of domestic regulation, including administration and development of measures as well as transparency.

Box II.3

The multilateral trading system and the 2030 Agenda: Insights from trade agreements

International trade can be used as a way to implement the 2030 Agenda for Sustainable Development. To harness its potential, trade policies need to be coherent with and supportive of the Sustainable Development Goals. Trade liberalization can foster economic growth, but we need to ensure that it does not lead to lower labour or environmental standards for the sake of competitiveness.

In the multilateral trading system, negotiations on sustainable development issues can be slow, as epitomized by the World Trade Organization (WTO) Doha Development Round. At the same time, bilateral and regional preferential trade agreements (PTAs) have recently made rapid advances towards addressing sustainable development concerns. For example, including stricter obligations on labour standards and environmental protection in PTAs has become increasingly common over the last years. That said, PTA provisions in both fields vary in terms of enforceability and aspirations.

Can countries build upon the experience of PTAs when addressing sustainable development concerns in multilateral trade negotiations? Comparing the texts of labour and environmental provisions across PTAs allows us to assess to what extent these can serve as building blocks for future WTO commitments.

To this end, we extract labour/environment chapters and labour/environment-related provisions from PTAs and compute an indicator of textual similarity between different treaties known as a Jaccard similarity (Alschner, Seiermann and Skougarevskiy, 2017). The results of this exercise are displayed in heat maps, where each cell represents the textual similarities between one pair of treaties. It is coloured red to identify similar textual patterns and bright yellow to identify differences.

Agreements are ordered along the axes according to the name, in alphabetical order, of the signatory party with the highest 2015 GDP in each respective agreement. For example, the first row and column in each graph represents the degree of similarity between the Free Trade Agreement (FTA) between Australia and the Republic of Korea and another treaty. The solid red diagonal reflects the perfect

Figure II.3.1

Heat maps of textual similarity of PTA chapters on sustainable development

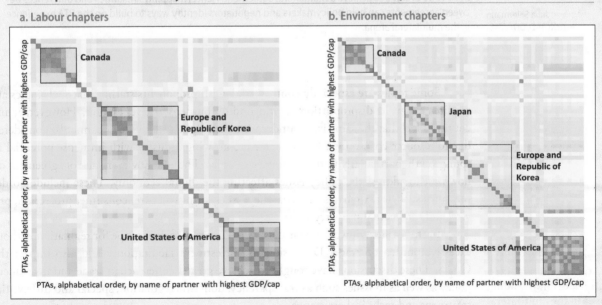

a. Labour chapters   b. Environment chapters

Source: Author's computations.

Note: Red = high similarity, bright yellow = low similarity.

(continued)

Box II.3 (*continued*)

overlap between identical treaty pairs (i.e., the top left corner simply represents the overlap between the FTA between Australia and the Republic of Korea with itself). The graph is symmetrical along the diagonal, as treaty pairs follow the same order along the vertical and horizontal axes. Within each figure, the treaties along the horizontal and vertical axes are the same and identically ordered. However, the included treaties differ between the two figures, as only treaties that contain provisions on labour are included in figure a, and those with provisions on environment are included in figure b. This explains why the location of treaty groups may differ between the two figures.

The key message to take away from the figure is that it is possible to identify certain countries that have considerable overlap on provisions related to labour standards and environmental protection among their bilateral and regional agreements. Canada and the United States have a relatively consistent treaty network concerning both labour and the environment. Different European groupings (the European Free Trade Association and the EU) and the Republic of Korea have concluded PTAs with similar labour provisions with different partners, but are heterogeneous in terms of environmental provisions. Japan's environmental provisions resemble each other across different treaties. Commonalities demonstrate that the content and formulation of these provisions is accepted across several partner countries, which can make it easier to introduce them at a multilateral level.

A large and growing number of recent agreements between other countries includes labour and/or environmental provisions. For example, more than 200 agreements stipulate the right to apply technical barriers to trade measures related to the environment (Morin, Pauwelyn and Hollway, 2017). PTAs with labour and/or environmental provisions include North-North, South-South and North-South agreements, regional and interregional, and with the participation of countries from different continents.

This broad willingness to consider sustainable development issues in the context of trade agreements by a wide range of countries is a promising precedent for multilateral negotiations. As stated by the ILO (2016) in a report on labour provisions, "regardless of the approach […], the objectives of countries are shared". While no single template of labour/environmental provisions has yet emerged, there is some evidence of convergence, such as between environmental clauses in agreements signed by the EU and the United States (Morin and Rochette, 2017). Sets of provisions that have already been accepted by several countries from different world regions may have a larger chance of being multilateralized. Where two or more templates exist, their texts need to be compared in more detail to determine whether the textual differences also reflect fundamental differences in the content and purpose of the provisions that need to be bridged to achieve a multilateral agreement. Hence, mapping similarities and differences between agreements can help policymakers and negotiators identify ways to build on the PTA experience in the multilateral arena.

Author: Julia Seiermann (UNCTAD/DITC/TAB)

Some topics are especially controversial, with proponents stating that such topics are required to avoid disproportionate and unduly burdensome regulation. However, many countries feel that the same issues undermine their right to regulate or cannot be considered due to resource constraints. E-commerce is a growing industry with immense potential to spur growth, particularly in developing economies. There is, however, lack of agreement on how best to address the policy issues affecting the digital economy. These include border measures such as tax rebates, transparency issues, infrastructure, consumer protection, privacy and intellectual property rights.

In this context, it would be necessary to ensure sufficient scope for regulation without excessive burden on trade. Discussions on investment facilitation could also impact the GATS. These discussions have sought to achieve greater coherence in trade and investment policy as well as in issues such as transparency, domestic regulation, special and differential treatment and technical assistance.

Special and differential treatment remains a central and longstanding issue in the multilateral trading system

The development dimension of the trading system relies heavily on special and differential treatment. This remains a central but also longstanding issue, where the implementation of past decisions continues to be an important concern. This includes the Duty Free and Quota Free market access and the preferential Rules of Origin for LDCs.

In this context, it is important to ensure the effective operationalization of the LDC services waiver and preferential treatment of LDC services and services suppliers. International support is required to address supply capacity constraints of LDCs, including infrastructure, skills, and technology, and should contribute to pro-development regulatory and institutional frameworks (Mashayekhi, 2017).

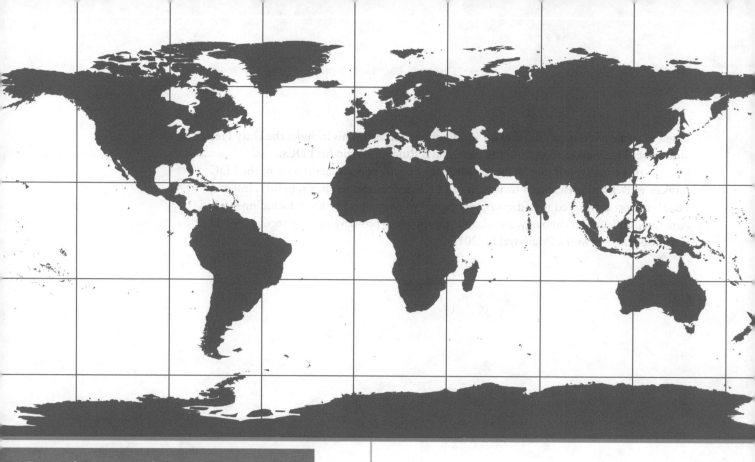

Snapshot: Developed economies

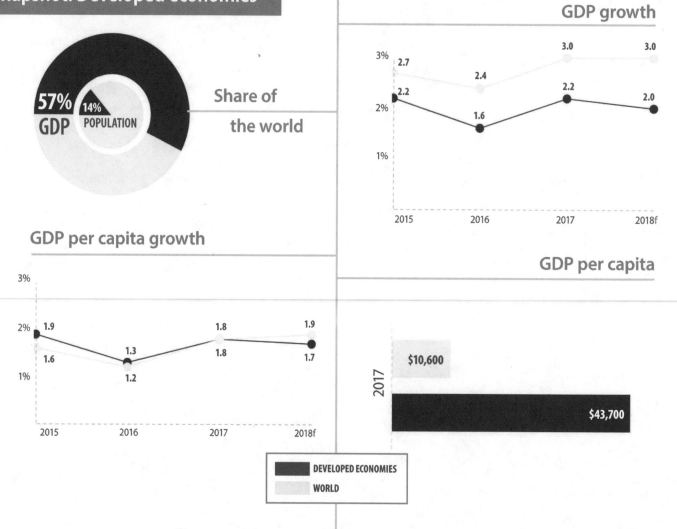

57% GDP

14% POPULATION

Share of the world

GDP growth

3% — 2.7

2.2

2.4

1.6

3.0

2.2

3.0

2.0

2%

1%

2015   2016   2017   2018f

GDP per capita growth

3%

2% — 1.9

1.6

1.3

1.2

1.8

1.8

1.9

1.7

1%

2015   2016   2017   2018f

GDP per capita

2017

$10,600

$43,700

■	DEVELOPED ECONOMIES
■	WORLD

Chapter III
Regional developments and outlook

Developed economies

United States: Stronger growth supported by an improvement in business investment

Following an estimated growth of 2.2 per cent in 2017, the United States of America is forecast to expand at a steady pace of 2.1 per cent in both 2018 and 2019. This marks a significant improvement compared to the 1.5 per cent growth recorded in 2016. The acceleration largely stems from shifting dynamics in business investment and, to a lesser extent, net trade.

Steady growth in the United States is underpinned by a sustained pace of expansion in household spending, estimated at 2.6 per cent in 2017, following growth of 2.7 per cent in 2016. However, over the same period, real personal disposable income growth averaged a mere 1.1 per cent. This indicates that consumers have drawn down savings in order to sustain expenditure growth, resulting in a deterioration of the savings rate by nearly 3 percentage points since 2015. In late 2017, household savings stood at 3.4 per cent of disposable personal income, compared to an average of 5.6 per cent since 1990.

Stable household spending sustained at the cost of depleting savings

Over a longer-term perspective, since 1940, the only other time when the household savings rate dropped below 4 per cent was just prior to the global financial crisis, when household spending was buoyed by excessive optimism and overinflated asset prices. Given that consumer spending cannot be financed indefinitely by a continued drawdown in savings, sustained strength in household demand going forward will depend on firmer growth in real disposable income.

The recent deterioration in savings raises concerns over whether the growth in household spending has been fuelled by inflated asset prices. House prices in the United States are nearly as high today as they were at the peak of the housing market bubble in 2006–2007 (figure III.1), which ultimately acted as one of the triggers of the global financial crisis. Underlying fundamentals in the housing market, however, are more closely aligned with house prices than they were in 2006–2007.

House prices approach pre-crisis levels, but supported by stronger fundamentals

The level of investment in housing remains nearly 15 per cent below pre-crisis peaks. Household indebtedness also remains below previous peaks due to a significant deleveraging process, although it has been on the rise since 2013. Mortgage delinquency rates continue to decline, and house prices, when viewed relative to income, remain well below pre-crisis levels (figure III.1). Collectively, these indicators suggest that the housing market does not pose an immediate threat to financial stability, but nonetheless merits monitoring over the forecast period. Further deterioration in household savings, combined with a rise in debt, could signal a buildup of excessive leverage in the household sector.

Despite strong job creation, growth in real personal disposable income has remained weak in the United States. This highlights the weak growth of average wages, which in part reflects stagnant wages at the lower end of the wage spectrum, resulting in a rise in the ratio of mean-to-median wages (figure III.2). The most recent data suggests that wage inequality

Wage inequality increased while unemployment rate declined

may have started to improve slightly, although it is premature to identify this as a trend. Going forward, stronger wage growth among lower income earners would help to sustain solid household spending growth, as those on the lower-end of the income scale tend to consume more from current income.

Labour market conditions have tightened

In mid-2017, the unemployment rate in the United States declined to its lowest level since 2001, and is hovering below what is considered its long-run equilibrium level. Nevertheless, pockets of higher unemployment persist in certain sectors and regions of the country. In addition, labour force participation rates of workers over the age of 55 have declined significantly since the global financial crisis. Notwithstanding these prevailing weaknesses, overall labour market conditions have clearly tightened. Given the forecast for steady GDP growth, the tighter labour market is expected to exert some upward pressure on wages in 2018, especially for lower-paid jobs. This should help redress the recent rise in wage

Figure III.1
House prices in the United States

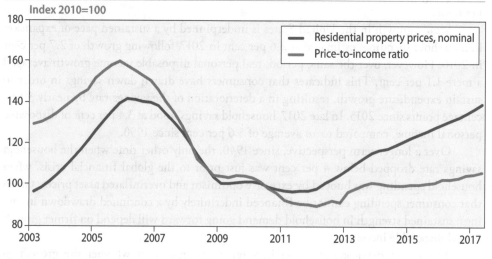

Index 2010=100

Source: UN/DESA, based on data from BIS Residential Property Price Database, U.S. Bureau of Economic Analysis, Table 2.1.

Figure III.2
Wage inequality in the United States

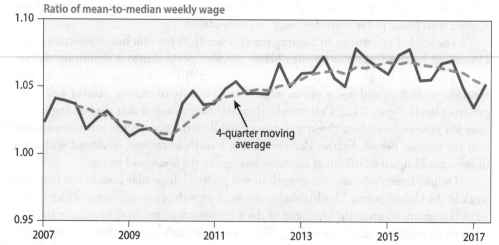

Source: UN/DESA, based on data from U.S. Bureau of Labor Statistics, Current Population Survey and Current Employment Statistics.

inequality. Shifts in income tax brackets and standard deductions expected in the 2018 budget[1] may partially offset any improvement in after-tax wage inequality, as independent estimates indicate that the bulk of tax relief would be directed towards households with the highest incomes (Tax Policy Center Urban Institute and Brookings Institution, 2017).

The core inflation measure closely monitored by the Federal Open Market Committee (FOMC) of the Fed averaged about 1.6 per cent in 2017, drifting slightly downward from March. This did not deter the FOMC from forging ahead with its balance sheet normalization plan in October 2017 (see further discussion in chapter II). Inflation is expected to rise towards the Fed target of 2 per cent over the course of 2018, contingent on an acceleration in wage growth.

Rise in inflation towards central bank target contingent on acceleration in wage growth

Non-residential investment saw a relatively broad-based revival in 2017, after contracting by 0.6 per cent in 2016. The rise in equipment investment, which accounted for 40 per cent of investment growth in the first three-quarters of the year, is particularly encouraging, as it lays the foundation for a revival in productivity growth.

Recovery in equipment investment lays foundation for a revival of productivity growth

While the United States' proposed infrastructure plan to support $1 trillion in infrastructure investment has not yet gained traction, a recovery in external demand coupled with expectations for stable domestic growth will continue to support moderate investment growth into 2018. Planned cuts to corporation tax may also encourage investment. However, lingering uncertainties regarding future trade relationships and the withdrawal of monetary stimulus are likely to hold back a more robust rebound in investment activity over the forecast horizon.

Canada: Sharp growth acceleration in 2017

GDP growth in Canada is estimated to have reached 3 per cent in 2017, placing the country among the fastest growing developed economies. The acceleration in growth was supported by fiscal stimulus measures, coupled with a sharp rise in household consumption and some revival in business investment. As in the United States, more than 40 per cent of Canada's business investment growth in the first half of 2017 was driven by investment in machinery and equipment, in particular computing equipment and transportation vehicles. (figure III.3). If sustained, the reorientation of investment towards machinery and equipment has the potential to underpin stronger productivity growth over the medium term.

Canada among the fastest growing large developed economies in 2017

The recent surge in consumer spending is partly attributable to strong gains in housing wealth. Canada's housing market was relatively unscathed by the global financial crisis, and house prices have continued to rise steadily nationwide, with particularly strong gains in cities such as Toronto and Vancouver. While mortgage arrears remain very low, the outstanding stock of residential mortgages has doubled in size since 2006. This prompted policymakers to introduce measures to moderate demand in major cities. These measures include a higher property-transfer tax on some non-resident investors, as speculative demand from foreign investors has partly driven house price growth in some large cities. By mid-2017, growth in housing starts had begun to moderate.

Housing market expected to moderate in 2018

The Bank of Canada is expected to continue to withdraw monetary stimulus from the economy, following interest rate rises of 25 basis points in both July and September 2017, pointing to further moderation in the housing market next year. As consumer spending becomes more closely aligned with income, GDP growth in Canada is forecast to moderate to 2.2–2.3 per cent per annum in 2018 and 2019.

---

1   See https://www.whitehouse.gov/the-press-office/2017/09/27/unified-framework-fixing-our-broken-tax-code

Figure III.3
Decomposition of investment growth in Canada

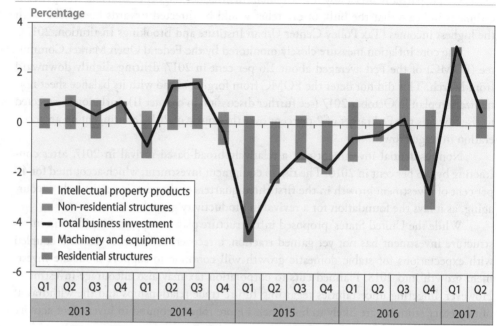

Source: Statistics Canada,
Table 380-0068.

Japan: Domestic demand growth leads the economic expansion

Economic growth in Japan accelerated to unexpectedly high levels in 2017, with GDP growth reaching an estimated 1.7 per cent. The robust economic growth is prompted by the continuously accommodative macroeconomic policy stance, and is led by a rapid expansion of domestic demand. Steady external demand growth from Asia and North America also contributed to the growth.

Exceptional growth momentum of 2017 expected to taper off

The present momentum is expected to taper off over 2018 and 2019, as the impact from fiscal stimulus measures ease. GDP is forecast to grow by 1.2 per cent in 2018 and 1.0 per cent in 2019. Consumer price inflation is estimated at 0.3 per cent in 2017, well below the Bank of Japan's (BoJ) inflation target of 2 per cent. Nevertheless, consumer price inflation is projected to rise to 1.4 per cent in 2018, and 1.8 per cent in 2019, due to upward pressure on wage levels as well as the proposed sales tax hike in October 2019.

Monetary and fiscal policy stance in Japan remains accommodative

Despite the Government's commitment to fiscal consolidation, particularly to lowering its debt dependency, the fiscal policy stance remained accommodative in 2017. The implementation of public investment projects introduced in the supplemental budgets in the 2016 fiscal year provided a significant stimulus to Japan's economic expansion over the first half of 2017.

The BoJ has continued to maintain a set of unconventional monetary easing measures — Quantitative and Qualitative Monetary Easing (QQE) — and is committed to using the balance sheet to expand the monetary base at the present pace. However, compared to the speed of monetary base expansion, the growth of broad money stock remains sluggish. The year-on-year growth rate of broad money stock, M2, has only gradually accelerated and reached the 4 per cent mark in February 2017 for the first time since August

2015. Nevertheless, the recovery in broad money growth reflects an accelerated growth in bank lending, particularly for investment purposes.

Through its intervention, the central bank effectively set an upper bound on the 10-year Japanese Government Bond (JGB) yield at 0.1 per cent. The BoJ asserted controls over rising yields in the market in February 2017 and July 2017 by announcing fixed-rate purchase operations. This intervention measure, known as the Yield Curve Control component of QQE, resulted in a widened yield spread between 10-year JGB and United States Treasury bonds. Over the first nine months in 2017, the yield spread averaged 226 basis points, up by 37 basis points from the 2016 average. This intervention has helped stabilize the value of the Japanese yen against the US dollar. The yen/dollar exchange rate was around 112 for the first nine months in 2017. In 2016, the exchange rate fluctuated between 121 and 100.

Yield curve control has helped stabilize the currency

Japanese industrial operating profits were strengthened by competitiveness gains related to the lower value of the Japanese yen (figure III.4). Industrial production continued to grow in 2017, albeit at a moderate pace. Estimates for inventories in the second quarter of 2017 signalled the start of an inventory buildup phase, which may last until mid-2018. Rising industrial production, inventory accumulation, and profit growth will support the growth momentum into the first quarter of 2018.

Competitiveness gains drive stronger profit growth

While consumer confidence improved during the first half of 2017, growth in household expenditure was held back by low growth in average real wages. Japanese labour markets have been in a paradoxical phase since 2011. The decline in the unemployment rate has coincided with a decline in the real wage rate (figure III.5). However, the real wage level bottomed out in 2016. The labour market has tightened, as the unemployment rate reached 2.8 per cent in July 2017, the lowest level since 1994. In light of the robust growth in industrial operating profits, real wages will likely come under increasing upward pressure in the coming quarters.

Real wage growth remains weak, but will come under increasing upward pressure

The main downside risk for the Japanese economy in the short run is an abrupt appreciation of the Japanese yen. Since the current exchange rate has been bolstered by the BoJ's intervention, abandoning its yield curve control measure, for either financial or political reasons, could lead to a rapid appreciation of the yen. This would reduce competitiveness, restrain industrial operating profits, and reverse progress towards defeating deflation, all of which would drive GDP growth down.

Risks to the outlook include a sharp appreciation of the yen

Japan also faces structural challenges that weigh on its potential growth. These include a declining population and persistently high public debt, with limited room to expand tax revenue.

Australia and New Zealand: More expansionary fiscal stance supports outlook

Australia and New Zealand both posted solid economic growth in 2017, estimated at 2.8 per cent and 2.5 per cent, respectively. In 2018, GDP growth is expected to reach 3 per cent in Australia and 2.9 per cent in New Zealand, supported by a more expansionary fiscal stance and solid consumer spending in both countries. While investment in Australia will be driven by a booming housing market, the housing cycle in New Zealand has started to turn, after house prices increased by more than 20 per cent compared to early 2015. Residential construction activity in New Zealand has slowed, and is expected to remain soft in 2018–2019.

Housing market cycle has turned in New Zealand, but risks of an abrupt adjustment in Australia remain

Figure III.4
Industrial production and operating profits in Japan

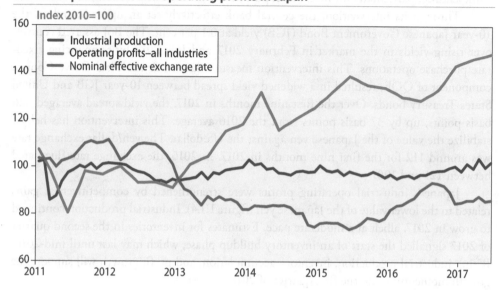

Sources: Japan Ministry of
Economy, Trade, and Industry;
Bank of Japan.

Figure III.5
Unemployment rate and real wages in Japan

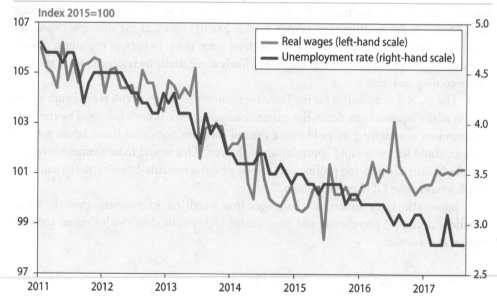

Sources: Japan Ministry
of Internal Affairs and
Communications; Ministry of
Health, Labour and Welfare.

As in Canada, both Australia and New Zealand have introduced several measures to restrict the role of speculative non-resident investors in the housing market. Nevertheless, house prices in Australia have continued to rise steadily and residential investment is projected to remain strong. The Reserve Bank of Australia has warned that some borrowers, especially those with lower income, may struggle to meet mortgage payments when interest rates rise from their prevailing low rates. While adjustment in the housing market may unfold gradually, there is a risk that Australia will experience an abrupt turn in the housing cycle, driving a sharp slowdown in economic growth.

Europe: Robust growth amid continued policy challenges

Economic activity in Europe remains robust, with real GDP growth forecast to reach 2.1 per cent in 2018. Household consumption will remain a major contributor to growth, underpinned by rising disposable incomes, falling unemployment, further upward pressure on wages and the continued low level of interest rates. The expansionary monetary policy stance will also continue to underpin business investment and construction activity. Nevertheless, the European Central Bank (ECB) decision to taper the pace of its asset purchases and eventually cease expansion of its balance sheet will have some dampening effect, contributing to a slight downtick in growth to 1.9 per cent in 2019.

This overall solid aggregate growth trajectory encompasses several economies with markedly higher growth rates. For example, Spain is forecast to see growth of 2.6 per cent in 2018 and 2.4 per cent in 2019, driven by private consumption, fixed investment — especially in construction and machinery — and solid external demand, including tourism.

A similar combination of solid domestic and external demand will drive growth in Ireland, with a growth forecast of 2.8 per cent and 3.1 per cent for 2018 and 2019, respectively. By contrast, Italy will register the lowest growth in the region, with 1.4 per cent and 1.1 per cent in 2018 and 2019, respectively. Slow employment growth and weak consumer sentiment related to political uncertainty will hinder private consumption growth, while weak public investment and limited access to bank lending will cap fixed investment.

In the United Kingdom of Great Britain and Northern Ireland, growth will decelerate to 1.4 per cent in both 2018 and 2019, as the economy will face increasing pressure from the effects of the decision to leave the EU. The weaker pound sterling has contributed to the rise in import cost pressures while taming domestic demand. At the same time, business investment is suffering from significant uncertainty regarding the future framework for the economic relations of the United Kingdom with the EU and the rest of the world. This includes, in particular, the looming loss for businesses located in the United Kingdom of the right to operate in EU member countries under the umbrella of unified EU regulations.

The outlook for Europe is subject to several downside risks. Negotiations over the exit of the United Kingdom from the EU remains a major source of uncertainty. Any negative surprises or perceived increase in the probability of a negotiation failure would further crimp business investment in the United Kingdom. In terms of euro area economic policy, the ECB has already shifted its policy stance by reducing the amount of its monthly asset purchases. Implementing the further reduction in its stimulus will be challenging in terms of both its precise design and communication to the public, creating important risks for actual or even perceived policy missteps.

In the area of fiscal policy, the euro area's lack of a stronger and more coherent institutional underpinning will remain a major weakness. The continued excessive reliance on targets for budget deficits leaves open the problem of enforceability and the risk of renewed tensions between member states, especially if there is a new economic downturn.

International trade will remain a major driver of growth for Europe. The overall positive economic trends within the region in terms of falling unemployment rates, rising incomes, stronger consumption and solid consumer and business confidence will lead to a continued strong expansion of trade between EU member states. In addition, steady expansion in other major global export markets such as the United States and China will also underpin solid external demand. Despite this positive baseline forecast, the trade trajectory for Europe will face a number of headwinds.

Private consumption is a major driver of solid economic growth

Spain and Ireland will lead growth performance in the European Union, while Italy and the United Kingdom will see slower growth rates

Downside risks include Brexit and economic policy

Both intra-EU trade and global demand will support growth

A major challenge for exporters lies in the appreciation of the euro against the US dollar, which makes European exports more expensive abroad and, thus, less competitive. However, past episodes of currency appreciation showed the capacity of many exporters to absorb the negative effects of a stronger currency by increasing their productivity or by using their pricing power based on quality and the provision of niche products. Second, negotiations over exact procedures for the exit of the United Kingdom from the EU not only create major uncertainties, but could also spark negative economic shocks if negotiations fail. Third, stronger protectionist tendencies in the global arena would kindle significant downside risks, especially for the heavily export-oriented sectors and companies in Europe, including many small and medium-sized enterprises.

Aggregate unemployment has been declining, but remains elevated in several economies

Against a backdrop of solid economic growth, unemployment has been on a downward trend across the EU, with the overall unemployment rate declining to 7.5 per cent in September 2017 compared to 8.5 per cent in the previous year. This solid aggregate trend masks significant dispersion among national labour markets. The Czech Republic, Germany and Malta registered the lowest unemployment rates, with 2.7 per cent, 3.6 per cent and 4.1 per cent, respectively. By contrast, unemployment was the highest in Greece, Spain and Italy, with rates of 21.0 per cent (July 2017), 16.7 per cent and 11.1 per cent, respectively, and stood at around 10 per cent in Croatia, Cyprus and France.

Youth unemployment remains a serious challenge. It reached 16.6 per cent EU-wide in 2017, and exceeded 35 per cent in Greece, Italy and Spain. Although employment should be boosted by the robust economic forecast, the spillover effects of this boost will not be fully exploited unless policymakers take action, for example, to reduce skill mismatches.

Drastic technology shifts could fundamentally change the automotive supply chain, with significant consequences for employment in some economies

In various European economies with significant automotive sectors such as the Czech Republic, Germany and Slovakia, drastic technology shifts in the automotive industry — tied to electric vehicles and autonomous driving — will cause significant economic and employment impacts. Notably, any meaningful adoption of electric vehicles stands to revolutionize the automotive supply sector, as entire subsystems and components needed for conventional engine technology will not be required anymore. While new technologies, including those linked to battery technology or autonomous driving, will create new opportunities in the automotive supply chain, this would still involve significant structural changes, for example regarding the skill profile of the workforce.

The solid macroeconomic picture will lead to further increases in inflation

Inflation in Europe has been on an upward trend and has remained solid. This is true even after the one-off effects from lower oil prices fade. The aggregate inflation rate is forecast to increase from 1.6 per cent in 2017 to 1.8 per cent in 2018, with a further acceleration in inflation to 2.1 per cent in 2019. A number of factors are driving this price trajectory.

In the United Kingdom, the still lingering effects of the depreciation of the pound sterling in 2016 has pushed up import prices, leading to inflation forecasts of 2.5 per cent and 2.9 per cent for 2018 and 2019, respectively. Unemployment has decreased in numerous economies, with some regions experiencing labour market conditions equivalent to full employment and real wages showing some solid increases, which, in turn, will underpin private consumption. On the other hand, the sharp appreciation of the euro against the dollar during 2017 will exert a moderating effect on inflation on the import side.

Monetary policy has reached a turning point

The ECB monetary policy stance has in large part driven financial market movements in 2017. The ECB reduced the amount of its monthly asset purchases, albeit with an extension of the purchase programme, and adjusted the language in its policy guidance by dropping the reference to possibly lower interest rates. These hints of a reduction in the monetary policy stimulus and some expectations of more pronounced moves by the ECB in this direction helped to support the sharp increase in the value of the euro against the dollar during 2017 (figure III.6) and underpinned higher yields on euro area benchmark bonds.

Notably, the yield on the German 10-year bond reached almost 0.60 per cent in July 2017, compared to around -0.19 per cent in the previous year. In view of robust economic growth and inflation trends, the elevated levels of consumer and business confidence indices, as well as the extremely loose current monetary policy stance, the ECB is likely to initiate additional steps to remove some of its stimulus in 2018. This includes further guidance on its path for reducing asset purchases, which are expected to continue until at least September 2018. Guidance regarding interest rate normalization may also be announced, which will begin well past the end of the asset purchase programme. At the same time, the ECB is expected to continue reinvesting maturing asset holdings for an extended period of time, bolstering support for financial markets.

Rising inflation pressure also underpinned an increase in interest rates by the Bank of England in November 2017, with policymakers stating that further interest rate hikes may be required.

Fiscal policy will have a less negative impact on growth compared to recent years that have been marked by fiscal consolidation. The implemented fiscal adjustments have led to measurable improvements in fiscal budget positions. In 2016, only France and Spain exceeded the EU limit for budget deficits of 3.0 per cent of GDP by registering a deficit of 3.4 per cent and 4.5 per cent, respectively.

Fiscal policy will have a less negative impact on growth

A number of countries, like Austria and Germany, will increase fiscal spending to integrate a large number of migrants. However, fiscal policy space will remain limited in the EU as a whole, with the aggregate debt-to-GDP ratio standing at 86 per cent and Belgium, Cyprus, France, Greece, Italy, Spain and Portugal featuring debt-to-GDP ratios around or in excess of 100 per cent. The current low level of interest rates reduces the costs

Figure III.6
Major developed market currencies' exchange rates against the US dollar

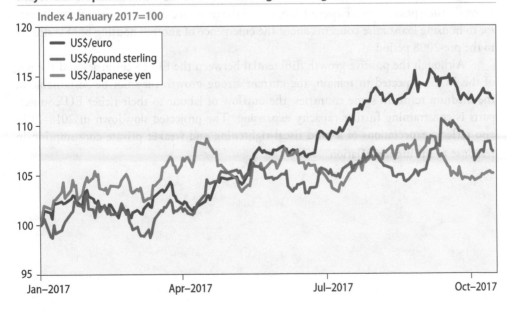

Source: IMF Exchange Rate Query Tool.

Note: A rise indicates an appreciation.

of servicing these debts, but the turn in monetary policy towards a normalization of interest rates points to higher levels of fiscal spending on servicing public debt in the future.

In the United Kingdom, the budget deficit will reach around 3.5 per cent of GDP in 2018. Fiscal policy will remain under pressure from the effects created by the decision to leave the EU. In the course of this process, the United Kingdom has to reorganize public support mechanisms and financial flows in a plethora of policy areas, and undertaking this administrative exercise alone already entails a major fiscal cost.

Economic growth in the EU members from Eastern Europe and the Baltic States continues to outpace the EU average

Economic growth in the EU members from Eastern Europe and the Baltic States continues to outpace the EU average, thanks to capital accumulation and productivity gains. The aggregate GDP of the group of EU-13 countries, which also includes Cyprus and Malta, is estimated to expand by 4.2 per cent in 2017, 3.6 per cent in 2018 and 3.5 per cent in 2019. As in 2016, Romania will remain the fastest-growing European economy over the forecast horizon, with GDP growth projected to approach 6 per cent in 2017.

Robust exports, investment and private consumption have been major drivers of growth

The expansion in the EU-13 in 2017 has been largely driven by the robust export performance of the manufacturing sector in Eastern Europe, and also a recovery of investment following the earlier slump (in particular, in construction activity) in 2015–2016 that was related to the interval between EU funding cycles.

Private consumption has also contributed notably to growth, supported by a surge in nominal wages amid tight labour market conditions. The Czech Republic in 2017 had the lowest unemployment rate in the EU, and in a number of countries, including Hungary, Poland and Slovakia, the unemployment rate has declined to record low levels. A rapid expansion in private credit, as well as an increase in social transfers also supported growth in some countries.

Some economies of the EU-13 may be operating above potential

There are signs that some EU-13 economies may be operating above potential, as reflected in the accelerating inflation — from negative or near zero figures in 2015–2016, inflation surged to around 2 per cent in most EU-13 countries and exceeded the target in the Czech Republic by almost 1 percentage point, prompting the central bank to become the first in the EU to start a gradual monetary tightening in 2017. In Lithuania, inflation accelerated to an alarming 4.8 per cent at the end of 2017.

Consumption-driven growth and rising private debt may hide numerous risks. The rising housing prices across Eastern Europe, and the increased exposure of the financial sector to housing loans raise concerns about the emergence of another housing bubble similar to the pre-2008 period.

Labour outflow, fiscal tightening and inflation likely to constrain growth

Although the positive growth differential between the EU-13 countries and the rest of the EU is expected to remain, the current strong growth may not be sustainable in the medium term. In some countries, the outflow of labour to their richer EU counterparts is constraining further capacity expansion. The projected slowdown in 2018–2019 also reflects expectations of a mild fiscal tightening and weaker private consumption in response to the higher inflation.

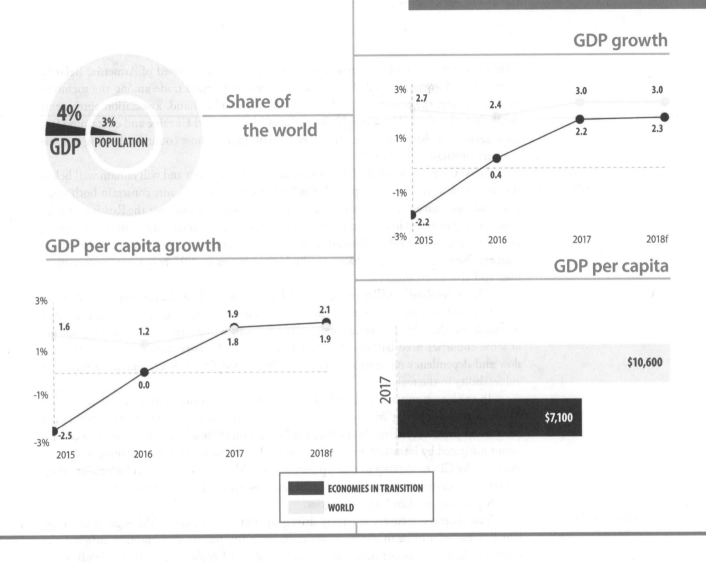

GDP growth

Share of the world

4% GDP

3% POPULATION

GDP per capita growth

GDP per capita

2017

$10,600

$7,100

ECONOMIES IN TRANSITION

WORLD

Economies in transition

The Commonwealth of Independent States and Georgia: Cyclical recovery, but uncertain long-run prospects

The pace of economic activity in the Commonwealth of Independent States (CIS) is accelerating, marked by the return to growth in the Russian Federation after a two-year contraction. Improved terms of trade, a more supportive external environment and less volatile macroeconomic conditions, including tapering inflation and stabilized exchange rates, have created a more favourable environment for the region's economies.

Belarus is exiting recession and growth has accelerated in Kazakhstan; Armenia, Kyrgyzstan and Uzbekistan have reported vibrant economic activity indicators. Aggregate GDP of the region, which remained practically flat in 2016, is expected to increase by around 2.2 per cent in 2017; growth is projected to accelerate to around 2.3 per cent in 2018 and 2.4 per cent in 2019. The Central Asian economies are expected to expand faster than other CIS economies, benefiting from stronger remittance inflows, the implementation of the "Belt and Road" initiative, and, in some cases, fiscal spending on development. Integration within the framework of the Eurasian Economic Union (composed of Armenia, Belarus, Kazakhstan, Kyrgyzstan and the Russian Federation) boosted trade among the members in 2017, despite the remaining trade barriers. On the other hand, association agreements concluded with the EU by Georgia, Republic of Moldova and Ukraine and containing free trade agreements have influenced the directions of trade of those countries, leading to some trade fragmentation in the CIS area.

Long-run growth faces structural constraints

However, for most of the CIS, projected growth is modest and will remain well below the rates seen in the pre-crisis period. Cyclical and structural factors constrain both near-term and long-run economic prospects. International sanctions against the Russian Federation, initially imposed in 2014, remain in place. They restrict access to certain technologies, including deep-water oil exploration and drilling equipment, and limit access to capital markets. New sanctions introduced by the United States in 2017 may target energy pipelines and also sovereign debt.

The unresolved conflict in the east of Ukraine weighs on the country's economy, as loss of control over the resources in the east has reduced export capacity. Room is limited for fiscal spending both in energy exporters and energy importers, while banking sectors in some countries need bailouts. Progress in economic diversification in the CIS remains slow and dependency on natural resources, albeit to varying degrees, remains a source of vulnerability in the region.

In the longer run, unfavourable demographic trends in the European part of the CIS will lead to a shrinking workforce and increased dependency ratios, putting additional burdens on pension systems. In the Russian Federation those adverse trends are to a certain extent mitigated by intra-CIS migration (box III.1). On the other hand, as younger workers leave smaller CIS economies to take up long-term residency in the Russian Federation, their departure undermines future growth prospects — even while alleviating current labour market pressures in their home countries.

Recovery is driven by domestic demand

The observed recovery is largely driven by domestic demand. Although in the Russian Federation, unlike in the previous crisis in 2009, private consumption suffered the brunt of the recent adjustment, the dynamics of retail trade and mortgage lending are improving amid positive real wage growth. However, consumption is still relatively weak. Inventory accumulation is expected to have made a large contribution to growth in 2017. Investment has been boosted by the 2018 FIFA World Cup preparations. However, numerous uncertainties and the high cost of capital are holding private investment back. Counter-sanctions adopted by the Russian Federation since 2014 — banning food imports from most OECD economies — have prompted expansion of some sectors, such as agriculture and food processing. In the outlook period, the country is expected to remain on a low-growth trajectory.

Among the other energy exporters, increasing oil production at the giant Kashagan field in Kazakhstan has contributed to higher exports. Further infrastructure development may help to sustain growth at above 3 per cent in the medium term.

Azerbaijan is the only CIS country where GDP is expected to have contracted in 2017, due to a contraction of oil production and problems in the financial sector. The launch of a new gas field will support a recovery in 2018–2019. In Uzbekistan, growth is likely to remain strong, as the liberalization of currency regulation and the ongoing shift to convertibility opens new investment opportunities.

Thanks to the relatively quick exchange rate reaction of the Russian Federation to the oil price decline (figure III.7), the recent recession has been milder compared to past

Figure III.7
Average monthly exchange rates of the CIS energy-exporters versus the US dollar

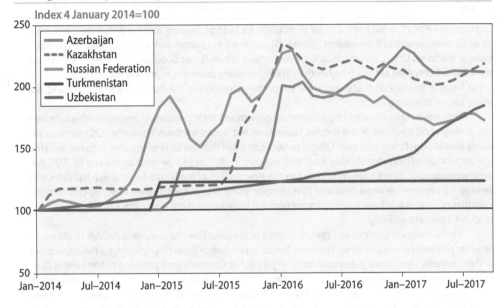

Index 4 January 2014=100

Legend:
- Azerbaijan
- Kazakhstan
- Russian Federation
- Turkmenistan
- Uzbekistan

Sources: IMF International Financial Statistics and United Nations estimates.

Note: A rise indicates a depreciation.

contractions. By contrast, in other energy exporters, there was an initial reluctance to let the currency depreciate and the adjustment is still ongoing.

Among the energy-importers, in Ukraine, after the cumulative 15 per cent fall in GDP in 2014–2015, the recovery continued for a second year, despite the company seizures and trade blockade in areas in the east of the country. The minimum wage was doubled in 2017 and private consumption is gaining momentum; gross fixed capital formation shows robust dynamism after its collapse in 2014–2015.

The reorientation of trade towards the EU, however, has been accompanied by a shift in production, with an increasing weight on agricultural products. Although external financing options have improved, low growth creates challenges for external debt sustainability. Belarus in 2017 has come out of recession, with strong industrial growth and a good harvest. The settlement of the dispute with the Russian Federation on oil deliveries and gas debts has boosted exports and improved economic prospects. In the medium term, these countries are expected to remain on a low-growth trajectory. They also face large debt servicing payments.

The recovery of remittances from the Russian Federation is contributing to the acceleration of economic activity in Central Asia and the Caucasus. In Armenia, the economy has bounced back strongly, amid rapid industrial growth and higher copper prices. In Kyrgyzstan, large increases in gold production boosted output and the economy expanded by over 6 per cent in the first half of 2017.

The region is benefiting from somewhat easier access to capital. A number of countries, including Belarus, the Russian Federation, Tajikistan and Ukraine have taken advantage of the search for yield among international investors to launch eurobonds. Belarus, in addition, has refinanced its debt with the Russian Federation following the agreement on payments for gas arrears and a new deal on energy deliveries.

Box III.1
Migration: Labour markets and remittances in the CIS

The Russian Federation has been a major destination for both permanent and temporary migrants from other Commonwealth of Independent States (CIS) countries. In contrast with the years following the collapse of the Soviet Union, economic considerations have driven recent population movements. Wages in the Russian Federation are much higher than in neighbouring countries, especially in Central Asia, which is the focus of this box. In these countries, temporary migration to the Russian Federation provides a major source of income.

Over the last two decades negative natural growth and rapid population ageing has characterized the demographic structure of the Russian Federation. Net migratory flows from other CIS countries explains overall population increases. Official projections show that the ratio of the elderly to the working age population will increase steadily, from 45.5 per cent in 2017 to 54.1 per cent by the end of 2035. Adverse demographic trends have contributed to the slow growth of the labour force, which has increased by only 1.5 per cent between 2010 and 2016, despite rising labour participation rates. By contrast, the countries of Central Asia have exhibited more favourable demographic trends, with natural growth rates of above 2 per cent annually.

Methodological changes and the persistence of irregular flows have made it difficult to obtain an accurate picture of migration levels. However, trends in remittance flows clearly highlight the importance of these revenues for Central Asian economies (figure III.1.1). Quarterly data provided by the Central Bank of the Russian Federation on cross-border monetary transfers by physical persons closely tracks remittance figures compiled on an annual basis by the World Bank. Overall remittances expressed in dollar terms peaked in 2013, before declining sharply as the Russian economy contracted and the rouble depreciated. As the recession came to an end in late 2016, this negative trend has now reversed (figure III.1.2).

Meanwhile, changes in Russian legislation were introduced in 2014–2015 to regularize migration and curb illegal work. After the creation of the Eurasian Economic Union (EEU) in 2015, a different access regime to the labour market of the Russian Federation emerged for members and for those outside the EEU. This helps explain the resilience of remittances to Kyrgyzstan, which joined the EEU in mid-2015, relative to other recipients in Central Asia.

Remittances remain a major transmitter of external shocks, as seen during the recent downturn. The large declines observed in 2015–2016 draw into question the general belief that these flows are relatively stable, and suggests a high degree of labour market flexibility for migrant workers, who provide a

Figure III.1.1
Remittances from the Russian Federation as a percentage of GDP

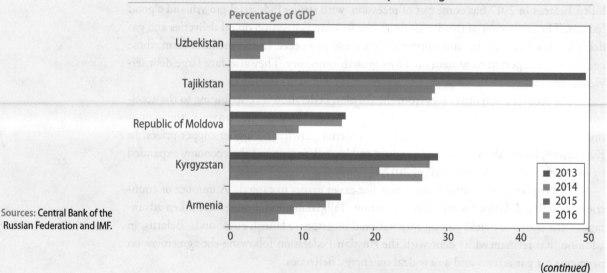

Sources: Central Bank of the Russian Federation and IMF.

(continued)

buffer for firms when adjusting to changes in demand conditions. In fact, migrants are especially represented in low-skill jobs in sectors such as construction and retail, which contracted the most during the recent downturn. In addition, the dynamics of remittances in the Russian Federation are closely associated with the evolution of non-tradable output and display a very seasonal pattern.

In receiving countries of the CIS, remittances are largely used to finance higher consumption. Stronger remittance flows also tend to provide an impetus to construction. Money transfers from migrants have also been a major source of liquidity for the banking sectors of the small Central Asian countries (the cost of sending remittances from the Russian Federation to other CIS countries are among the lowest in the world, which has encouraged the use of formal channels). Consequently, their decline contributed to the weakening of financial institutions, through both deteriorating asset quality and creating funding pressures. These patterns in general limit the contribution of migration to human capital accumulation and development in the region.

Given the projected demographic dynamics, large migratory flows are likely to continue, although these will not only be influenced by economic conditions but also by regulatory changes. Remittances will remain a major source of income for Central Asian countries. However, the recent large declines have exposed the underlying economic vulnerability of these economies and the continued need for economic diversification.

Box III.1 (continued)

Author: José Palacín (ECE)

Figure III.1.2
Remittances from the Russian Federation

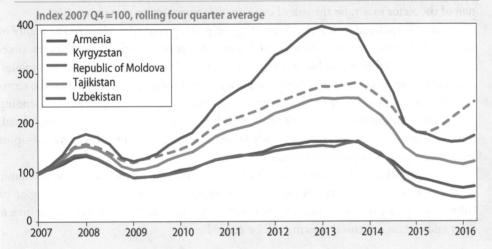

Index 2007 Q4 =100, rolling four quarter average

- Armenia
- Kyrgyzstan
- Republic of Moldova
- Tajikistan
- Uzbekistan

Source: Central Bank of the Russian Federation.

Inflation in the CIS exhibited large heterogeneity in 2017, ranging from a near-zero inflation in Armenia to double-digit price increases in Azerbaijan and Ukraine. In several countries, price pressures have eased amid the strengthening of exchange rates. By contrast, hikes to utility costs pushed inflation up in others. In the Russian Federation, lower food prices, driven by a good harvest and the resumption of imports from Turkey, have brought inflation to record low levels. Stronger domestic demand and the lifting of disinflationary pressures related to the exchange rate appreciation of 2016 may create some inflationary pressures next year. Inflation has fallen into single digits in Belarus, supported by a tight monetary policy and the reduction of directed lending, and in Kazakhstan, thanks to the stronger currency. On the other hand, inflation remains elevated in Azerbaijan and Ukraine, at 12 and 15 per cent, respectively. In late 2017, inflation subsided to a record low level in Belarus, at around 6 per cent. In Uzbekistan, the ongoing shift to currency con-

Inflation performances diverge

vertibility will push inflationary pressures. For the countries with relatively high inflation rates, further disinflation is expected in 2018–2019.

Labour markets
remained resilient
during the crisis

Employment held up well during the crisis, given wage flexibility and the use of part-time work. The recovery is resulting in growing wage gains, the reduction of involuntary adjustment mechanisms and declines in unemployment rates. In the Russian Federation, falling unemployment is being accompanied by a shrinking labour force. The economy of Kazakhstan continued to generate jobs, in part thanks to the ongoing urbanization.

Monetary loosening
continues, with some
exceptions

Declining price pressures allowed for a cautious loosening of monetary policies, although countries in the region are in different positions in this easing cycle. The National Bank of Ukraine sharply reversed its previous softening in view of accelerating inflation. In the Russian Federation, even after a series of policy rate cuts in 2017, real rates are high compared to other emerging markets. Lending, in particular to households, has picked up, but the banking sector in the region remains generally in poor shape.

State support has been substantial in recent years. However, more support will be required, despite tangible success in stabilizing the financial system. In 2017, the Central Bank of the Russian Federation intervened to rescue the largest private bank in response to a massive deposit withdrawal. The cost of restructuring the banking sector looms large for several CIS countries and will contribute to a rise in public debt. The ongoing consolidation of the sector may raise the risk of excessive concentration in some countries.

Fiscal stances
consolidating, but
gradually

Fiscal consolidation is gradual, as energy-exporting countries adapt to the reality of persistently low energy prices. New fiscal frameworks for the use of hydrocarbon resources are being deployed in Kazakhstan and the Russian Federation to reduce the economies' sensitivity to oil prices. In some energy importers, fiscal policy is constrained by the terms of IMF programmes. There is a heightened emphasis on the efficiency of public spending and its contribution to growth in the region. While fiscal consolidation is moving ahead, pension systems in some countries — where demographic conditions are adverse — post large deficits, requiring sizeable transfers.

The geopolitical situation in the CIS remains complicated and weighs on economic prospects. Once more, the recent downturn has exposed the vulnerability of the region to falling commodity prices. To take advantage of depreciated exchange rates, stronger investment and certain structural reforms will be needed.

South-Eastern Europe: Moderate, but relatively more balanced growth

Economic activity in South-Eastern Europe is supported by improved economic prospects in the EU and stronger domestic demand. Infrastructure-related investment continues to boost growth, in particular in Montenegro. Private consumption is playing an increasing role, in particular, in Albania, where employment and wages have increased. However, in Serbia, the largest economy of the region, a harsh winter has disrupted transport links and reduced construction activity. Later in the year, a drought caused a poor agricultural harvest. These factors dampened the growth outlook.

Domestic political uncertainties in the former Yugoslav Republic of Macedonia weigh on business investment and private consumption. Growth of the aggregate GDP of the region subsided from 2.9 per cent in 2016 to an estimated 2.5 per cent in 2017, but is expected to accelerate to 3.2 per cent in 2018. The region is seeing increased investment from

China, mostly in the form of construction projects, financed by loans from China. While these loans provide a welcome upgrade to infrastructure, they also drive up public debt.

The current growth pattern in the region is more balanced than in the pre-crisis period, when rapid expansion was accompanied by massive current account deficits (figure III.8) and increasing private and public indebtedness. Still, current account deficits continue to create external financing needs, making the region vulnerable to a deterioration in financing conditions. On the positive side, foreign direct investment (FDI) remains the main source of financing in the region and increased export capacity will reduce external imbalances in the future.

Current pattern of growth is more balanced, but stronger job creation is needed

To overcome the structural problems of the region, stronger growth is required. A more robust pace of job creation is needed to prevent people from leaving — especially youth. Unemployment remains high, particularly in Bosnia and Herzegovina and in the former Yugoslav Republic of Macedonia, despite the introduction of public sector programmes. Stronger regional integration within the Central European Free Trade Agreement (CEFTA) framework would also be welcome.

Despite progress in fiscal consolidation and some success in stabilizing public debt in Albania and Serbia, the two largest countries, debt burdens remain significant in the region. In the former Yugoslav Republic of Macedonia and in Montenegro, further infrastructure spending is planned, which can lead to further fiscal deficit widening.

Public debt remains a burden

Economic prospects of South-Eastern Europe depend on growth dynamics in the European Union. Geopolitical tensions are also a downside risk. The prospect of EU accession remains the most important policy anchor for the region, and in many aspects, developments on that front will determine both the political and economic outlook.

EU accession remains the most important policy anchor

Figure III.8
GDP growth and current account deficits in South-Eastern Europe

Sources: IMF International Financial Statistics and UN/DESA.

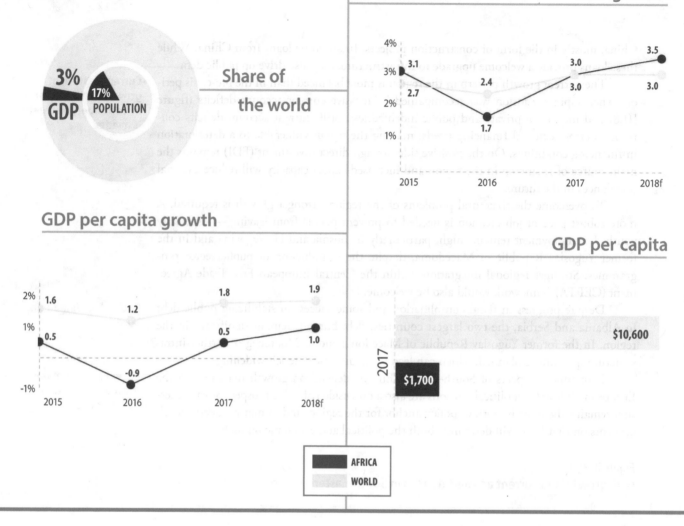

Share of the world

3% GDP

17% POPULATION

GDP growth

4%
3.1
3%
2.7
2.4
2%
1.7
1%

3.0 3.0
3.5
3.0

2015   2016   2017   2018f

GDP per capita growth

2%   1.6
1.8
1.9

1%   0.5
1.2
0.5
1.0

-1%   -0.9

2015   2016   2017   2018f

GDP per capita

2017

$10,600

$1,700

AFRICA
WORLD

Developing economies

Africa: Gradual cyclical improvement continues

Acceleration in growth driven mainly by cyclical improvements

Africa's economic growth is projected to pick up to 3.5 per cent in 2018 and 3.7 per cent in 2019 (or 3.3 per cent and 3.5 per cent in 2018 and 2019, respectively, excluding Libya). The projected modest improvement in growth is underpinned by strengthening external demand and a moderate increase in commodity prices. The improvement in growth will also be supported by more favourable domestic conditions, including the restoration of oil production in Algeria, Angola and Nigeria, the increase in oil production from new fields in Ghana and the Republic of Congo, and the recovery in agricultural production and mining in South Africa. The improvement in the region's aggregate growth in 2018–2019 is largely attributable to a recovery in Egypt, Nigeria and South Africa, three of Africa's largest economies.

Compared to forecasts made a year ago, there was an overall downward revision to growth for the continent as a whole, due to a slower than anticipated recovery in many commodity-exporting economies, especially fuel and mineral exporters. Looking ahead, growth in Africa remains constrained by several domestic obstacles, including foreign exchange controls in Angola and Nigeria, weather-related shocks especially in East Africa, and political uncertainty leading to low business confidence in countries such as the Democratic Republic of Congo, Kenya and South Africa. There are also security threats in East Africa, and in countries in the Sahel region.

Though growth appears to have firmed from very low levels in 2016, it remains barely higher than population growth, estimated at 2.5 per cent in 2018–2019. This means per capita GDP growth — projected to increase from 0.5 per cent in 2017 to 1.0 per cent in 2018 and 1.2 per cent in 2019 — will remain inadequate for Africa to make significant progress towards the Sustainable Development Goals (SDGs), in particular the eradication of poverty and hunger.

Current economic recovery is insufficient to raise living standards

The region's aggregate GDP masks considerable variation among its subregions (figure III.9). The less resource-dependent countries in East Africa, such as Djibouti, Ethiopia and the United Republic of Tanzania, and in West Africa, including Côte d'Ivoire, Ghana and Senegal, will continue to witness above average growth, supported by vigorous infrastructure investment, strong services sectors and a recovery in agricultural production. By contrast, many oil and minerals exporters will witness weak growth, as commodity prices remain well below their 2014 levels and fiscal consolidation efforts constrain public investment.

The strong headwinds that the region faced in 2016 eased in 2017. Moderately increasing commodity prices and recovering external demand have contributed to a narrowing of current account deficits, especially among the highly commodity-dependent economies. An improvement in external financing conditions has also led to a decline in borrowing costs and improved access to finance. This has enabled some countries to re-enter the eurobond market.

Headwinds to growth have subsided in 2017

Internally, drought conditions have eased in countries in East and Southern Africa. The security situation has also improved, particularly with regards to militant attacks on oil pipelines. Nonetheless, tensions remain high in several areas, especially in Somalia. In some countries, recent elections have been conducted without major incidents (e.g., Angola). By contrast, elections sparked political tensions in others, such as Kenya. Risks of heightened political tensions remain in advance of several elections lying ahead in 2018–2019, and a rapidly changing situation in Zimbabwe.

Figure III.9
Average annual GDP growth in Africa, by subregion

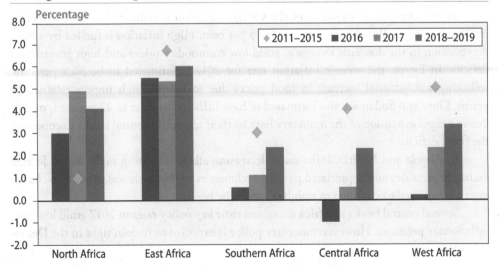

Source: UN/DESA.

In 2017, the African economies are estimated to have expanded in aggregate by 2.6 per cent (excluding Libya), following growth of 1.7 per cent in 2016, one of the slowest rates of expansion in the past two decades. The recovery was supported by improvement in large oil exporting economies, such as Angola and Nigeria, and by Morocco where the agricultural sector recovered from the devastating drought of 2016.

Nigeria contributed about half of the improvement in Africa's overall growth in 2017. In contrast, growth was restrained by adjustment to lower commodity revenues in countries such as Côte d'Ivoire (which saw world cocoa prices and fiscal revenues plummet in 2017). Ethiopia, Kenya and the United Republic of Tanzania, still among the fastest growing economies in Africa, also slowed compared to 2016, as did fuel exporters such as Algeria, Cameroon and Gabon. The drought in East Africa continued into early 2017 affecting agricultural production in Kenya and Uganda and worsening famine conditions in Somalia and South Sudan.

Current account deficits narrowed

Current account deficits have narrowed in many African countries, especially among the oil and mineral exporters, as a result of a partial recovery in some commodity prices. Mining companies throughout the continent have increased production and exports. The North African economies benefited as well from a recovery in the tourism sector and growing demand for exports from Europe. The improvement was particularly remarkable in Egypt where the current account deficit narrowed rapidly, and foreign reserves surpassed a level last seen in 2010 as a result of the decision to float the currency and lift most capital controls in November 2016.

In Nigeria, oil exports recovered as militant attacks on oil pipelines subsided and oil production slowly increased, although production has not returned to previous levels. However, the current account deficit remains high in oil-importing economies, particularly in East Africa where some countries sustain high capital imports for infrastructure projects and a higher cost of fuel imports driven by the increase in global oil prices. Also, the situation remains vulnerable in Libya, Sudan, and Tunisia where foreign reserves were in decline in the first half of 2017.

Stabilization of several currencies, after sharp depreciations in 2016, eased inflationary pressures in many countries across the continent in 2017. In addition, better weather conditions contributed to lower food price inflation, especially in areas previously damaged by drought, easing household budget constraints which have hampered domestic demand. However, the inflation rate remains high.

In the Democratic Republic of the Congo, inflation is estimated to have increased by 20 percentage points in 2017, to nearly 45 per cent. High inflation is fuelled by a steep depreciation in the domestic currency, amid low commodity prices and high government deficits. In Egypt, the average inflation rate for 2017 is estimated to be 30.5 per cent, reflecting a substantial increase in food prices due to Egypt's high import reliance on grains. Libya and Sudan are also estimated to have inflation of close to 27 per cent, mainly due to a rapid expansion of the monetary base by their respective central banks to cope with the fiscal deficit.

In Angola and Nigeria, inflation is decreasing albeit remaining high, due to foreign exchange pressures and depreciated parallel exchange rates. Nevertheless, overall, exchange rates are expected to continue to stabilize across the region.

Disinflationary pressures created monetary policy space

Several central banks in Africa decreased their key policy rates in 2017 amid lowering inflationary pressures. However, monetary policy is expected to remain tight in the Democratic Republic of the Congo, Egypt, Sierra Leone and Tunisia to stabilize the value of the national currency and halt accelerating inflationary pressure.

The fiscal policy stance should remain tight in the outlook period, even as rising commodity prices allow a moderate easing of fiscal pressures. Fiscal deficits remain high, particularly among oil and mineral exporters. For example, in Sudan, the fiscal deficit is expected to widen in 2017 due to a decline in oil transit fees from South Sudan and lower levels of oil production from aging oil fields. In most countries, fiscal stabilization has come at the expense of decreased expenditure as opposed to structural fiscal reforms. For example, cocoa exporters, including Côte d'Ivoire and Ghana announced cuts to government expenditure in 2017.

Significant fiscal adjustments lie on the horizon for commodity exporters

However, some countries have taken a notably different path. In North Africa, some fiscal authorities have started fiscal consolidation efforts in a framework of structural reforms. Examples include the new value-added tax (VAT) law in Egypt and Algeria's ambitious fiscal consolidation plan for 2017–2019, which sets out a long-term strategy to foster greater private sector activity and economic diversification. Coupled with sharp exchange rate depreciations in some countries, the elevated level of fiscal deficits has increased public debt in Africa. The deterioration in public finances forced Benin, Cameroon, Chad, Gabon, Niger, Sierra Leone and Togo to seek financial assistance from the IMF in 2017.

Capital inflows have improved from the very low levels of 2016 at the same time as borrowing costs have declined. Apart from Ghana and Mozambique, where the fiscal deficit remains considerably high, sovereign spreads have diminished. In the beginning of 2017, Nigeria and Senegal successfully returned to the eurobond market, benefiting from decreased risk aversion regarding investment in developing economies and low financial market volatility.

East Africa continues to host the fastest growing economies in Africa with an expected annual growth rate of 5.9 per cent in 2018 and 6.2 per cent in 2019. Ethiopia, Kenya, the United Republic of Tanzania and Uganda lead the growth performance of the subregion with average growth of 6 per cent per annum, supported by infrastructure investments and an improving business environment. In Ethiopia, fiscal stimulus, foreign investment in infrastructure and manufacturing, diversification of the economy towards tourism and strong internal demand will continue to support growth.

East African economies grow at the fastest pace in the continent

Strong fundamentals sustain the growth of the Kenyan economy with the services sector growing and infrastructure projects supporting development in the long term. The development of oil and gas sectors will be one of the main drivers for the next years in the United Republic of Tanzania, which should also benefit from oil investments in neighbouring Uganda as oil is going to be exported through a pipeline towards Tanzanian shipping port facilities. The performance of the Somalian economy will continue to depend heavily on how the security situation and drought conditions evolve. The Democratic Republic of the Congo is profiting from a higher price of cobalt, driven by policy shifts towards zero emissions vehicles in developed economies and China. However, unsolved political tensions largely offset this positive development.

Average growth in North Africa is estimated at 4.1 per cent in 2018 and 2019 (3.5 per cent in 2018 and 3.6 per cent in 2019, excluding Libya). Stable economic growth is forecast to continue in 2018 with a scenario of stable commodity prices, further improvement in the security situation, and continuing economic recovery in Europe.

North Africa benefits from increased tourism

Moreover, the decision by the United States to ease economic and trade sanctions against Sudan may positively impact the Sudanese economy in 2018. In 2017, the economies in North Africa began to rebound due to robust growth in tourism, owing to the improving security situation, and to a recovery in commodity prices. In addition, the economic recovery of European economies also supported exports, as Europe remains the region's largest trading partner.

The recovery in oil and gas prices pushed real GDP growth in Algeria and Libya. The higher price of iron ore in 2017 versus 2016 sustained the economic expansion of Mauritania. Stable gold prices positively impacted Sudan. A substantial jump in crop yields in Morocco and Tunisia, after a severe drought in the previous crop year, contributed to the economic expansion in both economies along with the phosphate rock industry. Overall, the improvement in the region's business sentiment and consumer confidence in 2017 is revealed by the rising number of tourists visiting North Africa. The positive impact from recovering tourism was particularly felt in Egypt and Tunisia.

Nigerian economy will recover oil production and output performance

The West African economies are projected to grow by 3.3 per cent in 2018 and 3.4 per cent in 2019. Growth in Nigeria will propel the regional average forward. The country exited recession in 2017 due largely to a rebound in oil production and increase in fiscal expenditure. Looking ahead, returning business confidence is evidenced by improvement in the Purchasing Managers' Index. Improved prospects are also demonstrated by a stable foreign exchange rate for importers and exporters, convergence of the parallel and official exchange rates, improved foreign exchange reserves, decreasing inflation and improving oil prices — all paving the way for output recovery.

However, structural challenges remain, as evidenced by Moody's Investors Service cut to Nigeria's sovereign issuer rating. Challenges include a possible return of militants' attacks on oil pipelines as the country heads into its presidential campaign season, and a failure to broaden the non-oil revenue base.

Average growth in West Africa masks some of Africa's fastest growing economies, including Benin, Burkina Faso, Côte d'Ivoire and Senegal. Growth will remain supported by robust infrastructure project implementation. Côte d'Ivoire was particularly hit by the decline in cocoa prices, since 40 per cent of its export revenues originate from this commodity. However, strong private investment will compensate for shortfalls in government spending. Ghana, which also saw its export revenues drop due to lower prices for gold, cocoa and oil exports, is projected to see stronger economic growth in 2018, as new oil fields nearly double oil output. The economies of the Sahel continue to face serious threat from violent conflict, weighing on growth prospects.

Previously delayed fiscal adjustment has started amid security concerns

The Central African economies are projected to grow by 2.1 per cent in 2018 and 2.5 per cent in 2019, supported by the increase in oil prices. Looking ahead, the security situation in the region will continue to hamper its prospects for investment and GDP growth. In Cameroon, growth will be driven by the implementation of large infrastructure projects and a rise in gas production in 2018 which should compensate the decline in oil production since 2016, although significant political tensions and security threats pose risks to the outlook.

Despite vulnerabilities to the spread of terrorist activities from Nigeria, an easing of fiscal austerity will improve growth in Chad, along with a stronger oil sector performance. Equatorial Guinea joined the Organization of the Petroleum Exporting Countries (OPEC) in May 2017 and is taking steps to stem the decline in its oil production. Nevertheless, the economy is expected to remain in recession over the forecast period, as it adjusts to a lower oil price.

Political uncertainty weighs on prospects in Southern Africa

In Southern Africa, growth is expected to average 2.3 per cent in 2018 and 2.5 per cent in 2019, supported by increasing agricultural production. However, an infestation of armyworm might pose a substantial risk to crops in the region and possibly beyond. Additionally, investment is expected to remain subdued mainly due to political uncertainties, further constrained by a lack of reforms, an unfavourable institutional environment, and slowly addressed infrastructure gaps.

In South Africa, net exports will rebound but fail to compensate weak growth in private consumption and investment. Borrowing costs have risen after the country's credit rating was downgraded to sub-investment level in April 2017 due to heightened political uncertainty. In Angola, growth will rise, sustained by increased industrial activity and improving energy supplies. Developments in mineral prices and the mining sector will determine growth in Botswana and Namibia. Growth in Zambia remains dependent on the price of copper, and will be held back by deficiencies in the electricity supply, 97 per cent of which is generated by hydropower.

In Zimbabwe, high debt levels, structural and institutional constraints, lack of liquidity, and a challenging environment as the country undergoes political transition, will continue to constrain the economy. Prospects have improved in Malawi since it re-established relations with foreign donors. Investment in Mozambique is being hampered by the government's default in January 2017 and the high level of debt. Growth in Mozambique will additionally be held back by political tensions.

The outlook for Africa remains subject to a number of risks. Externally, a sharper than expected increase in global interest rates or an increase in the premium for sovereign bonds could decrease sovereign access to financing, which has become an increasingly important source for domestic investment in recent years, and endanger debt sustainability.

Outlook clouded by external and internal factors

Further downgrades to sovereign ratings could hinder investment confidence. Moreover, lower export demand (for instance, from a less gradual moderation in Chinese growth) or a reversal in commodity price growth (as seen for some commodities in early 2017), could decrease FDI and remittance flows and generally threaten the recovery momentum. In certain least developed countries (LDCs), a decrease in the amount of aid received could have significant negative implications.

Internally, an absence of policies of fiscal adjustment to a lower commodity price level could jeopardize macroeconomic stability and the growth trend in many countries. Other risks are posed by potential escalation of the security threat, especially in the Sahel region and in Somalia, and political instability ahead of key elections in Egypt, Nigeria and South Africa. At the same time, economic reform measures in North Africa, including the introduction of new taxes, might destabilize the political and social situation, in a region which

Figure III.10
Growth of commodity prices and real GDP per capita growth in Africa

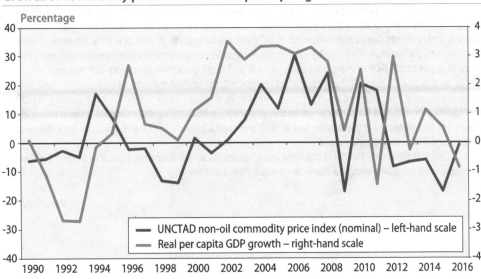

Sources: UN/DESA and UNCTADstat.

Debt, fiscal reform, drought and conflict among the greatest challenges

continues to post high unemployment rates, particularly among youth and women. Finally, several agricultural economies remain exposed to weather-related shocks.

Considerable policy challenges lie ahead for Africa. Large fiscal deficits, growing interest payments and valuation changes from exchange rate depreciation are contributing to a rapid accumulation of debt, especially in oil-exporting countries.

Fiscal adjustment plans should be developed and strictly implemented to avoid the high rate of debt accumulation of recent years. The adjustment could benefit from increased and sustained efforts in domestic resource mobilization, rather than expenditure compression. Over-reliance on commodity revenues must be curbed, through economic diversification and structural transformation, to avoid the pass-through of commodity price volatility to macroeconomic conditions (figure III.10).

In the medium-term, investments in human capital and transparent governance and institutions could help support economic diversification. Acute malnutrition must be urgently addressed in the conflict-affected areas of northeast Nigeria and South Sudan and in the dry areas of East Africa, especially in Somalia. The current growth momentum should be strengthened in sustainable and inclusive ways, so that everyone can gain, and poverty can be reduced (see Box III.2).

Box III.2
Inclusive growth in Africa

Since the turn of the century, Africa's growth performance has been unprecedentedly strong, with an average annual growth rate of 4.7 per cent between 2000 and 2015, compared to 2.4 per cent between 1980 and 2000, thus rekindling hope for more rapid development on the continent. However, between 2000 and 2014, income inequality measured by the Gini coefficient fell only slightly from 44.7 to 42.5. This has spawned concern over whether the recent growth has been inclusive.

Based on a sample of 42 countries for the period 1990–2014, Hussein, Mukungu and Awel (2017) explore the current state of inclusiveness of Africa's growth and highlight the factors that drive inclusive growth in Africa. The study relies on a unified single measure of inclusiveness that integrates growth and income distribution (GDP per capita growth, and income equity growth) following a methodology developed by Anand, Mishra and Peiris (2013). While developments clearly differ across countries, in general the modest rise in inclusiveness (estimated to have increased by 25 per cent over the sample period) has been driven by economic growth raising the level of GDP per capita, while inequality measures have remained largely stagnant.

In figure III.2.1, quadrant I shows countries where growth was inclusive through a rise in both average income per capita and equity. Notably, countries such as Burkina Faso, Ethiopia and Mali recorded greater inclusiveness due to improvements in GDP per capita growth as well as equity. However, Kenya and Uganda, for instance, registered greater inclusiveness by ensuring more equity growth and marginal growth in per capita GDP or marginal equity growth and more growth in per capita GDP, respectively.

In quadrant II, since GDP per capita has contracted, the unified measure of inclusiveness will only have improved if the observed equity growth exceeds in absolute value the percentage decline in GDP per capita. Burundi and Madagascar are in this quadrant. In both cases, the marginal growth in equity could not compensate for the contraction in GDP per capita growth, hence in both cases inclusiveness deteriorated over the sample period.

Quadrant III clearly indicates a decline in inclusiveness in two countries, Côte d'Ivoire and Guinea-Bissau, since both GDP per capita and income equity have declined.

(continued)

In quadrant IV, since income equity has declined, inclusiveness will only have improved if GDP per capita growth exceeds in absolute value the percentage decline in income equity. Several countries registered inclusive growth while growth was non-inclusive for some. For instance, Mozambique and Rwanda have clearly seen improvements in inclusiveness despite declines in equity, due to rising GDP per capita. In contrast, growth in Benin and Togo has been non-inclusive since the decline in income equity eclipsed the marginal GDP per capita growth in these countries.

Hussein, Mukungu and Awel (ibid.) show that investment, government spending, loose monetary policy, competitive and efficient financial institutions, better ICT infrastructure as well as better institutions help to promote more inclusive growth. Therefore, in pursuit of achieving the SDGs and Africa's Agenda 2063, African countries must strive to implement macro policies and strategies aimed at achieving both higher economic growth and improved equity.

Box III.2 (continued)

Authors: Khaled Hussein, Allan Mukungu and Yesuf Awel (ECA)

Figure III.2.1
Inclusiveness matrix for a sample of African countries, 1990–2014

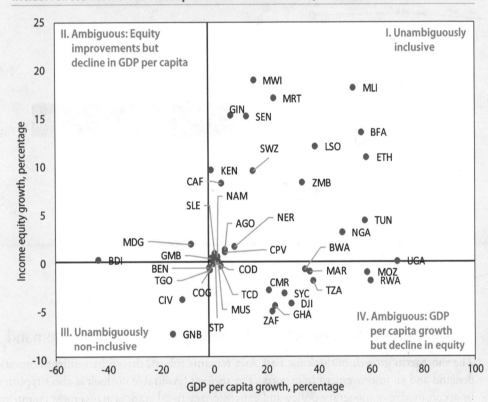

Sources: Authors' computations based on World Development Indicators 2016.

Note: Both the horizontal and vertical axes represent cumulative percentage changes over the sample period. See Table J in the Statistical annex for definitions of country codes.

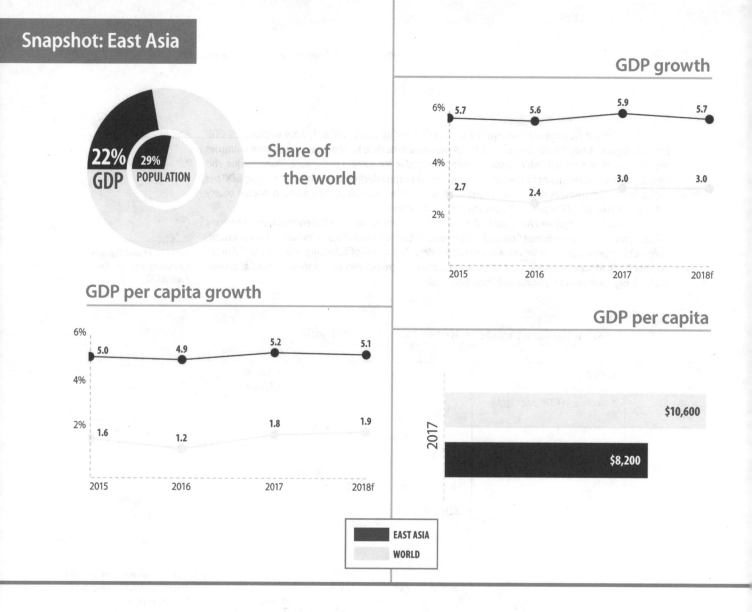

Share of the world

22% GDP

29% POPULATION

GDP growth

2015	2016	2017	2018f
5.7	5.6	5.9	5.7
2.7	2.4	3.0	3.0

GDP per capita growth

2015	2016	2017	2018f
5.0	4.9	5.2	5.1
1.6	1.2	1.8	1.9

GDP per capita

2017

$10,600

$8,200

EAST ASIA

WORLD

East Asia: Steady growth supported by robust domestic demand

The short-term growth outlook for East Asia remains robust, driven by resilient domestic demand and an improvement in exports. The region's favourable outlook is also supported by accommodative monetary policy and expansionary fiscal stances across most countries. Following growth of 5.9 per cent in 2017, the East Asian region is projected to expand at a steady pace of 5.7 per cent in 2018 and 5.6 per cent in 2019 (figure III.11). Nevertheless, the region faces several downside risks, arising mainly from high uncertainty in the international policy environment and elevated debt levels.

Private consumption remains key driver of growth for the region

Private consumption will remain the key driver of growth in East Asia, supported by modest inflationary pressures, low interest rates and favourable labour market conditions. In addition, public investment is likely to remain strong in most countries as governments continue to embark on large infrastructure projects, aimed at alleviating structural bottlenecks. Amid rising capacity utilization rates, private investment activity is also expected to pick up, particularly in the export-oriented sectors.

Figure III.11
GDP growth and inflation in East Asia

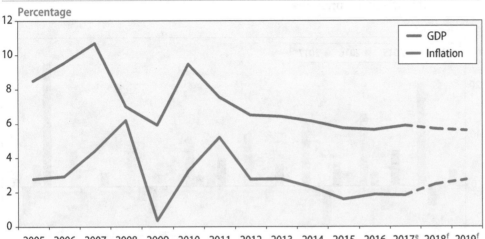

Source: UN/DESA.

Given the region's high trade openness, growth in East Asia is benefiting from the ongoing recovery in global trade activity. The recovery in the region's exports is being largely driven by growing intraregional demand. Improving demand from the developed countries, particularly the United States and Europe, is also providing an impetus to regional exports, amid the gradual revival in investment in these economies.

More specifically, the region is experiencing a strong rebound in exports of electrical and electronic goods (figure III.12), amid the upturn in the global electronics cycle. In Malaysia, the Republic of Korea, Taiwan Province of China and Thailand, shipments of semiconductors and consumer electronics grew at a double-digit pace in 2017, reflecting rising external demand and the strong integration of these economies into global and regional production networks in the electronics industry.

In the outlook period, export growth is expected to temper, given waning base effects. However, a continued expansion in external demand will generate positive spillovers to the domestic economy through the income and investment channels.

Despite robust economic activity, inflationary pressures are expected to remain subdued across most of the region, amid moderate growth in global oil prices. In 2017, higher agriculture production weighed down on food prices in countries such as China, Indonesia and Thailand. In Indonesia, Malaysia and the Philippines, adjustments to energy or transportation subsidies during the year exerted some upward pressure on overall prices. However, the effect of these one-off factors on headline inflation rates is expected to dissipate going forward. Furthermore, core inflation remains low in many economies, reflecting limited capacity pressures in the region.

Amid subdued inflation and high uncertainty in the external environment, monetary policy is likely to remain accommodative over the forecast period. In 2017, Indonesia and Viet Nam reduced their key policy rates, in efforts to stimulate bank lending and boost growth. For many countries, however, there is limited room for further rate cuts. Policy rates are at historic lows in several countries, with rates in the Republic of Korea, Taiwan Province of China and Thailand currently below 2 per cent. Furthermore, as developed economies normalize monetary policy, central banks in East Asia are faced with the poten-

Strong global demand for electrical and electronic goods has been driving the rebound in exports

Inflationary pressures expected to remain subdued across the region

Figure III.12
**Annual growth in electrical and electronic exports
in selected East Asian economies**

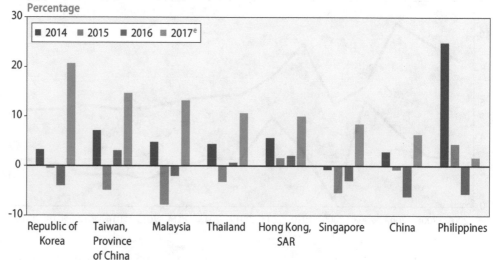

Source: National authorities.
Note: Electrical & electronic
(E&E) products refer to those
listed under HS codes 84 and
85. 2017ᵉ refers to year-on-year
growth in E&E exports from
January–September 2017 for
the Republic of Korea, January–
July 2017 for Malaysia and the
Philippines, and January–August
2017 for all other countries.

tial risk of managing large capital outflows. Elevated private sector debt in several countries also poses a constraint to the effectiveness of lower interest rates.

Fiscal policy to play a more active role in supporting domestic demand

Against this backdrop, fiscal policy in the East Asian economies is expected to play a more active role in supporting domestic demand. In 2017, several countries including China, the Philippines, the Republic of Korea, Taiwan Province of China and Thailand announced a range of fiscal and pro-growth measures, including accelerating infrastructure investment, improving access to finance for small and medium enterprises, and enhancing corporate tax incentives.

Growth in China to remain solid, as fiscal measures provide support to domestic demand

In China, growth is expected to remain solid, underpinned by favourable domestic demand and accommodative fiscal measures. Amid ongoing economic rebalancing efforts, growth will moderate at a gradual pace from 6.8 per cent in 2017 to 6.5 per cent in 2018 and 6.3 per cent in 2019. In 2017, the Chinese economy expanded at a faster pace compared to the previous year, marking the first acceleration in growth since 2010. The stronger than expected growth was in part attributed to the implementation of policy stimulus measures, including higher infrastructure spending. Private consumption remains the main driver of growth, as reflected in the continued strong increase in sales of consumer goods in 2017. Looking ahead, household spending in China is expected to remain robust, supported by healthy wage growth, rising disposable income and steady job creation.

Manufacturing activity in China also strengthened in 2017, buoyed by an improvement in both domestic and external demand, as well as rising business confidence. Coupled with a stronger rise in producer prices, these developments also contributed to double-digit growth in industrial profits during the year. On the investment front, however, overall fixed asset investment growth eased, despite continued strong infrastructure investment. This in part reflects ongoing structural reform measures to reduce excess capacity in several heavy industries, such as steel and coal.

In 2017, the Chinese authorities announced a range of monetary, macroprudential and regulatory measures aimed at mitigating rising financial sector vulnerabilities, which include elevated corporate debt, rapid credit growth and high property prices. Notably, policymakers are prioritizing the deleveraging of state-owned enterprises, including through tighter controls on debt acquisition as well as accelerating the debt-for-equity swap programme.

In addition, some measures to cool the property sector are expected to weigh on real estate investment going forward. Nevertheless, while efforts to address financial imbalances will contribute to more sustainable medium-term growth, the Chinese authorities are faced with the policy challenge of ensuring that these measures do not derail the economy's short-term growth prospects. In this environment, fiscal policy is expected to remain supportive of growth.

The Republic of Korea is projected to grow at a sustained pace of 2.8 per cent in 2018 and 2019, following an estimated growth of 3.0 per cent in 2017. Growth is expected to be broad-based across demand components, supported by policy measures and a favourable external environment. Exports grew at a double-digit pace in 2017, driven primarily by strong demand for semiconductors and petrochemical products. Amid an improvement in business sentiment and dissipating political uncertainty, private investment growth also rebounded in 2017, as capital spending in the information and technology sector picked up. Looking ahead, investment activity is projected to remain on an upward trend, buoyed by improving demand. In addition, the Government's supplementary budget, aimed at expanding welfare benefits and promoting stronger job creation, is expected to spur consumer spending. Nevertheless, geopolitical tensions in the Korean Peninsula will continue to adversely affect investor sentiments and domestic financial markets. Trade tensions with China also pose a risk to the exports outlook.

The growth outlook in the Republic of Korea, Taiwan Province of China and Singapore has strengthened

Stronger global demand for electronics has also boosted the growth outlook of the other economies in the region that are closely integrated into global and regional electronics production networks. Following subdued growth of 1.5 per cent in 2016, growth in Taiwan Province of China picked up to 2.2 per cent in 2017, and is projected to strengthen further to 2.4 per cent in 2018. In 2017, the surge in electronics and machinery exports generated positive spillovers to domestic demand, particularly in private investment. The favourable growth outlook is also reinforced by the announcement of a fiscal stimulus programme in early 2017. The plan includes the implementation of large infrastructure projects and measures to promote job creation.

Meanwhile, growth in Singapore accelerated from 2.0 per cent in 2016 to 3.0 per cent in 2017, as the strong expansion in exports boosted activity in the manufacturing and logistics sectors. Private investment however, remained sluggish, while consumer spending continued to be weighed down by weak job creation, slower wage growth and declining house prices. In 2018 and 2019, the Singaporean economy is projected to expand at a steady pace of 2.7 per cent. The projected gradual recovery in the housing market will lend support to consumption and investment activity, while improved external demand conditions are likely to spur more investment in the trade-oriented sectors.

Growth in the ASEAN economies underpinned by robust domestic demand

The favourable growth outlook for the large economies in the Association of Southeast Asian Nations (ASEAN)[2] is underpinned by robust domestic demand conditions, amid improving external demand and a modest recovery in commodity prices. In the Philippines, growth is projected to gain further traction, rising from 6.7 per cent in 2017 to 6.9 per cent in 2018 and 2019. Private consumption, which accounts for nearly 70 per cent

---

2   ASEAN member countries consist of Brunei Darussalam, Cambodia, Indonesia, Lao People's Democratic Republic, Malaysia, Myanmar, the Philippines, Singapore, Thailand and Viet Nam.

of GDP, is expected to sustain a healthy momentum, driven by large remittance inflows and buoyant consumer confidence. Fixed investment growth is also projected to remain strong, as the authorities continue to embark on large infrastructure development projects. In addition, the planned introduction of tax reform measures is expected to support the increase in public expenditure.

Following stronger than expected growth of 5.4 per cent in 2017, growth in Malaysia is projected to remain relatively steady at 4.9 per cent in 2018 and 5.0 per cent in 2019. In tandem with the growth recovery in key trading partners, Malaysia's exports saw a broad-based rebound in 2017, driven primarily by double-digit increase in demand for electrical and electronic products and an improvement in exports of commodities, particularly crude oil, palm oil and natural gas. While this strong export momentum is likely to moderate in the outlook period, growth in the Malaysian economy will be underpinned by robust domestic demand. Private consumption will be supported by continued wage and employment growth, as well as higher welfare payments. The investment outlook in Malaysia also remains strong, amid ongoing infrastructure projects and capacity expansion in the manufacturing and services sectors. In Thailand, GDP growth picked up to 3.5 per cent in 2017, as a robust expansion in private consumption and exports more than offset the weakness in private investment. Going forward, the Thai economy is projected to register growth of 3.4 per cent in 2018, supported by a pickup in public investment that largely offsets weaker investment in the private sector. Lingering political uncertainty will continue to weigh on investor sentiments. In Indonesia, the growth outlook remains stable, against a backdrop of steady growth in private consumption and public expenditure. Growth is projected to improve slightly from an estimated 5.2 per cent in 2017 to 5.3 per cent in 2018, as additional monetary policy easing measures lend support to businesses and private investment activity. In addition, a series of policy reforms to improve the business climate, progressively introduced since late 2015, will bolster future investment prospects of the Indonesian economy. Meanwhile, the positive growth outlook for Viet Nam is underpinned by buoyant FDI inflows, particularly in the electronics sector, as well as strong tourism revenue.

ASEAN LDCs to continue growing at a rapid pace, but structural challenges remain

The LDCs in ASEAN, namely Cambodia, Lao People's Democratic Republic and Myanmar, are projected to continue achieving growth rates of above 7.0 per cent in 2018 and 2019, as incomes rise from relatively low bases. Alongside vigorous private consumption growth, strong infrastructure investment, particularly in the energy and transportation sectors, is also boosting growth in these economies. Growth is also benefiting from the improvement in external demand, especially from within the Asian region. Nevertheless, low levels of productivity, amid shortfalls in essential infrastructure continue to pose a challenge to medium-term growth prospects and to making significant progress towards the SDGs.

Steady growth in the Pacific Island economies

Meanwhile, the Pacific Island economies, including Kiribati, Papua New Guinea, the Solomon Islands and Vanuatu, are expected to grow at a steady pace in the forecast period. The positive outlook is supported by continued growth in revenues from the agriculture, mining, fisheries and tourism industries. Given high commodity dependence, however, the growth prospects of these economies remain highly susceptible to commodity price and weather-related shocks.

East Asia faces downside risks, particularly rising trade protectionism

Looking ahead, the region faces considerable downside risks to its growth outlook, mainly arising from high uncertainty in the external environment. In particular, a potential sharp escalation in trade protectionism measures by the United States could disrupt regional production networks, harming the region's growth prospects. In addition, faster-than-expected monetary policy normalization in developed economies may trigger sudden and large capital outflows from the region, potentially disrupting domestic financial conditions. Furthermore, rising geopolitical tensions, notably in the Korean Peninsula, continue to weigh on investor sentiments.

On the domestic front, financial sector vulnerabilities, particularly high corporate and household debt, will continue to weigh on investment prospects in several countries. In China, the country's high debt, particularly relative to the level of its GDP per capita (figure III.13), has raised concerns over financial stability risks arising from a possible sharp deleveraging process. While ongoing policy measures to contain financial vulnerabilities is expected to result in a gradual growth moderation in China, the risk of a sharper-than-expected growth slowdown remains. The materialization of such a risk would have considerable ramifications on the rest of East Asia, given the region's high trade exposure to the Chinese economy.

Given the favourable macroeconomic environment in the short term, policymakers in the region have more policy space to make progress on structural reforms aimed at enhancing economic resilience and improving the quality of growth. Policy strategies geared towards raising productivity growth are vital in boosting the region's dynamism and medium-term growth prospects. This includes placing greater focus on addressing critical infrastructure gaps, upskilling of the workforce and initiatives to foster innovation as well as research and development investment. In addition, stronger redistribution policies and social safety nets will not only invigorate domestic demand, but also contribute to more sustainable and inclusive growth.

Measures to boost productivity growth are needed to strengthen East Asia's medium-term growth prospects

Figure III.13

Private non-financial debt and nominal GDP per capita of selected East Asian and developed economies, 2016

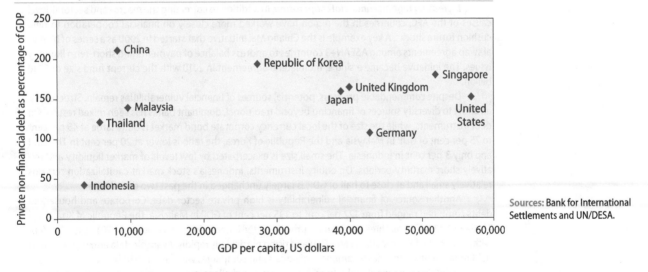

Sources: Bank for International Settlements and UN/DESA.

Box III.3

20 years after the Asian financial crisis

The year 2017 marks the 20th anniversary of the Asian financial crisis (AFC). Major crisis-affected econ-omies often cited include Indonesia, Malaysia, the Republic of Korea and Thailand, although the AFC also dampened economic growth in several other East Asian economies, such as Hong Kong SAR, the Philippines and Singapore.

This box shows that the region's macroeconomic fundamentals have improved in the past two decades, partly aided by enhanced policy management following the AFC. This has helped emerging Asian economies to benefit from a long period of financial stability, including during the global financial crisis. However, pockets of domestic financial vulnerabilities remain today, particularly rising private sector debt amid a high degree of global policy uncertainty.

Macroeconomic fundamentals and financial stability in the crisis-affected economies have strengthened amid policy adjustments and reforms. At a macro level, the AFC was primarily caused by burgeoning external imbalances, such as large current account deficits amid foreign debt-fuelled busi-ness investment. At a sectoral level, loose prudential regulation and supervision resulted in the build-up of financial and corporate vulnerabilities. Given the unprecedented scale of economic turmoil that the AFC brought, the crisis triggered policymakers in the region to spend considerable effort in addressing these issues. Some examples of policy measures include:

Enhancing macroeconomic management. The crisis-affected economies have adopted a more flexible exchange rate regime and inflation targeting framework, which helped reduce external account imbalances and increased the effectiveness of monetary policy in managing inflation. In 1996, the year before the AFC began, the current account deficit in the crisis-affected economies amounted to 3.4 per cent to 8 per cent of GDP, while foreign exchange reserves were equivalent to only two to five months of imports. In recent years, these economies have enjoyed sizeable current account surpluses or much smaller deficits, while reserves are currently worth at least seven months of imports.

Strengthening macroprudential regulation and supervision. To achieve greater financial stability, the crisis-affected economies shut down and merged financial institutions, introduced new financial su-pervisory agencies, and promoted transparency and data disclosure. Among several other factors, such policy changes helped reduce the share of non-performing loans from its peak of 19 per cent to 49 per cent of total loans in Indonesia, Malaysia and Thailand in 1998 to below 3 per cent in recent years.

Increasing regional financial cooperation. In addition to correcting the macro- and sectoral-level causes of the AFC, countries in the region have worked more closely on financial cooperation to help cushion future shocks. A key example is the Chiang Mai Initiative that started in 2000 as a series of bilater-al swap agreements among ASEAN+3 countries to address balance of payments and short-term liquidity issues. The initiative became a single, multilateral agreement in 2010 with the current fund size of $240 billion.

Despite commendable progress, potential sources of financial vulnerabilities remain. Structurally, an effort to diversify sources of financing beyond traditional, dominant banks has seen mixed results. On debt instruments, while the size of the local currency corporate bond market is quite large at 45 per cent to 75 per cent of GDP in Malaysia and the Republic of Korea, the ratio is lower at 20 per cent in Thailand and only 3 per cent in Indonesia. The small size is exacerbated by low levels of market liquidity and rel-atively short maturity periods. On equity instruments, Indonesia's stock market capitalization remains relatively small and at close to half of GDP, is largely unchanged in the past two decades.

Another source of financial vulnerability is high private sector debt. Corporate and household debts combined ranged from 122 per cent to 195 per cent of GDP in Malaysia, the Republic of Korea and Thailand in 2016. In all three economies, private sector indebtedness was higher in 2016 than in 2007, with household debt in Malaysia and Thailand rising particularly rapidly. Available data also suggests that debt repayment ability is lower among individuals and companies with larger debt burdens.

Maintaining financial stability in Asia remains a challenging task. Rising private sector debt in the region comes at a time when global policy uncertainty is high and interest rates in major developed economies, particularly the United States, are on an upward trend. The risk of sharp reversal of portfolio capital inflows remains, especially if geopolitical tensions in the region intensify. Finally, rising intrar-egional trade and financial linkages call for greater vigilance and cooperation among policymakers in the region.

Authors: Sara Holttinen and
Vatcharin Sirimaneetham
(ESCAP)

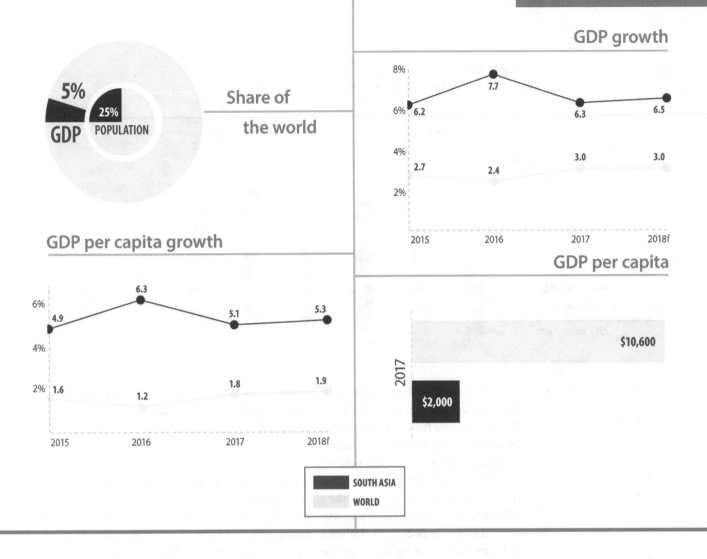

Share of the world

5% **GDP**

25% **POPULATION**

GDP growth

8%

7.7

6% 6.2

6.3 6.5

4%

3.0 3.0

2.7 2.4

2%

2015   2016   2017   2018f

GDP per capita growth

6.3

6% 5.1 5.3

4.9

4%

1.8 1.9

2% 1.6 1.2

2015   2016   2017   2018f

GDP per capita

2017

$10,600

$2,000

SOUTH ASIA

WORLD

South Asia: A favourable short-term outlook with significant medium-term challenges

The economic outlook remains steady and largely favourable in South Asia, driven by robust private consumption and sound macroeconomic policies. Monetary policy stances are moderately accommodative, while fiscal policies in several economies maintain a strong emphasis on infrastructure investment. The recovery of external demand is also buttressing growth. Against this backdrop, regional GDP growth is expected to strengthen to 6.5 per cent in 2018 and 7.0 per cent in 2019, following an estimated expansion of 6.3 per cent in 2017.

The positive economic outlook is widespread across the region, with most economies projected to see stronger growth rates in 2018 compared to 2017. In addition, regional inflation is expected to remain stable and at relatively low levels. The favourable prospects for inflation, coupled with mostly sustainable current account deficits, will facilitate macroeconomic policy management across the region in the near term. Overall, this positive outlook is a continuation of the improvement in economic conditions in South Asia over the past several years (figure III.14), and will contribute to gradual progress in labour market indicators and a reduction in poverty rates.

South Asia remains the fastest-growing developing region…

Figure III.14
South Asia: GDP growth and consumer-price inflation

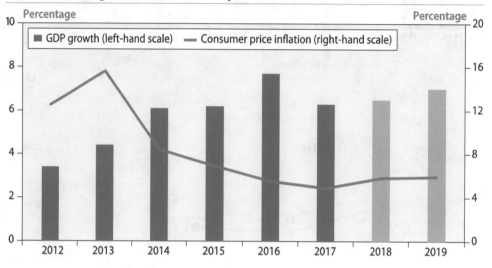

Source: UN/DESA.

Note: Figures for 2017 are partly estimated; figures for 2018 and 2019 are forecasts.

...but there are several downside risks that can affect the short-term outlook

Notwithstanding this short-term outlook, South Asian economies face several downside risks and uncertainties, which could significantly alter the projected growth trajectory. On the domestic front, the reform agenda, a crucial element of higher productivity growth, could experience setbacks in some countries, while heightened regional geopolitical tensions may restrain investment projects.

On the external front, the monetary normalization process in the United States poses risks to financial stability across the region. Tighter global liquidity conditions could significantly affect capital flows into the region, leading to a spike in financing costs, depreciation in exchange rates and a decline in equity prices. This could adversely impact banking and corporate sector balance sheets as well as the capacity to roll over debt, especially in countries with relatively low financial buffers and high dollar denominated debt.

Despite the growth slowdown in 2017, the outlook for India remains positive

Despite the slowdown observed in early 2017 and the lingering effects from the demonetization policy, the outlook for India remains largely positive, underpinned by robust private consumption and public investment as well as ongoing structural reforms. Hence, GDP growth is projected to accelerate from 6.7 per cent in 2017 to 7.2 per cent in 2018 and 7.4 per cent in 2019.

Nevertheless, the anaemic performance of private investment remains a key macroeconomic concern. Gross fixed capital formation as a share of GDP has declined from about 40 per cent in 2010 to less than 30 per cent in 2017, amid subdued credit growth, low capacity utilization in some industrial sectors and balance sheet problems in the banking and corporate sectors. In this environment, vigorous public investment in infrastructure has been critical in propping up overall investment growth.

Meanwhile, the economic situation in the Islamic Republic of Iran has improved visibly in recent years. In 2017, GDP growth remained relatively robust at 5.3 per cent, after surging by an estimated 12.5 per cent in 2016 due to a strong expansion of oil production and exports. GDP growth is expected to remain above 5.0 per cent in 2018 and 2019, supported by easing monetary conditions and an improving external sector. However, the moderately favourable outlook is contingent on the capacity to attract foreign investments and is subject to significant geopolitical risks and uncertainties.

Among the smaller economies in the region, economic activity in Pakistan is expected to remain vigorous, with GDP growth projected to reach 5.5 per cent and 5.2 per cent in 2018 and 2019, respectively. Economic activity will be supported by a pickup in exports and rising investment demand, which is expected to benefit from an improving business sentiment, the China-Pakistan Economic Corridor (CPEC) and other infrastructure initiatives. However, a rising current account deficit coupled with a recent deterioration of fiscal accounts, pose risks to the baseline projection.

Meanwhile, the Bangladesh economy is set to continue expanding at a rapid pace, underpinned by strong domestic demand, especially large infrastructure projects and new initiatives in the energy sector. GDP growth is expected to remain above 7.0 per cent in 2018 and 2019. Following several years of subdued economic activity and balance of payment problems, growth in Sri Lanka is gradually gaining momentum. The recovery has been supported by stronger external demand and moderate investment growth. In Nepal, economic growth is projected to slow from the peak of 7.5 per cent observed in 2017, but to remain above 4.5 per cent, closer to its medium-term potential (figure III.15).

Inflation prospects remain benign across the region. Consumer price inflation reached a multi-year record low of 4.9 per cent in 2017, due to relatively low commodity prices, waning depreciation pressures and good harvest seasons in most countries that have supported lower food prices, notably in India. In 2017, inflation declined to record lows in India and Nepal, while it remained relatively muted in comparison to historical figures in Pakistan, Bangladesh and the Islamic Republic of Iran.

By contrast, inflation in Sri Lanka tended to increase throughout 2017, pushed by depreciation pressures, relatively high credit expansion and the drought's impact on food prices. In the outlook, consumer price inflation in South Asia is expected to rise moderately to 5.8 per cent in 2018 and 5.9 per cent in 2019, still well-below historical levels in the region.

Against this backdrop, monetary policy stances are mostly accommodative in the region, following an easing cycle initiated in previous years. In 2017, monetary conditions

GDP growth in Bangladesh remains robust, while economic activity in Sri Lanka is slowly picking up

Monetary policy stance remains mostly accommodative…

Figure III.15
South Asia: GDP growth, 2018 and 2012–2017 (*average*)

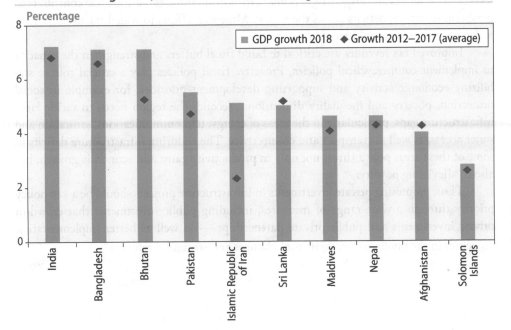

Source: UN/DESA.
Note: Figures for 2018 are forecasts.

were eased further in countries such as India, the Islamic Republic of Iran and Nepal. In India, the key policy rate was cut by an additional 25 basis points in August, while monetary authorities in the Islamic Republic of Iran reduced reserve requirements from 13 per cent to 10 per cent to encourage lending to small and medium-size enterprises.

Yet, credit growth remains moderately subdued across the region, particularly so in industrial sectors in India. In response, the Indian Government has implemented a range of policy measures to address the relatively elevated levels of non-performing loans, for instance through a large recapitalization plan for State-owned banks and by implementing new insolvency proceedings.

Looking ahead, there exists some degree of uncertainty over the monetary policy stance in India. Subdued inflation, coupled with a good monsoon season, offers scope for additional monetary easing. However, if inflation accelerates faster than anticipated, the loosening cycle could end abruptly. Meanwhile, the Central Bank of Sri Lanka is modifying its monetary policy and exchange rate framework, moving towards an inflation-targeted policy approach.

...while fiscal policies are moderately tight but with significant degrees of freedom

Amid relatively high levels of public debt, fiscal policies are officially in a moderately tight stance in most economies. Ongoing fiscal consolidation efforts, however, have yielded different levels of progress, as public budgets have been in reality more expansionary. In India, the fiscal deficit has declined visibly, and it is expected to narrow further to 3.2 per cent of GDP in 2018. In Sri Lanka, the fiscal deficit has also narrowed, amid strong consolidation pressures under the Extended Fund Facility arrangement with the IMF. By contrast, the fiscal deficit has recently expanded in Pakistan, and it continues to be moderately high in Bangladesh, at about 5 per cent of GDP. Given the large development needs across the region, budget deficits are expected to remain relatively high but manageable in the outlook period. Several economies have introduced new initiatives to strengthen the tax base, including comprehensive tax reforms in India and Sri Lanka.

Tackling structural issues should be a key priority to promote stronger productivity gains, more inclusive growth and greater poverty reduction

Beyond the favourable economic situation and its short-term risks and uncertainties, there are crucial areas that South Asia needs to address to unleash its growth potential and to promote a more sustained and inclusive development path in the medium term. First, strengthening the fiscal accounts constitutes a key challenge for most economies. The low level of tax revenues and largely rigid public expenditure throughout the cycle contribute to persistent structural deficits across the region. Moreover, efforts to widen the tax base have so far exerted only partial success.

Improved tax revenues are critical to build fiscal buffers and strengthen the capacity to implement countercyclical policies. Proactive fiscal policies play a crucial role in stabilizing economic activity and supporting development priorities, for example in social protection, poverty and inequality dimensions. Second, the region needs to tackle large infrastructure gaps, particularly in the areas of energy, telecommunications, sanitation and water access, as well as transport and connectivity. The enduring infrastructure deficits in some of these areas pose a threat not only to productivity gains and economic growth, but also to alleviating poverty.

Thus, promoting private investments in infrastructure projects should be a key policy priority through a wide range of measures, including public investments that crowd-in private investments and public-private partnerships — as well as better implementation capacities in the public sector, regulatory changes and structural reforms.

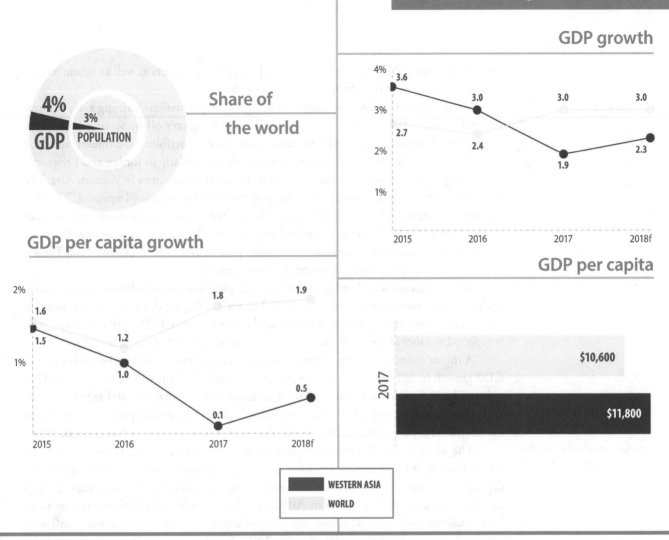

GDP growth

Share of the world

4% GDP

3% POPULATION

GDP per capita growth

GDP per capita

2017

$10,600

$11,800

WESTERN ASIA

WORLD

Western Asia: Outlook mixed, overshadowed by oil market and geopolitical factors

The economic outlook for Western Asia remains mixed, overshadowed by oil market developments and geopolitical factors. GDP growth for Western Asia slowed to an estimated 1.9 per cent in 2017. A slow recovery is projected, with GDP growth forecast to be 2.3 per cent for 2018, and 2.7 per cent for 2019.

Oil market developments remained the most influencing factor to the region's economies in 2017, particularly in the major oil exporting economies of Bahrain, Iraq, Kuwait, Oman, Qatar, Saudi Arabia and the United Arab Emirates. As oil prices are forecast to recover gradually (see discussion in Chapter I), the GDP growth of the member states of the Cooperation Council for the Arab States of the Gulf (GCC), namely Bahrain, Kuwait, Oman, Qatar, Saudi Arabia and the United Arab Emirates, is forecast to bottom out in 2018, followed by a gradual acceleration. Despite a significant negative contribution of the oil sector to real GDP growth in 2017, a resilient domestic demand expansion prevented the GCC economies from a severe contraction. Domestic demand in GCC economies has been supported by the stabilizing value of financial and real estate assets as well as strong foreign investors interest — mainly from South and East Asia.

Intraregional resource flows decline as a regional repercussion of the slowdown in GCC economies

Weaker growth in GCC economies had regional repercussions, causing a dip in intraregional resource flows from GCC economies to the region's oil importing economies. Stagnation in intraregional trade, workers' remittances, portfolio investments and FDI posed less favourable external conditions for growth, particularly in Jordan and Lebanon.

The geopolitical situation continues to influence the economies in Western Asia. The Iraqi economy regained a degree of stability as the security situation improved. The dire economic situation in the Syrian Arab Republic and Yemen continues as both countries face humanitarian crises due to ongoing armed violence. While geopolitical tensions continued to impact negatively on neighbouring economies, particularly Jordan, Lebanon and Turkey, several signs of resilience were observed in those economies.

After exhibiting a resilient growth in 2016 despite political turbulences, the expansion of the Turkish economy accelerated in 2017. The real GDP growth for 2017 is estimated at 3.3 per cent, supported by strong domestic and external demand. The present momentum is expected to taper off as GDP growth is forecast to slow to 2.1 per cent in 2018.

A robust economic expansion continued in Israel despite a deceleration in the rate of GDP growth in 2017 from the previous year. The real GDP growth of Israel for 2017 is estimated at 2.9 per cent. Growth in both domestic and external demand led the present strong expansion, supported by accommodative fiscal and monetary policies. The present momentum is expected to continue, as GDP growth is forecast to be 3.1 per cent in 2018.

Inflation trends vary for country-specific factors

The average annual consumer price inflation of Western Asia is estimated to be 4.8 percent in 2017. However, inflation trends varied among Western Asian economies depending on country-specific factors. Average consumer price inflation is forecast to drop to a moderate pace of 4.5 per cent in 2018 and 3.9 per cent in 2019. Inflationary pressures have remained weak in GCC economies, particularly on food prices. By contrast, inflation rates in Jordan and Lebanon picked up in 2017 after deflation in 2016. Conflict-related inflationary pressures were well contained in Iraq.

Hyperinflation continued in the Syrian Arab Republic and Yemen, but the inflation rate is expected to drop significantly in Syria with the stabilizing value of the Syrian pound. In 2018, the economic recovery in GCC countries is expected to produce mild inflationary pressure, which could be reinforced by the expected introduction of a unified VAT in 2018.

The consumer price inflation rate in Turkey is estimated to be 10.8 per cent in 2017, in part reflecting a rise in import prices due to the depreciation of the Turkish lira. The rapid growth of the broad money stock continued well into 2017. The inflation rate is forecast to be 8.3 per cent in 2018 as the pass-through impact of the Turkish lira's steep devaluation in 2016 dissipates.

Consumer price inflation in Israel is estimated to be 0.2 per cent in 2017. The appreciation of the shekel put the economy into deflationary territory. However, overheating domestic demand and upward pressure on wage rates are expected to create inflationary pressures in Israel — with inflation forecast to rise to 2.3 per cent for 2018.

Policy interest rate in GCC economies and Jordan rise in line with the Fed

Financing costs in GCC economies and in Jordan and Lebanon have been rising, which suppressed the growth of the broad money stock. As the majority of economies in the region peg their national currencies to the US dollar, central banks in Bahrain, Jordan, Kuwait, Qatar, Saudi Arabia and the United Arab Emirates increased their respective policy interest rates in line with the federal funds rate hikes in the United States.

Despite the ongoing armed conflict, central banks in Iraq, the Syrian Arab Republic and Yemen remained functioning, and have endeavoured to exert some economic order by stabilizing the foreign exchange rates and maintaining money circulation.

The Central Bank of the Republic of Turkey tightened its policy stance by raising its policy rate, aiming to stabilize the Turkish lira. Its late liquidity window rate had reached 12.25 per cent in April 2017 and stood at the same rate as in November 2017. The Central Bank of Israel maintained a record low level of its policy rate at 0.1 per cent.

Due to a moderate increase in fiscal revenues in GCC economies, and in Jordan and Lebanon, deficits are expected to edge down in those economies over 2017 and 2018. However, fiscal authorities remained cautious against loosening the policy stance, instead proposing tax reforms to strengthen the revenue base and to reduce public debt. The introduction of the VAT has been legislated in Saudi Arabia and the United Arab Emirates and will become effective on 1 January 2018. Other GCC economies are expected to follow. If implemented, a 5 per cent VAT will be imposed on a wide variety of goods and services (see Box III.4).

Fiscal authorities remain cautious against loosening fiscal stance

The Turkish Government is expected to maintain fiscal prudence by taking a tighter stance after having increased expenditure as part of stimulus measures introduced in 2017. This will keep both deficits and debts at a manageable level.

The fiscal policy stance remained accommodative in Israel due to its strong fiscal position. Fiscal expenditures are expected to grow, despite the planned introduction of tax cutting measures over 2017 and 2018.

External balances improved in some Western Asian economies, particularly in major oil exporting economies as oil export revenues recovered from the lows of 2016. A moderate recovery in tourism also supported the improvement. For 2017 and 2018, Kuwait, Qatar, Saudi Arabia and the United Arab Emirates are projected to record current account surpluses. Bahrain and Oman will continue to see current account deficits in 2017 before reaching surpluses in 2018. Growth in non-oil trade is expected in Bahrain and the United Arab Emirates, but the trade structure of the GCC economies remains highly oil-dependent.

External balances improve in major oil exporting economies

Current account deficits are expected to edge down in Jordan and Lebanon over 2017 and 2018. Stagnating resource inflows, such as FDI and workers' remittances, constrain the range of trade deficits that can be financed by financial account surpluses. The Syrian Arab Republic appears to have regained a stable external balance, as the value of the Syrian pound stabilized since August 2016. The Syrian pound even edged up against the US dollar, and stood at SYP 498/$ in November 2017.

The depreciation of the Turkish lira continued in 2017 albeit at a slower pace than in the previous year. Due to an improving trade balance, the central bank's foreign reserves rebounded in the second quarter of 2017. Despite active interventions by the central bank, the Israeli shekel continued to appreciate in 2017, impacting the price competitiveness of exports to Europe. However, strong growth in service trade kept the current account in surplus, accelerating foreign reserves accumulation.

The employment situation remain mixed in the region. A large share of the population is out of work due to armed conflicts in the region, and the chronically high unemployment situation in Jordan and Lebanon has not improved. However, national employment conditions have moderately improved in GCC economies along with the labour force nationalization policies. More GCC nationals took up private sector jobs that had been traditionally tasked to foreign workers.

The unemployment rate, particularly for women, remains high in some Western Asian economies

A gradually rising female labour participation rate in GCC economies also supported labour force nationalization. Nevertheless, due to a large number of new entrants to labour markets, unemployment rates remained high as indicated by available national data. The

Box III.4

A preliminary assessment of the economic implications of GCC-wide VAT

In an effort to reduce their fiscal dependency on oil revenue, the Cooperation Council for the Arab States of the Gulf (GCC) countries have attempted to implement various tax reforms over the last decades. The income and corporate taxes mostly targeting foreigners have been introduced during times of low oil prices, and have been occasionally abandoned by a recovery in oil prices. In particular, the introduction of value-added tax (VAT) has been discussed extensively but not implemented yet as many GCC countries would want to remain a tax-free area to attract foreign investment and maintain the status of an international service hub.[a]

Meanwhile, the recent drop in oil prices and its implications in terms of fiscal deficit and indebtedness and dwindled foreign reserves reinforce a further robust basis for the VAT introduction in GCC countries. Recently, a decision has finally been made to implement a GCC-wide VAT at 5 per cent starting January 2018 in Saudi Arabia and the United Arab Emirates, and by the end of 2018 for the rest of the GCC States. In effect, a newly introduced VAT could have substantial socioeconomic implications for household consumption paths by raising consumer prices. Its effect on growth, trade and sectoral production could depend significantly on how governments utilize the generated revenues.

A preliminary assessment using the MIRAGE global computable general equilibrium (CGE) model[b] shows that the net impact of a GCC-wide VAT at 5 per cent could generate a considerable fiscal revenue (countries varying between 0.9 per cent and 3.1 per cent of GDP). If these revenues are only used to improve the fiscal balance, this could generate a slowdown in growth, an increase in unemployment, a rise in inflation and a reduction of household consumption. This further implies a reduction in imports under an assumption that public spending remains unchanged, which in a modelling-context of fixed balance of payments can be associated with a real depreciation of exchange rates and an increase of total exports.

In contrast, the results could completely change if these revenues were utilized for public expenditure while leaving the public deficit unchanged.[c] Model estimates suggest that the net impact of the VAT shock on growth will be positive, as government expenditure could bring about cycles of spending that would positively affect employment creation and domestic demand (known as the Keynesian multiplier). The estimated job creation would increase household revenue and consumption and pull in additional imports from the rest of the world. The rise in economic activity and domestic demand would raise fiscal revenue over and above the direct impact of the VAT rise.

While successful implementation of VAT is important as a revenue generator, its socioeconomic effects depend on the use of these revenues, which is even more critical, as demonstrated by the preliminary assessment. If the revenue generated by VAT is used only to improve fiscal balances, the implementation could hinder sustainable growth and employment. Meanwhile, both growth and job creation could be positive if the revenue is allocated to public spending. Not only should policymakers effectively implement the new taxation, they should also consider its broad implications and distributive effects.

a Abed and Davoodi (2003).

b The GCC-wide VAT at 5 per cent rate is modelled for four years (2018-2021) to estimate its distributive effects of two broad policy options—the generated revenue by VAT is simulated to utilize to either reduce fiscal deficit or increase government expenditure. The impacts are averaged across six countries.

c Based on IMF country reports and Article IV missions, reports and consultations.

Author: Seung-Jin Baek (ESCWA)

Figure III.4.1

Macroeconomic implications from introducing VAT in GCC countries

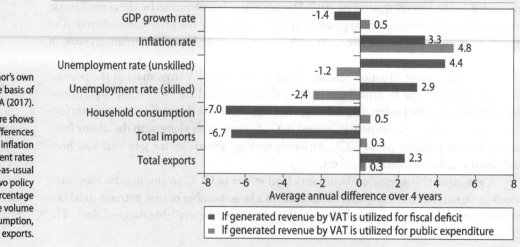

Source: Author's own elaboration on the basis of ESCWA (2017).

Note: The figure shows percentage point differences for GDP growth rate, inflation rate and unemployment rates between the business-as-usual scenario and the two policy scenarios, and percentage differences in the volume of household consumption, imports and exports.

	If generated revenue by VAT is utilized for fiscal deficit	If generated revenue by VAT is utilized for public expenditure
GDP growth rate	-1.4	0.5
Inflation rate	3.3	4.8
Unemployment rate (unskilled)	4.4	-1.2
Unemployment rate (skilled)	2.9	-2.4
Household consumption	-7.0	0.5
Total imports	-6.7	0.3
Total exports	2.3	0.3

Average annual difference over 4 years

unemployment rate in Jordan stood at 18.2 per cent (13. 9 per cent for male and 33.0 per cent for female) in the first quarter of 2017. The unemployment rate among Saudi nationals stood at 12.8 per cent (7.4 per cent for male and 33.1 per cent for female) in the second quarter of 2017. After registering a seven-year high in January with 13 per cent, the unemployment rate in Turkey came down to 10.2 per cent in June 2017. Male unemployment has quickly come down to 8.6 percent, whereas the female unemployment rate rose moderately to 13.5 per cent. Employment dynamics in Israel bucked the regional trend as the unemployment rate continued to drop to 4.1 per cent (4.1 per cent for male and 4.2 per cent for female) in August 2017.

Geopolitical tensions, political instability and oil market developments persist as the main downside risks for Western Asian economies. Oil prices are expected to stay between $50 per barrel and $60 per barrel over 2017 and 2019. However, energy-saving measures as well as the expanded use of renewables may slow the growth in crude oil demand earlier than projected. Major oil exporting economies may need to expedite reform measures in order to diversify their economies before oil prices level off in response to the structural shift in energy markets.

Geopolitical tensions and oil market developments continue to dominate economic prospects

Snapshot: Latin America and the Caribbean

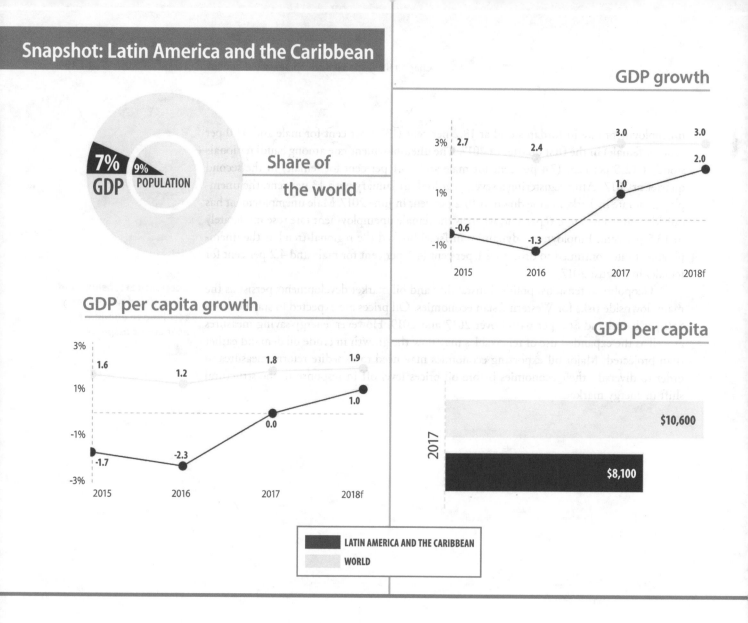

7% GDP   **9% POPULATION**

Share of the world

GDP growth

3%   2.7   2.4   3.0   3.0

2.0

1%   1.0

-0.6   -1.3

-1%

2015   2016   2017   2018f

GDP per capita growth

3%   1.6   1.2   1.8   1.9

1.0

1%

0.0

-1%

-1.7   -2.3

-3%

2015   2016   2017   2018f

GDP per capita

2017

$10,600

$8,100

LATIN AMERICA AND THE CARIBBEAN

WORLD

Latin America and the Caribbean:
The recovery is projected to strengthen

Against a backdrop of favourable global conditions, the economic recovery in Latin America and the Caribbean[3] is set to gain further traction during the forecast period. After growing by an estimated 1.0 per cent in 2017, the region's economy is projected to expand by 2.0 per cent in 2018 and 2.5 per cent in 2019. These growth rates would be the strongest that the region has seen since 2013. The recovery will be largely driven by a broad-based improvement in economic activity in South America, including in the two largest economies Argentina and Brazil. While average growth in the region is projected to strengthen gradually, it will remain well below rates observed during the commodity boom of the 2000s. A prolonged period of subpar growth would hamper the region's progress towards achieving the SDGs.

---

3   The country classification is based on United Nations Economic Commission for Latin America and the Caribbean (ECLAC). The region of Latin America and the Caribbean comprises three subregions: South America; Mexico and Central America (which includes Caribbean countries that are considered part of Latin America, namely, Cuba, the Dominican Republic and Haiti); as well as the Caribbean.

The economies of South America, many of which are specialized in the production of primary goods (particularly oil, minerals and food), were heavily affected by the negative terms of trade shock in 2015–2016. In 2017, these economies benefited from a combination of stronger global growth — and thus stronger external demand — and a modest recovery in commodity prices. This not only helped the terms of trade and export earnings, but also fiscal revenues.

At the same time, domestic demand started to recover in 2017. Total investment has expanded for the first time since 2013 and private consumption has picked up, supported by lower inflation and looser monetary policy. Despite solid growth in exports, the external sector constituted a drag to growth in 2017 as the rise in domestic demand drove imports up. On average, South America's economy has grown by an estimated 0.4 per cent in 2017, after two consecutive years of economic contraction. Notably, Argentina, Brazil and Ecuador, which all saw contractions in economic activity in 2016, have returned to growth in 2017.

In 2018, South American economies are forecast to see a further pickup in growth to 1.8 per cent. The economic recoveries in Argentina and Brazil are expected to strengthen as investment accelerates and labour markets improve; Paraguay and the Plurinational State of Bolivia are projected to post robust growth rates well above the subregional average; Chile and Peru will likely see notable improvements in their economic performance as some of the factors that dragged growth down in 2017 ease (including a copper mine strike and forest fires in Chile and floods in Peru). Meanwhile, Colombia's economic slowdown appears to have bottomed out and a mild recovery is expected in 2018. The Bolivarian Republic of Venezuela will likely see a further contraction in economic activity in 2018 amid continuing disruptions to the productive base.

The economic recoveries in Argentina and Brazil are projected to gain momentum

The subregion of Mexico and Central America is expected to grow by 2.5 per cent in 2017 and 2.6 per cent in 2018. The countries in this subregion continue to benefit from higher remittances and stronger global growth, including that of its main trading partner, the United States. Private consumption continues to be the main driver of growth, supported by low inflation rates and strong remittance inflows.

The Dominican Republic, Nicaragua and Panama will remain among the region's fastest-growing economies, benefiting from buoyant private consumption, robust public investment and a strong tourism sector. Growth in Mexico is projected to pick up slightly in 2018 to 2.4 per cent. Assuming NAFTA renegotiations are concluded in the first quarter of 2018 as scheduled, this will ease uncertainty regarding future trade relations, and support a slight recovery in private investment. A positive growth impulse is also likely to come from reconstruction spending following the two devastating earthquakes that hit Mexico in September 2017.

In English-speaking Caribbean economies, GDP growth averaged only 0.2 per cent in 2017. This weak performance reflects several factors: ongoing contractions in some of the subregion's commodity exporters, in particular Suriname and Trinidad and Tobago; the damage caused by Hurricanes Irma and Maria in several countries in September 2017, including losses in tourism; and persistent structural barriers, such as elevated unemployment, high debt burdens, insufficient access to finance and weak infrastructure. In 2018, economic growth is projected to accelerate to 1.8 per cent, supported by increased reconstruction spending and stronger private investment.

The forecasts for 2018 and 2019 are contingent on a continued benign international environment

Amid abundant global liquidity and reduced risk aversion, portfolio capital flows to Latin America continued to rise in 2017 and this positive trend is expected to continue in 2018. While financial volatility remains very low, indicators of global policy uncertainty are still elevated as risks related to protectionism, monetary tightening and geopolitical issues prevail. A marked growth slowdown in China presents an additional risk, especially for South America's commodity-exporting countries.

Slow growth in parts of Latin America and the Caribbean continues to weigh on labour markets, affecting both the quantity and quality of employment. The region's average urban unemployment is estimated to have increased for a third consecutive year, rising from 8.9 per cent in 2016 to 9.4 per cent in 2017. This reflects both a decline in the urban occupation rate and an increase in the labour force participation rate. Job creation has mainly occurred in the self-employment category, which is often associated with lower quality jobs. Total wage employment, by contrast, has seen only a modest increase.

Trends in the crisis-hit countries of South America and the rest of the region differ significantly. In fact, much of the year-on-year increase in regional unemployment can be attributed to Brazil, where unemployment surged in 2016. After peaking at a record level of 13.7 per cent in March 2017, the country's unemployment rate has started to decline — a trend that is expected to continue in 2018 and 2019. The labour market performance in Mexico and Central America has generally been more favourable. In Mexico, the unemployment rate has remained near a decade-low of 3.2 per cent amid robust job creation in the private sector. Looking ahead, average urban unemployment in the region is projected to decline slightly in 2018 and 2019 as the recovery in Brazil and other South American economies gains momentum.

The average fiscal deficit in Latin America remained steady at an estimated 3.1 per cent of GDP in 2017, albeit with significant differences across subregions (figure III.16). Following three consecutive years of improvement, the unweighted average fiscal deficit in Mexico and Central America is expected to have widened to 2.4 per cent of GDP, owing mainly to a deceleration in public revenue growth.

Similarly, in the Caribbean, where countries on average are running primary surpluses, the average fiscal deficit is estimated to have risen from 2.1 per cent of GDP in 2016 to 2.3 per cent of GDP in 2017. By contrast, in South American countries, the average deficit

> **Average urban unemployment increased further in 2017, but a mild decline is expected for 2018**

> **Recovery of fiscal space in Latin America and the Caribbean remains slow...**

Figure III.16
Latin America and the Caribbean: Central government balances, 2015–2017

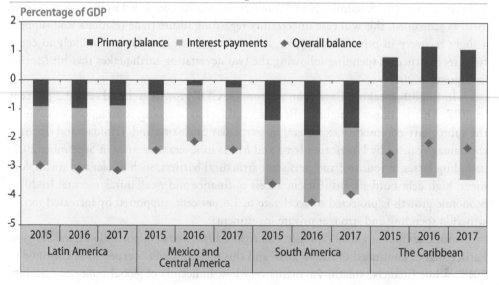

Source: ECLAC, based on official figures.

Note: Figures reflect simple (unweighted) averages of country data; Latin America and South America exclude the Plurinational State of Bolivia and the Bolivarian Republic of Venezuela; the Caribbean includes: Antigua and Barbuda, Bahamas, Barbados, Belize, Granada, Guyana, Jamaica, Saint Kitts and Nevis, Saint Vincent and the Grenadines, Santa Lucia, Suriname and Trinidad and Tobago.

is expected to have narrowed slightly, from 4.2 per cent of GDP in 2016 to 3.9 per cent of GDP in 2017, as fiscal consolidation efforts, including public spending cuts, continued.

The persistence of fiscal deficits in the post-crisis period has put upward pressure on public debt levels. The average public debt level of central governments in Latin America reached a simple average of 37.3 per cent of GDP by the end of 2016, up from 30.7 per cent in 2009. The consolidation efforts seen in South America over the past few years have helped to stabilize public debt. The regional average, however, masks significant differences between countries, with central government debt ranging from about 20 per cent of GDP in Peru to more than 70 per cent of GDP in Brazil. In the Bolivarian Republic of Venezuela (excluded in the regional average), the Government announced plans in November 2017 to refinance and restructure its external debt. However, there is immense uncertainty about what this process would entail and how it could eventually play out. In the Caribbean, high levels of public debt that entail an average annual interest burden in excess of 3 per cent of GDP remain a key fiscal constraint and a significant development barrier, although some progress has been made in recent years.

Public revenue growth has remained relatively weak in Latin America in 2017, in contrast with an upturn in the Caribbean. In Latin America, total revenues as share of GDP have decreased slightly, reflecting lower tax revenues. The unexpected increase in tax revenues in 2016 was partly the result of exceptional factors. These include the implementation of new tax administration measures in some countries, particularly in Mexico and Central America, and extraordinary income from tax amnesty programmes in South America, which mitigated the fall in public revenue. Total public revenue in the Caribbean is estimated to have risen slightly in 2017, but with large variation between countries.

Due to fiscal consolidation efforts in several countries, public spending is expected to have declined marginally in South America. The spending cuts have disproportionately affected capital expenditures. In Mexico and Central America, public spending is expected to remain stable relative to output, at close to 19 per cent of GDP. Public spending is estimated to have risen slightly in the Caribbean to about 30 per cent of GDP in 2017, with a certain shift towards higher capital expenditure, in part related to reconstruction efforts in the aftermath of natural disasters.

...despite continuing fiscal consolidation efforts, especially in South America

While consolidation measures are likely to continue during the outlook period, gains in fiscal space will take longer to materialize. Modest economic growth and moderate commodity prices will continue to weigh on fiscal revenue growth. Efforts to cut or to constrain growth in public expenditure threaten to worsen the already large structural deficits in the provision of public services, particularly in the areas of education, health and social security, possibly lowering potential growth in the future.

Against the backdrop of declining inflation, weak economic activity and improved financial stability, several South American central banks, including those in Brazil, Chile, Colombia and Peru, have eased monetary policy during 2017. The Central Bank of Brazil cut its main policy rate aggressively from 14.25 per cent in October 2016 to a current level of 8.25 per cent, the lowest level since 2013. In Argentina, by contrast, the central bank raised its reference rates in 2017 as inflation has remained above target. As South America's recovery gains momentum and economic slack diminishes, the monetary easing cycle is expected to come to an end. In the absence of negative shocks, policy rates are projected to remain largely unchanged over the next year. A moderate tightening of monetary policy is possible in the later part of the forecast period.

Monetary authorities in South America have utilized available policy space to stimulate domestic demand

In Mexico and Central America, monetary authorities generally had less scope to stimulate economic activity, partly due to elevated inflation pressures and exchange-rate volatility. Policy rates were raised in Costa Rica, the Dominican Republic and Mexico. In Mexico, the protracted tightening cycle, which started in late 2015 and saw the main policy rate rise from 3 per cent to 7 per cent, has likely come to an end. In 2018, the central bank is expected to pursue a broadly neutral stance as inflation will start to come down, albeit remaining above the 3 per cent target rate.

In countries that are dollarized (Ecuador, El Salvador and Panama) or have a pegged exchange rate against the dollar (e.g., Bahamas, Barbados and Belize), monetary policy is essentially imported from the United States. As such, local interest rates are projected to rise in line with those of the Fed.

Box III.5
The rise of the international bond market and corporate debt in Latin America

Since the start of the global financial crisis (2007–2009), the international bond market has become a major source of funding for emerging market economies including those of Latin America. The decomposition of the stock of debt issued by sector shows the rapid rise in importance of the debt of the financial and, more prominently, of the non-financial corporate sector. The increased debt of the non-financial corporate sector has been accompanied by a decline in firms' profitability, amid lower commodity prices and slower growth. This has had a negative effect on investment, and may continue to restrain investment in 2018–2019. Following the global financial crisis, the deleveraging process witnessed by global banks and other large financial institutions was accompanied by a significant decline in their profitability levels. On average, between the pre- and post-global financial crisis period, profitability measured by the rate of return on equity (ROE), which measures the amount of net income returned as a percentage of shareholders' equity, declined by 50 per cent (from 15.5 per cent to 7.7 per cent on average) in the United States.

Meanwhile, for Europe, ROE declined from 14.4 per cent to 4.9 per cent. Moreover, in the case of both Europe and the United States, the largest decline in profitability occurred in banks with the largest asset levels. Deleveraging by global banks contributed to the decline in cross-border bank lending throughout the world. Between the periods 2001 and 2008 and 2010 and 2015, the rate of growth of cross-border bank lending declined from an average of 14.6 per cent to 7.5 per cent for the United States, 16.0 per cent to 4.8 per cent for Japan, and 16.7 per cent to -1.0 per cent for the euro area.

Part of the slack in lending was filled by the bond market, which became a major source of funding for emerging market economies including those of Latin America. In the case of Latin America, the total stock of outstanding international debt securities issued, which averaged $332 billion between 2000 and 2007, increased to $881 billion in 2017. The stock of debt is concentrated in Mexico and the larger countries of South America (Argentina, Brazil, Chile, Colombia, Peru and the Bolivarian Republic of Venezuela), which account for 89 per cent of the total international debt stock in Latin America and the Caribbean.

The decomposition of the stock of debt issued by sector (including the government, the central bank, financial corporations and commercial banks) for the period 2000–2017 shows several stylized facts. First, although the government is the most important issuer of international debt, its importance has declined over time.

A second stylized fact is the rapid rise in importance of the debt of the financial and, more prominently, of the non-financial corporate sector. The stock of international debt securities of the financial sector rose, on average, from $47 billion to $241 billion between 2000–2007 and 2017. The decomposition between the private and public sector components also shows that the former explains the bulk of the rise in debt. For its part, at the regional level, the stock of the non-financial corporate sector expand-

(continued)

Box III.5 *(continued)*

Table III.5.1
Stock of international debt securities

	In US$ billions						As percentage of the total						As percentage of GDP			
Latin America and the Caribbean	2000-2007	2009	2012	2015	2016	2017	2000-2007	2009	2012	2015	2016	2017	2000-2007	2009	2012	2015
Government	235	228	255	287	334	351	70.8	58.8	40.2	36.3	38.8	39.8	9.7	5.7	4.4	6.1
Central banks	0	0	0	0	0	0	0.1	0.0	0.0	0.0	0.0	0.0	1.5	0.0	0.0	0.0
Financial corporations	24	43	106	126	121	120	7.3	11.0	16.7	15.9	14.1	13.7	1.1	1.1	1.8	2.7
Commercial banks	10	21	61	61	57	56	3.0	5.5	9.6	7.7	6.6	6.3	0.9	0.6	1.2	1.4
Other financial corporations (private)	7	18	33	39	40	40	2.2	4.5	5.1	5.0	4.6	4.5	0.3	0.4	0.6	0.8
Public banks	5	3	11	19	18	18	1.6	0.8	1.7	2.4	2.1	2.1	0.3	0.2	0.4	0.9
Non financial corporations	49	74	167	254	284	289	14.8	19.1	26.3	32.0	33.0	32.9	2.4	1.9	3.0	5.5
Other financial corporations (public)	1	1	2	6	6	6	0.3	0.2	0.4	0.8	0.7	0.7	0.7	0.2	0.2	0.3
TOTAL	332	387	634	792	860	881	100.0	100.0	100.0	100.0	100.0	100.0	17.0	10.1	11.5	17.7

Source: BIS (2017c).

ed from $49 billion to $289 billion for the same period. The data also shows that the stock of corporate debt is more important for South America than Central America.

The countries that are most exposed to corporate debt in the international bond market include Mexico and, within South America, Brazil, Chile, Colombia and Peru. Available data between 2000 and 2015 shows that for Mexico, the stock of debt of the non-financial corporate sector increased visibly from 3.1 per cent to 11.9 per cent of GDP. During the same period, the stock of debt of the non-financial corporate sector in Brazil expanded from 2.2 per cent to 8.5 per cent, from 3.3 per cent to 16.1 per cent in Chile, from 1.0 per cent to 6.3 per cent in Colombia and from 0 per cent to 4.9 per cent in Peru. Other countries in South America such as Argentina and Paraguay have, in comparative terms, smaller corporate debt ratios.

Companies that have issued debt in the international bond market have registered, on average, high levels of indebtedness and declining levels of profitability. The available evidence for Argentina, Brazil, Chile, Colombia, Mexico and Peru shows that the leverage (measured by the debt-to-equity ratio) of the companies that have issued debt in the international bond market increased from 116 per cent to 141 per cent between 2009 and 2015. At the same time, profitability measured by the ROE fell from 11.5 per cent to 1.4 per cent

Against a backdrop of higher corporate borrowing, a drop in returns implies rising financing costs and a weaker capacity to meet obligations. This may lead to a decline in production levels and capital spending, with macroeconomic repercussions as these firms represent a large percentage of total assets for the economy as a whole, whether considered at the country level, or by sector of economic activity. The firms that have issued debt in the international bond market are also among those that have the highest capitalization ratios. While only 3.7 per cent of large listed companies have issued debt in the international bond market, their share of total assets, and of fixed-asset spending and long-term investment, is quite high (figure III.5.1).

Author: Esteban Pérez Caldentey, ECLAC

(continued)

Box III.5 (*continued*)   **Figure III.5.1**
Latin America (*selected countries*)**: Non-financial firms that issued debt in
international bond markets, 2015**

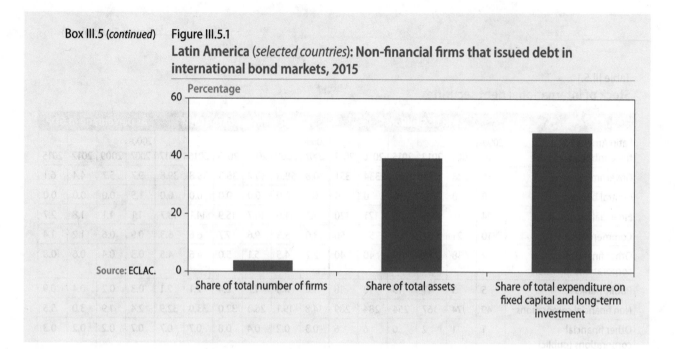

Source: ECLAC.

Statistical annex

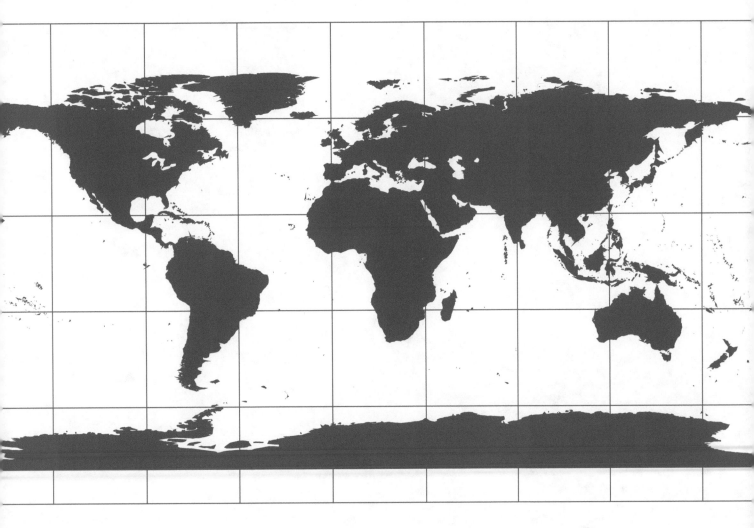

Country classifications

Data sources, country classifications and aggregation methodology

Data sources

The annex was prepared by the Development Policy and Analysis Division (DPAD) of the Department of Economic and Social Affairs of the United Nations Secretariat (UN/DESA). It is based on information obtained from the Statistics Division and the Population Division of UN/DESA, as well as from the five United Nations regional commissions, the United Nations Conference on Trade and Development (UNCTAD), the United Nations World Tourism Organisation (UNWTO), the International Monetary Fund (IMF), the World Bank, the Organisation for Economic Co-operation and Development (OECD), and national and private sources. Estimates for the most recent years were made by DPAD in consultation with the regional commissions, UNCTAD, UNWTO and participants in Project LINK, an international collaborative research group for econometric modelling coordinated jointly by DPAD and the University of Toronto. Forecasts for 2018 and 2019 are primarily based on the World Economic Forecasting Model of DPAD, with support from Project LINK.

Data presented in *WESP* may differ from those published by other organizations for a series of reasons, including differences in timing, sample composition and aggregation methods. Historical data may differ from those in previous editions of *WESP* because of updating and changes in the availability of data for individual countries.

Country classifications

For analytical purposes, *WESP* classifies all countries of the world into one of three broad categories: developed economies, economies in transition and developing economies. The composition of these groupings, specified in tables A, B and C, is intended to reflect basic economic country conditions. Several countries (in particular the economies in transition) have characteristics that could place them in more than one category; however, for purposes of analysis, the groupings have been made mutually exclusive. Within each broad category, some subgroups are defined based either on geographical location or on ad hoc criteria, such as the subgroup of "major developed economies", which is based on the membership of the Group of Seven. Geographical regions for developing economies are as follows: Africa, East Asia, South Asia, Western Asia, and Latin America and the Caribbean.[1]

The term 'emerging economies' used throughout the Report is not a formal definition, but refers to mainly middle-income developing and transition countries that are integrated into the global financial system.

---

1   Names and composition of geographical areas follow those specified in the statistical paper entitled "Standard country or area codes for statistical use" (ST/ESA/STAT/SER.M/49/Rev), available from https://unstats.un.org/unsd/publication/SeriesM/Series_M49_Rev4(1999)_en.pdf.

In parts of the analysis, a distinction is made between fuel exporters and fuel importers from among the economies in transition and the developing countries. An economy is classified as a fuel exporter if the share of fuel exports in its total merchandise exports is greater than 20 per cent and the level of fuel exports is at least 20 per cent higher than that of the country's fuel imports. This criterion is drawn from the share of fuel exports in the total value of world merchandise trade. Fuels include coal, oil and natural gas (table D).

For other parts of the analysis, countries have been classified by their level of development as measured by per capita gross national income (GNI). Accordingly, countries have been grouped as high-income, upper middle income, lower middle income and low-income (table E). To maintain compatibility with similar classifications used elsewhere, the threshold levels of GNI per capita are those established by the World Bank. Countries with less than $1,005 GNI per capita are classified as middle-income countries, those with between $1,006 and $3,955 as lower middle-income countries, those with between $3,956 and $12,235 as upper middle-income countries, and those with incomes of more than $12,235 as high-income countries. GNI per capita in dollar terms is estimated using the World Bank Atlas method,[2] and the classification in table E is based on data for 2016.

The list of the least developed countries (LDCs) is decided upon by the United Nations Economic and Social Council and, ultimately, by the General Assembly, on the basis of recommendations made by the Committee for Development Policy. The basic criteria for inclusion require that certain thresholds be met with regard to per capita GNI, a human assets index and an economic vulnerability index.[3] As of June 2017, there were 47 LDCs (table F).

WESP also makes reference to the group of heavily indebted poor countries (HIPCs), which are considered by the World Bank and IMF as part of their debt-relief initiative (the Enhanced HIPC Initiative).[4] In February 2017, there were 39 HIPCs (see table G).

Aggregation methodology

Aggregate data are either sums or weighted averages of individual country data. Unless otherwise indicated, multi-year averages of growth rates are expressed as compound annual percentage rates of change. The convention followed is to omit the base year in a multi-year growth rate. For example, the 10-year average growth rate for the decade of the 2000s would be identified as the average annual growth rate for the period from 2001 to 2010.

WESP utilizes exchange-rate conversions of national data in order to aggregate output of individual countries into regional and global totals. The growth of output in each group of countries is calculated from the sum of gross domestic product (GDP) of individual countries measured at 2010 prices and exchange rates. Data for GDP in 2010 in national currencies were converted into dollars (with selected adjustments) and extended forwards and backwards in time using changes in real GDP for each country. This method supplies a reasonable set of aggregate growth rates for a period of about 15 years, centred on 2010.

---

2   See http://data.worldbank.org/about/country-classifications.

3   *Handbook on the Least Developed Country Category: Inclusion, Graduation and Special Support Measures* (United Nations publication, Sales No. E.07.II.A.9), available from http://www.un.org/en/development/desa/policy/cdp/cdp_publications/2008cdphandbook.pdf.

4   IMF, Debt relief under the Heavily Indebted Poor Countries (HIPC) Initiative, available from http://www.imf.org/About/Factsheets/Sheets/2016/08/01/16/11/Debt-Relief-Under-the-Heavily-Indebted-Poor-Countries-Initiative?pdf=1

The exchange-rate based method differs from the one mainly applied by the IMF and the World Bank for their estimates of world and regional economic growth, which is based on purchasing power parity (PPP) weights. Over the past two decades, the growth of world gross product (WGP) on the basis of the exchange-rate based approach has been below that based on PPP weights. This is because developing countries, in the aggregate, have seen significantly higher economic growth than the rest of the world in the 1990s and 2000s and the share in WGP of these countries is larger under PPP measurements than under market exchange rates.

Table A
Developed economies

North America	Europe		Major developed economies (G7)
	European Union	Other Europe	
Canada	**EU-15**	Iceland	Canada
United States	Austria[a]	Norway	Japan
	Belgium[a]	Switzerland	France
	Denmark		Germany
	Finland[a]		Italy
	France[a]		United Kingdom
	Germany[a]		United States
	Greece[a]		
	Ireland[a]		
	Italy[a]		
	Luxembourg[a]		
	Netherlands[a]		
	Portugal[a]		
	Spain[a]		
	Sweden		
	United Kingdom		
Developed Asia and Pacific	**EU-13**[b]		
Australia	Bulgaria		
Japan	Croatia		
New Zealand	Cyprus[a]		
	Czech Republic		
	Estonia[a]		
	Hungary		
	Latvia[a]		
	Lithuania[a]		
	Malta[a]		
	Poland		
	Romania		
	Slovakia[a]		
	Slovenia[a]		

a Member of Euro area.
b Used in reference to the 13 countries that joined the EU since 2004.

Table B
Economies in transition

South-Eastern Europe	Commonwealth of Independent States and Georgia[a]	
Albania	Armenia	Republic of Moldova
Bosnia and Herzegovina	Azerbaijan	Russian Federation
Montenegro	Belarus	Tajikistan
Serbia	Georgia[a]	Turkmenistan
The former Yugoslav Republic of Macedonia	Kazakhstan	Ukraine[b]
	Kyrgyzstan	Uzbekistan

a Georgia officially left the Commonwealth of Independent States on 18 August 2009. However, its performance is discussed in the context of this group of countries for reasons of geographic proximity and similarities in economic structure.
b Starting in 2010, data for the Ukraine excludes the temporarily occupied territory of the Autonomous Republic of Crimea and Sevastopol.

Table C
Developing economies by region[a]

Africa		Asia	Latin America and the Caribbean
North Africa	**Southern Africa**	**East Asia**[b]	**Caribbean**
Algeria	Angola	Brunei Darussalam	Bahamas
Egypt	Botswana	Cambodia	Barbados
Libya	Lesotho	China	Belize
Mauritania	Malawi	Fiji	Dominican Republic
Morocco	Mauritius	Hong Kong SAR[c]	Guyana
Sudan	Mozambique	Indonesia	Jamaica
Tunisia	Namibia	Kiribati	Suriname
	South Africa	Lao People's Democratic Republic	Trinidad and Tobago
Central Africa	Swaziland	Malaysia	**Mexico and Central America**
Cameroon	Zambia	Mongolia	
Central African Republic	Zimbabwe	Myanmar	Costa Rica
Chad		Papua New Guinea	Cuba
Congo	**West Africa**	Philippines	Dominican Republic
Equatorial Guinea		Republic of Korea	El Salvador
Gabon	Benin	Samoa	Guatemala
Sao Tome and Prinicipe	Burkina Faso	Singapore	Haiti
	Cabo Verde	Solomon Islands	Honduras
East Africa	Côte d'Ivoire	Taiwan Province of China	Mexico
	Gambia (Islamic Republic of the)	Thailand	Nicaragua
Burundi	Ghana	Timor-Leste	Panama
Comoros	Guinea	Vanuatu	**South America**
Democratic Republic of the Congo	Guinea-Bissau	Viet Nam	
Djibouti	Liberia	**South Asia**	Argentina
Eritrea	Mali		Bolivia (Plurinational State of)
Ethiopia	Niger	Afghanistan	Brazil
Kenya	Nigeria	Bangladesh	Chile
Madagascar	Senegal	Bhutan	Colombia
Rwanda	Sierra Leone	India	Ecuador
Somalia	Togo	Iran (Islamic Republic of)	Paraguay
Uganda		Maldives	Peru
United Republic of Tanzania		Nepal	Uruguay
		Pakistan	Venezuela (Bolivarian Republic of)
		Sri Lanka	
		Western Asia	
		Bahrain	
		Iraq	
		Israel	
		Jordan	
		Kuwait	
		Lebanon	
		Oman	
		Qatar	
		Saudi Arabia	
		Syrian Arab Republic	
		Turkey	
		United Arab Emirates	
		Yemen	

a Economies systematically monitored by the Global Economic Monitoring Unit of DPAD.

b Throughout the report the term 'East Asia' is used in reference to this set of developing countries, and excludes Japan.

c Special Administrative Region of China.

Table D
Fuel-exporting countries

Economies in transition	Developing countries				
	Latin America and the Caribbean	Africa	East Asia	South Asia	Western Asia
Azerbaijan	Bolivia (Plurinational State of)	Algeria	Brunei Darussalam	Iran (Islamic Republic of)	Bahrain
Kazakhstan	Colombia	Angola	Indonesia		Iraq
Russian Federation	Ecuador	Cameroon	Viet Nam		Kuwait
Turkmenistan	Trinidad and Tobago	Chad			Oman
Uzbekistan	Venezuela (Bolivarian Republic of)	Congo			Qatar
		Côte d'Ivoire			Saudi Arabia
		Egypt			United Arab Emirates
		Equatorial Guinea			Yemen
		Gabon			
		Libya			
		Nigeria			
		Sudan			

Table E
Economies by per capita GNI in June 2017[a]

High-income		Upper middle income		Lower middle income	
Australia	Lithuania	Albania	Kazakhstan	Angola[b]	Mongolia
Austria	Luxembourg	Algeria	Lebanon	Armenia	Morocco
Bahamas	Malta	Argentina	Libya	Bangladesh	Myanmar
Bahrain	Netherlands	Azerbaijan	Malaysia	Bhutan	Nicaragua
Barbados	New Zealand	Belarus	Maldives	Bolivia (Plurinational	Nigeria
Belgium	Norway	Belize	Mauritius	State of)	Pakistan
Brunei	Oman	Bosnia and	Mexico	Cambodia	Papua New Guinea
Darussalam	Poland	Herzegovina	Montenegro	Cameroon	Philippines
Canada	Portugal	Botswana	Namibia	Cabo Verde	Republic of Moldova
Chile	Qatar	Brazil	Panama	Congo	São Tomé and
Cyprus	Republic of Korea	Bulgaria	Paraguay	Côte d'Ivoire	Principe
Czech Republic	Saudi Arabia	China	Peru	Djibouti	Solomon Islands
Denmark	Singapore	Colombia	Romania	Egypt	Sri Lanka
Estonia	Slovak Republic	Costa Rica	Russian Federation	El Salvador	Sudan
Finland	Slovenia	Croatia[b]	Samoa[c]	Ghana	Swaziland
France	Spain	Cuba	Serbia	Georgia[b]	Syrian Arab Republic
Germany	Sweden	Dominican Republic	South Africa	Guatemala	Tajikistan
Greece	Switzerland	Ecuador	Suriname	Honduras	Timor-Leste
Hong Kong SAR[d]	Taiwan Province of	Equatorial Guinea	Thailand	India	Tunisia
Hungary	China	Fiji	The former Yugoslav	Indonesia	Ukraine
Iceland	Trinidad and Tobago	Gabon	Republic of	Jordan[b]	Uzbekistan
Ireland	United Arab Emirates	Guyana	Macedonia	Kenya	Vanuatu
Israel	United Kingdom	Iran (Islamic Republic	Turkey	Kiribati	Viet Nam
Italy	United States	of)	Turkmenistan	Kyrgyz Republic	Yemen
Japan	Uruguay	Iraq	Venezuela (Bolivarian	Lao People's	Zambia
Kuwait		Jamaica	Republic of)	Democratic	
Latvia				Republic	
				Lesotho	
				Mauritania	

Low-income	
Afghanistan	Liberia
Benin	Madagascar
Burkina Faso	Malawi
Burundi	Mali
Central African	Mozambique
Republic	Nepal
Chad	Niger
Comoros	Rwanda
Democratic Republic	Senegal
of the Congo	Sierra Leone
Eritrea	Somalia
Ethiopia	Togo
Gambia	Uganda
Guinea	United Republic of
Guinea-Bissau	Tanzania
Haiti	Zimbabwe

a Economies systematically monitored for the World Economic Situation and Prospects report and included in the United Nations' global economic forecast.

b Indicates the country has been shifted downward by one category from previous year's classification.

c Indicates the country has been shifted upward by one category from previous year's classification.

d Special Administrative Region of China.

Table F
Least developed countries (*June 2017*)

Africa		East Asia	South Asia	Western Asia	Latin America and the Caribbean
Angola	Malawi	Cambodia	Afghanistan	Yemen	Haiti
Benin	Mali	Kiribati	Bangladesh		
Burkina Faso	Mauritania	Lao People's	Bhutan		
Burundi	Mozambique	Democratic	Nepal		
Central African Republic	Niger	Republic			
Chad	Rwanda	Myanmar			
Comoros	Sao Tome and Principe	Solomon			
Democratic Republic of	Senegal	Islands			
the Congo	Sierra Leone	Timor Leste			
Djibouti	Somalia	Tuvalu[a]			
Eritrea	South Sudan[a]	Vanuatu			
Ethiopia	Sudan				
Gambia	Togo				
Guinea	Uganda				
Guinea-Bissau	United Republic				
Lesotho	of Tanzania				
Liberia	Zambia				
Madagascar					

a Not included in the WESP discussion because of insufficient data.

Table G
Heavily indebted poor countries (*as of February 2017*)

Post-completion point HIPCs[a]		Pre-decision point HIPCs[b]
Afghanistan	Haiti	Eritrea
Benin	Honduras	Somalia
Bolivia	Liberia	Sudan
Burkina Faso	Madagascar	
Burundi	Malawi	
Cameroon	Mali	
Central African Republic	Mauritania	
Chad	Mozambique	
Comoros	Nicaragua	
Congo	Niger	
Côte D'Ivoire	Rwanda	
Democratic Republic of the Congo	Sao Tomé and Principe	
Ethiopia	Senegal	
Gambia	Sierra Leone	
Ghana	Togo	
Guinea	Uganda	
Guinea-Bissau	United Republic of Tanzania	
Guyana	Zambia	

a Countries that have qualified for irrevocable debt relief under the HIPC Initiative.

b Countries that are potentially eligible and may wish to avail themselves of the HIPC Initiative or the Multilateral Debt Relief Initiative (MDRI).

Table H
Small island developing States

United Nations members		Non-UN members/Associate members of the Regional Commissions
Antigua and Barbuda	Marshall Islands	American Samoa
Bahamas	Mauritius	Anguilla
Bahrain	Nauru	Aruba
Barbados	Palau	Bermuda
Belize	Papua New Guinea	British Virgin Islands
Cabo Verde	Saint Kitts and Nevis	Cayman Islands
Comoros	Saint Lucia	Commonwealth of Northern Marianas
Cuba	Saint Vincent and the Grenadines	Cook Islands
Dominica		Curaçao
Dominican Republic	Samoa	Curaçao
Federated States of Micronesia	São Tomé and Príncipe	French Polynesia
	Seychelles	Guadeloupe
Fiji	Singapore	Guam
Grenada	Solomon Islands	Martinique
Guinea-Bissau	Suriname	Montserrat
Guyana	Timor-Leste	New Caledonia
Haiti	Tonga	Niue
Jamaica	Trinidad and Tobago	Puerto Rico
Kiribati	Tuvalu	Turks and Caicos Islands
Maldives	Vanuatu	U.S. Virgin Islands

Table I
Landlocked developing countries

Landlocked developing countries		
Afghanistan	Kyrgystan	South Sudan
Armenia	Lao People's Democratic Republic	Swaziland
Azerbaijan		Tajikistan
Bhutan	Lesotho	The former Yugoslav Republic of Macedonia
Bolivia (Plurinational State of)	Malawi	
Botswana	Mali	Turkmenistan
Burkina Faso	Mongolia	Uganda
Burundi	Nepal	Uzbekistan
Central African Republic	Niger	Zambia
Chad	Paraguay	Zimbabwe
Ethiopia	Republic of Moldova	
Kazakhstan	Rwanda	

Table J
International Organization for Standardization Country Codes

ISO Code	Country	ISO Code	Country	ISO Code	Country	ISO Code	Country
AFG	Afghanistan	DZA	Algeria	LBN	Lebanon	ROU	Romania
AGO	Angola	ECU	Ecuador	LBR	Liberia	RUS	Russian Federation
ALB	Albania	EGY	Egypt	LBY	Libya	RWA	Rwanda
AND	Andorra	ERI	Eritrea	LCA	Saint Lucia	SAU	Saudi Arabia
ARE	United Arab Emirates	ESP	Spain	LIE	Liechtenstein	SDN	Sudan
ARG	Argentina	EST	Estonia	LKA	Sri Lanka	SEN	Senegal
ARM	Armenia	ETH	Ethiopia	LSO	Lesotho	SGP	Singapore
ATG	Antigua and Barbuda	FIN	Finland	LTU	Lithuania	SLB	Solomon Islands
AUS	Australia	FJI	Fiji	LUX	Luxembourg	SLE	Sierra Leone
AUT	Austria	FRA	France	LVA	Latvia	SLV	El Salvador
AZE	Azerbaijan	FSM	Micronesia (Federated States of)	MAR	Morocco	SMR	San Marino
BDI	Burundi			MCO	Monaco	SOM	Somalia
BEL	Belgium	GAB	Gabon	MDA	Republic of Moldova	SRB	Serbia
BEN	Benin	GBR	United Kingdom of Great Britain and Northern Ireland	MDG	Madagascar	SSD	South Sudan
BFA	Burkina Faso			MDV	Maldives	STP	Sao Tome and Principe
BGD	Bangladesh			MEX	Mexico		
BGR	Bulgaria	GEO	Georgia	MHL	Marshall Islands	SUR	Suriname
BHR	Bahrain	GHA	Ghana	MKD	The former Yugoslav Republic of Macedonia	SVK	Slovakia
BHS	Bahamas	GIN	Guinea			SVN	Slovenia
BIH	Bosnia and Herzegovina	GMB	Gambia			SWE	Sweden
		GNB	Guinea Bissau	MLI	Mali	SWZ	Swaziland
BLR	Belarus	GNQ	Equatorial Guinea	MLT	Malta	SYC	Seychelles
BLZ	Belize	GRC	Greece	MMR	Myanmar	SYR	Syrian Arab Republic
BOL	Bolivia (Plurinational State of)	GRD	Grenada	MNE	Montenegro	TCD	Chad
		GTM	Guatemala	MNG	Mongolia	TGO	Togo
BRA	Brazil	GUY	Guyana	MOZ	Mozambique	THA	Thailand
BRB	Barbados	HND	Honduras	MRT	Mauritania	TJK	Tajikistan
BRN	Brunei Darussalam	HRV	Croatia	MUS	Mauritius	TKM	Turkmenistan
BTN	Bhutan	HTI	Haiti	MWI	Malawi	TLS	Timor-Leste
BWA	Botswana	HUN	Hungary	MYS	Malaysia	TON	Tonga
CAF	Central African Republic	IDN	Indonesia	NAM	Namibia	TTO	Trinidad and Tobago
		IND	India	NER	Niger	TUN	Tunisia
CAN	Canada	IRL	Ireland	NGA	Nigeria	TUR	Turkey
CHE	Switzerland	IRN	Iran (Islamic Republic of)	NIC	Nicaragua	TUV	Tuvalu
CHL	Chile			NLD	Netherlands	TZA	United Republic of Tanzania
CHN	China	IRQ	Iraq	NOR	Norway		
CIV	Côte D'Ivoire	ISL	Iceland	NPL	Nepal	UGA	Uganda
CMR	Cameroon	ISR	Israel	NRU	Nauru	UKR	Ukraine
COD	Democratic Republic of the Congo	ITA	Italy	NZL	New Zealand	URY	Uruguay
		JAM	Jamaica	OMN	Oman	USA	United States of America
COG	Congo	JOR	Jordan	PAK	Pakistan		
COL	Colombia	JPN	Japan	PAN	Panama	UZB	Uzbekistan
COM	Comoros	KAZ	Kazakhstan	PER	Peru	VCT	Saint Vincent and the Grenadines
CPV	Cabo Verde	KEN	Kenya	PHL	Philippines		
CRI	Costa Rica	KGZ	Kyrgyzstan	PLW	Palau	VEN	Venezuela (Bolivarian Republic of)
CUB	Cuba	KHM	Cambodia	PNG	Papua New Guinea		
CYP	Cyprus	KIR	Kiribati	POL	Poland	VNM	Viet Nam
CZE	Czech Republic	KNA	Saint Kitts and Nevis	PRK	Democratic People's Republic of Korea	VUT	Vanuatu
DEU	Germany	KOR	Republic of Korea			WSM	Samoa
DJI	Djibouti	KWT	Kuwait	PRT	Portugal	YEM	Yemen
DMA	Dominica	LAO	Lao People's Democratic Republic	PRY	Paraguay	ZAF	South Africa
DNK	Denmark			QAT	Qatar	ZMB	Zambia
DOM	Dominican Republic					ZWE	Zimbabwe

Annex tables

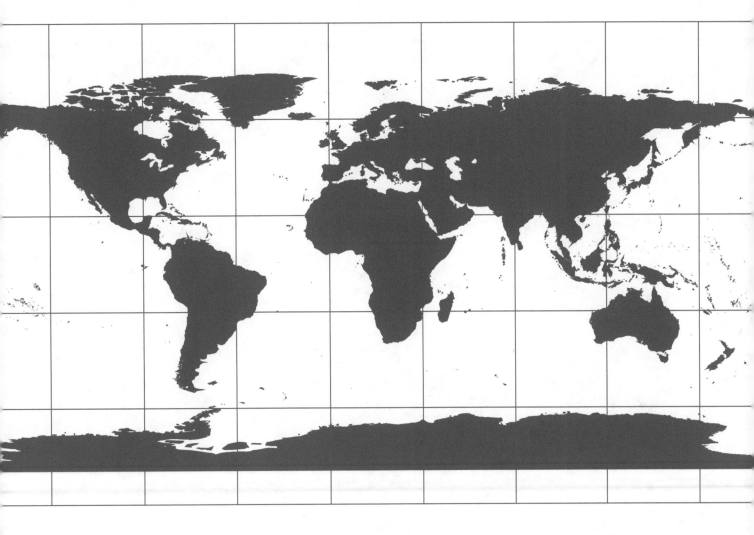

Table A.1
Developed economies: rates of growth of real GDP, 2009–2019

Annual percentage change

	2009-2016[a]	2009	2010	2011	2012	2013	2014	2015	2016	2017[b]	2018[c]	2019[c]
Developed economies	1.0	-3.7	2.6	1.5	1.0	1.2	1.9	2.2	1.6	2.2	2.0	1.9
United States	1.5	-2.8	2.5	1.6	2.2	1.7	2.6	2.9	1.5	2.2	2.1	2.1
Canada	1.5	-2.9	3.1	3.1	1.7	2.5	2.6	0.9	1.5	3.0	2.3	2.2
Japan	0.5	-5.4	4.2	-0.1	1.5	2.0	0.3	1.1	1.0	1.7	1.2	1.0
Australia	2.5	1.7	2.3	2.7	3.6	2.1	2.8	2.4	2.4	2.8	3.0	2.4
New Zealand	2.3	0.4	2.0	1.9	2.5	2.1	2.9	3.1	3.6	2.5	2.9	2.6
European Union	0.6	-4.4	2.2	1.7	-0.5	0.2	1.7	2.2	1.9	2.2	2.1	1.9
EU-15	0.5	-4.5	2.2	1.5	-0.5	0.1	1.6	2.1	1.8	2.0	1.9	1.8
Austria	0.6	-3.8	1.9	2.8	0.7	0.1	0.6	1.0	1.5	2.7	2.4	2.1
Belgium	0.8	-2.3	2.7	1.8	0.1	-0.1	1.6	1.5	1.2	1.7	1.6	1.6
Denmark	0.5	-4.9	1.9	1.3	0.2	0.9	1.7	1.6	1.7	2.0	1.9	1.8
Finland	-0.5	-8.3	3.0	2.6	-1.4	-0.8	-0.6	0.0	1.9	2.9	1.7	1.4
France	0.6	-2.9	2.0	2.1	0.2	0.6	0.9	1.1	1.2	1.7	1.8	1.8
Germany	1.1	-5.6	4.1	3.7	0.5	0.5	1.9	1.7	1.9	2.0	2.1	1.9
Greece	-3.7	-4.3	-5.5	-9.1	-7.3	-3.2	0.4	-0.2	0.0	1.3	1.8	1.9
Ireland	4.4	-4.6	2.0	0.0	0.0	1.6	8.3	25.6	5.1	2.2	2.8	3.1
Italy	-0.8	-5.5	1.7	0.6	-2.8	-1.7	0.1	0.8	0.9	1.5	1.4	1.1
Luxembourg	2.4	-5.4	5.8	2.0	-0.4	4.0	5.6	4.0	4.2	3.3	3.1	3.0
Netherlands	0.5	-3.8	1.4	1.7	-1.1	-0.2	1.4	2.3	2.2	2.8	2.4	2.1
Portugal	-0.5	-3.0	1.9	-1.8	-4.0	-1.1	0.9	1.6	1.4	1.6	1.4	1.2
Spain	-0.2	-3.6	0.0	-1.0	-2.9	-1.7	1.4	3.2	3.2	2.9	2.6	2.4
Sweden	1.7	-5.2	6.0	2.7	-0.3	1.2	2.6	4.1	3.2	2.7	2.4	2.3
United Kingdom	1.2	-4.3	1.9	1.5	1.3	1.9	3.1	2.2	1.8	1.7	1.4	1.4
EU-13	1.6	-3.6	1.9	3.1	0.5	1.2	2.9	3.8	2.9	4.2	3.6	3.5
Bulgaria	0.9	-4.2	0.1	1.6	0.2	1.3	1.4	3.6	3.4	3.6	3.6	3.8
Croatia	-1.0	-7.4	-1.7	-0.3	-2.2	-1.1	-0.1	2.3	3.0	3.1	3.3	2.7
Cyprus	-0.8	-1.8	1.3	0.3	-3.2	-6.0	-1.5	1.7	2.8	3.1	2.2	2.0
Czech Republic	1.1	-4.8	2.3	2.0	-0.8	-0.5	2.7	5.3	2.6	4.4	2.8	2.4
Estonia	0.7	-14.7	2.4	7.6	4.3	1.4	2.8	1.4	1.6	4.0	3.4	3.0
Hungary	0.6	-6.6	0.7	1.7	-1.6	2.1	4.0	3.1	2.0	3.6	3.2	3.2
Latvia	0.0	-14.3	-3.8	6.2	4.0	2.9	2.1	2.7	2.0	4.0	3.5	3.6
Lithuania	0.8	-14.8	1.6	6.0	3.8	3.5	3.5	1.8	2.3	3.6	3.5	3.5
Malta	3.8	-2.5	3.5	1.8	2.9	4.5	8.3	7.5	5.1	3.1	2.9	2.9
Poland	3.0	2.8	3.6	5.0	1.6	1.4	3.3	3.9	2.6	4.0	3.9	3.6
Romania	1.1	-7.1	-0.8	1.1	0.6	3.5	3.0	4.0	4.8	5.9	4.5	4.5
Slovakia	1.9	-5.4	5.0	2.8	1.7	1.5	2.6	3.8	3.3	3.3	3.6	3.9
Slovenia	-0.2	-7.8	1.2	0.6	-2.7	-1.1	3.1	2.3	3.1	4.6	4.2	4.0
Other Europe	1.1	-2.0	1.9	1.5	1.7	1.5	2.0	1.4	1.3	1.4	1.7	1.9
Iceland	1.2	-6.9	-3.6	2.0	1.2	4.4	1.9	4.1	7.2	5.1	3.4	3.1
Norway	1.1	-1.6	0.6	1.0	2.7	1.0	2.0	2.0	1.1	1.4	1.8	2.0
Switzerland	1.2	-2.1	3.0	1.8	1.0	1.8	2.0	0.8	1.3	1.2	1.7	1.7
Memorandum items												
North America	1.5	-2.8	2.6	1.8	2.2	1.8	2.6	2.7	1.5	2.3	2.1	2.1
Developed Asia and Pacific	0.9	-4.1	3.8	0.4	1.9	2.0	0.8	1.4	1.4	1.9	1.6	1.3
Europe	0.6	-4.3	2.1	1.7	-0.3	0.3	1.8	2.2	1.9	2.1	2.0	1.9
Major developed economies	1.1	-3.9	2.9	1.6	1.3	1.4	1.9	2.0	1.4	2.0	1.8	1.8
Euro area	0.4	-4.5	2.1	1.5	-0.9	-0.3	1.3	2.0	1.8	2.1	2.0	1.9

Source: UN/DESA, based on data of the United Nations Statistics Division and individual national sources.
Note: Regional aggregates calculated at 2010 prices and exchange rates.
a Average percentage change.
b Partly estimated.
c Baseline scenario forecasts, based in part on Project LINK and UN/DESA World Economic Forecasting Model.

Table A.2
Economies in transition: rates of growth of real GDP, 2009–2019

Annual percentage change

	2009–2016[a]	2009	2010	2011	2012	2013	2014	2015	2016	2017[b]	2018[c]	2019[c]
Economies in transition	0.9	-6.6	4.8	4.6	3.4	2.4	0.9	-2.2	0.4	2.2	2.3	2.4
South-Eastern Europe	1.0	-2.0	1.5	1.7	-0.7	2.4	0.2	2.0	2.9	2.5	3.2	3.3
Albania	2.5	3.4	3.7	2.5	1.4	1.1	2.0	2.6	3.5	3.8	3.8	3.7
Bosnia and Herzegovina	0.9	-2.9	0.8	0.9	-0.9	2.4	1.1	3.1	3.0	3.0	3.0	3.0
Montenegro	1.1	-5.7	2.5	3.2	-2.7	3.5	1.8	3.4	2.9	4.0	3.8	3.5
Serbia	0.2	-3.1	0.6	1.4	-1.0	2.6	-1.8	0.7	2.8	2.0	3.0	3.3
The former Yugoslav Republic of Macedonia	2.2	-0.4	3.4	2.3	-0.5	2.9	3.6	3.8	2.4	1.6	3.0	3.3
Commonwealth of Independent States and Georgia[d]	0.9	-6.8	4.9	4.7	3.6	2.4	1.0	-2.4	0.3	2.2	2.3	2.4
Commonwealth of Independent States and Georgia - net fuel exporters	1.1	-6.3	4.9	4.6	3.9	2.5	1.4	-1.9	0.2	2.2	2.2	2.2
Azerbaijan	2.5	9.4	4.6	-1.6	2.1	5.9	2.7	0.7	-3.1	-1.0	1.8	2.3
Kazakhstan	4.1	1.2	7.3	7.4	4.8	6.0	4.2	1.2	0.9	4.0	3.0	3.0
Russian Federation	0.4	-7.8	4.5	4.3	3.7	1.8	0.7	-2.8	-0.2	1.8	1.9	1.9
Turkmenistan	9.3	6.1	9.2	14.7	11.1	10.2	10.3	6.5	6.2	6.0	4.8	5.0
Uzbekistan	8.1	8.1	8.5	8.3	8.2	8.0	8.1	7.9	7.8	6.5	6.4	6.1
Commonwealth of Independent States and Georgia - net fuel importers	-0.8	-10.5	5.0	5.5	1.3	1.2	-2.6	-6.0	1.2	2.4	2.8	3.5
Armenia	1.0	-14.1	2.2	4.7	7.2	3.3	3.6	3.0	0.2	5.8	3.8	3.6
Belarus	1.4	0.2	7.7	5.5	1.7	1.0	1.7	-3.9	-2.7	1.5	2.0	2.3
Georgia[d]	3.7	-3.7	6.2	7.2	6.4	3.4	4.6	2.9	2.7	4.8	4.3	4.3
Kyrgyzstan	3.8	2.9	-0.5	6.0	-0.1	10.5	4.3	3.5	3.8	6.1	5.8	4.7
Republic of Moldova	3.0	-6.0	7.1	6.8	-0.7	9.4	4.8	-0.7	4.3	3.2	4.0	4.0
Tajikistan	5.7	4.0	6.5	2.4	7.5	7.4	6.7	4.2	6.9	5.5	6.0	6.0
Ukraine[e]	-2.7	-15.1	4.1	5.4	0.2	0.0	-6.6	-9.9	2.2	1.8	2.5	3.6

Source: UN/DESA, based on data of the United Nations Statistics Division and individual national sources.

Note: Regional aggregates calculated at 2010 prices and exchange rates.

a Average percentage change.

b Partly estimated.

c Baseline scenario forecasts, based in part on Project LINK and the UN/DESA World Economic Forecasting Model.

d Georgia officially left the Commonwealth of Independent States on 18 August 2009. However, its performance is discussed in the context of this group of countries for reasons of geographic proximity and similarities in economic structure.

e Starting in 2010, data for the Ukraine excludes the temporarily occupied territory of the Autonomous Republic of Crimea and Sevastopol.

Table A.3
Developing economies: rates of growth of real GDP, 2009–2019

Annual percentage change

	2009–2016[a]	2009	2010	2011	2012	2013	2014	2015	2016	2017[b]	2018[c]	2019[c]
Developing countries[d]	4.9	2.8	7.7	6.2	5.1	4.9	4.4	3.9	3.8	4.3	4.6	4.7
Africa	3.3	3.1	5.2	1.4	6.0	2.2	3.8	3.1	1.7	3.0	3.5	3.7
North Africa	1.9	3.2	4.0	-5.0	8.5	-2.9	1.9	3.2	2.8	4.8	4.1	4.1
Algeria	3.1	1.6	3.6	2.9	3.4	2.8	3.8	3.8	3.1	2.8	2.6	2.2
Egypt[e]	3.3	4.7	5.1	1.8	2.2	2.1	2.2	4.2	4.3	3.7	3.8	4.2
Libya	-14.5	-0.7	4.3	-61.3	124.7	-52.1	-24.0	-10.2	-3.0	45.9	16.2	12.3
Mauritania	3.8	-1.0	4.8	4.4	6.0	6.2	5.6	3.1	1.7	3.8	5.2	5.2
Morocco	3.7	4.2	3.8	6.3	2.3	4.9	2.7	4.5	1.2	4.2	4.1	4.0
Sudan[e]	3.5	9.5	6.9	-0.3	-2.2	5.3	1.6	4.9	3.0	4.2	4.1	4.2
Tunisia	1.8	3.1	3.0	-1.9	3.9	2.4	2.3	0.8	1.0	2.8	3.2	3.3
East Africa	6.5	5.0	7.9	7.2	5.9	6.9	7.0	6.7	5.4	5.3	5.8	6.2
Burundi	2.7	3.8	5.1	4.0	4.4	4.9	4.7	-4.1	-1.0	0.0	0.0	2.9
Comoros	4.8	4.4	3.8	4.9	3.1	9.6	5.9	2.6	4.5	2.8	3.0	3.7
Democratic Republic of the Congo	6.4	2.9	7.1	6.9	7.1	8.5	9.5	6.9	2.5	3.0	3.0	4.2
Djibouti	5.2	5.0	3.5	4.5	4.8	5.0	6.0	6.5	6.7	6.8	6.8	6.7
Eritrea	4.7	3.9	2.2	8.7	7.0	3.1	5.0	4.8	3.5	3.2	3.4	3.8
Ethiopia	10.2	10.7	12.9	10.8	9.6	10.4	9.9	9.6	7.6	6.5	7.3	7.5
Kenya	5.6	3.3	8.4	6.1	4.6	5.7	5.3	5.6	5.8	5.2	5.9	6.0
Madagascar	1.7	-4.1	0.4	1.5	3.0	2.3	3.3	3.0	4.1	4.3	4.5	4.8
Rwanda	6.8	6.3	7.3	7.9	8.8	4.7	7.0	6.9	5.9	6.1	6.7	7.0
Somalia	2.6	2.6	2.6	2.6	2.6	2.6	2.6	2.6	2.6	2.5	3.3	3.9
Uganda	5.2	6.9	8.2	5.9	3.2	4.7	4.6	5.7	2.3	5.2	5.7	6.0
United Republic of Tanzania	6.6	5.4	6.4	7.9	5.1	7.3	7.0	7.0	7.0	6.5	6.8	6.9
Central Africa	3.5	3.0	6.3	5.2	6.3	0.6	4.4	1.7	0.6	0.7	2.1	2.5
Cameroon	5.7	1.9	14.3	4.1	4.5	5.4	5.9	5.7	4.5	3.8	4.4	4.7
Central African Republic	-4.9	1.9	3.6	2.0	2.9	-36.7	1.0	4.8	-10.3	4.7	5.0	5.2
Chad	4.8	9.1	13.4	6.3	12.5	-5.9	3.4	4.4	-3.4	0.1	3.0	3.8
Congo	4.8	7.5	8.7	3.4	3.8	3.3	6.8	1.2	3.8	-0.6	2.6	0.1
Equatorial Guinea	-2.0	1.3	-8.9	6.5	8.3	-4.1	0.4	-9.0	-8.9	-5.9	-5.9	-3.6
Gabon	4.5	-0.5	6.8	7.1	5.3	5.6	5.0	4.0	3.2	1.1	2.7	3.5
Sao Tome and Principe	4.0	2.4	6.7	4.4	3.1	4.8	6.5	3.8	0.1	5.0	5.3	5.3
West Africa	4.9	6.1	7.3	5.0	5.3	5.8	6.1	3.2	0.3	2.4	3.3	3.4
Benin	4.4	2.3	2.1	3.0	4.6	6.9	6.5	5.0	5.0	5.4	6.0	6.2
Burkina Faso	5.5	3.0	8.4	6.6	6.5	5.8	4.3	3.9	5.9	6.4	6.4	6.3
Cabo Verde	1.6	-1.3	1.5	4.0	1.1	0.8	1.9	1.5	3.8	3.9	3.8	4.0
Côte D'Ivoire	5.7	3.3	2.0	-4.4	10.7	9.2	8.5	9.1	8.1	7.0	6.9	6.8
Gambia (Islamic Republic of the)	3.3	6.4	6.5	-4.3	5.9	4.8	0.9	4.7	2.1	2.6	3.6	3.9
Ghana	6.8	4.8	7.9	14.0	9.3	7.3	4.0	3.8	3.7	6.8	7.5	5.9
Guinea	3.9	-1.5	4.2	5.6	5.9	3.9	3.7	4.5	5.2	5.6	5.4	5.0
Guinea Bissau	3.5	3.4	4.6	8.1	-1.7	3.3	0.2	5.1	5.2	5.4	4.8	5.1
Liberia	5.4	12.3	10.8	5.8	8.2	8.1	0.7	0.3	-1.6	2.9	4.3	5.3
Mali	9.0	11.7	10.9	7.7	11.2	7.0	7.8	7.6	7.9	5.3	5.1	4.8
Niger	5.4	-0.7	8.4	2.3	11.8	5.3	7.5	4.0	5.0	5.2	5.5	5.9
Nigeria	4.6	6.9	7.8	4.9	4.3	5.4	6.3	2.7	-1.6	0.9	2.1	2.4
Senegal	4.2	2.4	4.2	1.8	4.4	3.5	4.3	6.5	6.6	6.4	6.4	6.4
Sierra Leone	4.5	3.2	5.3	6.3	15.2	20.7	4.6	-20.3	6.1	5.5	5.7	6.4
Togo	5.2	3.4	4.0	4.9	6.5	6.1	6.1	5.5	5.1	5.0	5.3	5.5

Table A.3
Developing economies: rates of growth of real GDP, 2009–2019 (*continued*)

Annual percentage change

	2009–2016[a]	2009	2010	2011	2012	2013	2014	2015	2016	2017[b]	2018[c]	2019[c]
Southern Africa	2.5	0.0	4.0	3.8	3.8	3.5	2.6	1.9	0.6	1.2	2.3	2.5
Angola	3.5	0.5	4.7	3.5	8.5	5.0	4.1	3.0	-0.7	1.9	2.7	2.7
Botswana	3.5	-7.7	8.6	6.0	4.5	11.3	4.1	-1.7	4.3	4.0	3.8	4.0
Lesotho	4.2	2.2	6.5	6.6	5.9	2.2	2.3	5.6	2.9	2.9	3.6	3.8
Malawi	4.7	8.3	6.9	4.9	-0.6	6.3	6.6	2.8	3.0	3.8	4.4	5.1
Mauritius	3.5	3.0	4.1	3.9	3.2	3.2	3.6	3.5	3.6	3.5	3.7	3.9
Mozambique	6.5	6.4	6.7	7.1	7.2	7.1	7.4	6.6	3.8	4.1	3.8	3.9
Namibia	4.4	0.3	6.0	5.1	5.1	5.6	6.4	6.0	1.1	-1.0	3.2	3.2
South Africa	1.6	-1.5	3.0	3.3	2.2	2.5	1.7	1.3	0.3	0.6	1.8	2.1
Swaziland	2.3	2.6	1.8	1.9	3.4	4.6	2.7	1.7	0.0	1.0	1.9	1.6
Zambia	6.1	9.2	10.3	5.6	7.6	5.1	4.7	2.9	3.6	3.2	4.2	4.1
Zimbabwe	11.4	55.5	11.4	11.9	10.6	4.5	3.8	1.1	0.7	0.0	1.5	1.0
Africa - net fuel exporters	3.0	4.1	5.5	-1.4	7.6	0.4	4.0	3.0	1.1	3.0	3.2	3.4
Africa - net fuel importers	3.7	1.8	4.9	4.9	4.0	4.4	3.6	3.3	2.4	3.0	3.8	4.0
East and South Asia	6.5	5.9	9.2	7.3	5.9	6.0	6.1	5.8	6.0	6.0	5.8	5.9
East Asia	6.7	5.9	9.5	7.6	6.5	6.4	6.1	5.7	5.6	5.9	5.7	5.6
Brunei Darussalam	-0.3	-1.8	2.6	3.7	0.9	-2.1	-2.3	-0.4	-2.5	0.5	2.3	2.7
Cambodia	6.1	0.1	6.0	7.1	7.3	7.4	7.1	7.0	7.2	7.0	7.1	7.0
China	8.3	9.4	10.6	9.5	7.9	7.8	7.3	6.9	6.7	6.8	6.5	6.3
Fiji	2.5	-1.4	3.1	2.8	1.4	4.7	5.6	3.6	0.4	3.9	3.5	3.3
Hong Kong SAR[f]	2.6	-2.5	6.8	4.8	1.7	3.1	2.7	2.4	2.0	3.5	2.8	3.0
Indonesia	5.4	4.6	6.2	6.2	6.0	5.6	5.0	4.9	5.0	5.2	5.3	5.4
Kiribati	2.8	1.1	-1.6	0.6	5.1	5.0	0.4	7.5	4.2	2.0	1.8	1.9
Lao People's Democratic Republic	7.7	7.5	8.1	8.0	7.9	8.0	7.6	7.6	7.0	7.2	7.3	7.2
Malaysia	4.5	-1.5	7.4	5.3	5.5	4.7	6.0	5.0	4.2	5.4	4.9	5.0
Mongolia	7.0	-1.3	6.4	17.3	12.3	11.6	7.9	2.4	1.0	4.0	3.2	4.5
Myanmar[e]	7.8	10.6	10.2	5.6	7.3	8.4	8.0	7.0	5.7	7.3	7.2	7.4
Papua New Guinea	5.6	6.1	11.2	3.4	4.0	3.6	7.4	6.6	2.5	2.8	2.9	2.7
Philippines	5.6	1.1	7.6	3.7	6.7	7.1	6.2	6.1	6.9	6.7	6.9	6.9
Republic of Korea	3.1	0.7	6.5	3.7	2.3	2.9	3.3	2.8	2.8	3.0	2.8	2.8
Samoa	1.0	-4.1	4.3	3.6	-2.3	0.5	1.9	2.8	1.7	2.9	1.5	2.0
Singapore	4.6	-0.6	15.2	6.2	3.9	5.0	3.6	1.9	2.0	3.0	2.7	2.7
Solomon Islands	3.7	0.2	10.6	6.4	2.6	3.0	2.0	1.8	3.2	3.0	2.8	3.2
Taiwan Province of China	2.9	-1.6	10.6	3.8	2.1	2.2	4.0	0.7	1.5	2.2	2.4	2.5
Thailand	3.0	-0.7	7.5	0.8	7.2	2.7	0.9	2.9	3.2	3.5	3.4	3.3
Timor-Leste	-1.3	-6.6	-1.3	11.9	4.8	-10.9	-26.0	20.9	5.0	5.1	5.5	5.8
Vanuatu	1.9	3.3	1.6	1.2	1.8	2.0	2.3	-1.0	4.0	4.2	3.8	3.5
Viet Nam	5.9	5.4	6.4	6.2	5.2	5.4	6.0	6.7	6.2	6.3	6.4	6.4
South Asia	6.0	5.7	8.1	6.5	3.4	4.4	6.1	6.2	7.7	6.3	6.5	7.0
Afghanistan[e]	6.3	17.2	3.2	8.7	10.9	6.5	3.1	-1.8	3.6	3.2	4.0	3.6
Bangladesh[e]	6.2	5.0	5.6	6.5	6.5	6.0	6.1	6.6	7.1	7.2	7.1	7.2
Bhutan	6.3	6.7	11.7	7.9	5.1	2.1	5.5	5.2	6.7	6.9	7.1	7.3
India[e]	7.4	8.5	10.3	6.6	5.6	6.6	7.2	7.6	7.1	6.7	7.2	7.4
Iran (Islamic Republic of)[e]	2.5	2.3	6.6	3.7	-6.6	-1.9	4.3	0.4	12.5	5.3	5.1	5.0
Maldives	3.7	-5.3	7.2	8.7	2.5	4.7	6.0	2.8	3.9	4.5	4.6	4.5

Table A.3
Developing economies: rates of growth of real GDP, 2009–2019 (*continued*)

Annual percentage change

	2009–2016[a]	2009	2010	2011	2012	2013	2014	2015	2016	2017[b]	2018[c]	2019[c]
Nepal[e]	3.9	4.5	4.8	3.4	4.8	4.1	6.0	2.7	0.6	7.5	4.6	4.9
Pakistan[e]	3.8	2.8	1.6	2.7	3.5	4.4	4.7	4.7	5.7	5.3	5.5	5.2
Sri Lanka	5.8	3.5	8.0	8.4	9.1	3.4	4.9	4.8	4.4	4.5	5.0	4.7
East and South Asia - net fuel exporters	4.5	3.7	6.0	5.5	2.4	2.8	4.4	3.9	7.5	5.3	5.3	5.4
East and South Asia - net fuel importers	6.8	6.1	9.6	7.6	6.3	6.4	6.3	6.0	5.9	6.0	5.9	5.9
Western Asia	**4.0**	**-1.6**	**6.1**	**7.5**	**4.6**	**5.9**	**3.3**	**3.6**	**3.0**	**1.9**	**2.3**	**2.7**
Net fuel exporters	3.9	-1.0	4.6	8.3	6.1	5.7	2.6	2.6	3.0	1.0	2.5	2.6
Bahrain	3.5	2.5	4.3	2.0	3.7	5.4	4.4	2.9	3.0	1.8	1.9	2.1
Iraq	8.2	5.8	5.5	10.2	12.6	26.0	-0.6	-2.4	11.0	1.8	3.7	3.1
Kuwait	1.5	-7.1	-2.4	9.6	6.6	1.1	0.5	1.8	2.5	0.8	2.5	2.9
Oman	4.3	6.1	4.8	-1.1	9.3	4.4	2.5	5.7	3.1	1.2	2.7	2.1
Qatar	7.4	12.0	16.7	13.0	4.7	4.4	4.0	3.6	2.2	1.3	3.3	2.9
Saudi Arabia	3.7	-2.1	5.0	10.0	5.4	2.7	3.7	4.1	1.4	0.4	1.8	2.1
United Arab Emirates	2.9	-5.2	1.6	6.4	5.1	5.8	3.3	3.8	3.0	2.1	2.8	3.1
Yemen	-6.9	4.1	5.7	-12.8	2.0	-1.6	-9.6	-28.1	-9.8	-7.5	-4.3	0.2
Net fuel importers	4.1	-2.2	7.8	6.7	2.8	6.1	4.2	4.8	3.1	3.0	2.2	2.9
Israel	3.6	1.4	5.7	5.1	2.4	4.4	3.2	2.5	4.0	2.9	3.1	3.2
Jordan	2.9	5.5	2.3	2.6	2.7	2.8	3.1	2.4	2.0	2.5	2.8	2.9
Lebanon	3.6	10.1	8.0	0.9	2.8	3.0	1.8	1.5	1.0	2.0	2.5	2.5
Syrian Arab Republic	-9.3	5.9	3.4	-6.3	-22.4	-24.8	-11.6	-8.0	-5.8	-3.9	-2.3	0.4
Turkey	5.0	-4.8	9.2	8.8	4.8	8.5	5.2	6.1	3.2	3.3	2.1	3.0
Latin America and the Caribbean	**1.7**	**-1.7**	**6.0**	**4.5**	**2.9**	**2.8**	**0.9**	**-0.6**	**-1.3**	**1.0**	**2.0**	**2.5**
South America	**1.4**	**-1.0**	**6.4**	**4.7**	**2.6**	**3.2**	**0.3**	**-1.9**	**-2.7**	**0.4**	**1.8**	**2.4**
Argentina	1.1	-6.0	10.4	6.1	-1.0	2.4	-2.5	2.6	-2.2	2.4	2.7	3.1
Bolivia (Plurinational State of)	4.9	3.4	4.1	5.2	5.1	6.8	5.5	4.9	4.3	4.0	4.0	3.8
Brazil	1.1	-0.1	7.5	3.9	1.9	3.0	0.5	-3.8	-3.6	0.7	2.0	2.5
Chile	3.2	-1.0	5.8	5.8	5.3	4.0	1.9	2.3	1.6	1.5	2.8	3.0
Colombia	3.8	1.7	4.0	6.6	4.0	4.9	4.4	3.1	2.0	1.8	2.6	3.0
Ecuador	3.0	0.6	3.5	7.9	5.6	4.9	3.7	0.1	-1.6	0.7	1.0	1.5
Paraguay	4.6	-4.0	13.1	4.3	-1.2	14.0	4.7	3.0	4.0	4.0	4.0	3.8
Peru	4.6	1.1	8.3	6.3	6.1	5.9	2.3	3.3	3.9	2.5	3.5	3.8
Uruguay	3.8	4.2	7.8	5.2	3.5	4.6	3.2	0.4	1.5	3.0	3.2	2.9
Venezuela (Bolivarian Republic of)	-1.8	-3.2	-1.5	4.2	5.6	1.3	-3.9	-6.2	-9.7	-8.0	-4.0	-1.0
Mexico and Central America	**2.4**	**-3.8**	**5.0**	**4.0**	**4.0**	**1.8**	**2.6**	**3.1**	**2.5**	**2.5**	**2.6**	**2.6**
Costa Rica	3.5	-1.0	5.0	4.3	4.8	2.0	3.7	4.7	4.3	3.9	4.0	4.0
Cuba	2.1	1.5	2.4	2.8	3.0	2.7	1.0	4.4	-0.9	0.5	0.5	1.9
Dominican Republic	5.0	0.9	8.3	2.8	2.6	4.8	7.3	7.0	6.6	4.9	5.1	4.7
El Salvador	1.3	-3.1	1.4	2.2	1.9	1.8	1.4	2.5	2.4	2.4	2.4	2.2
Guatemala	3.2	0.5	2.9	4.2	3.0	3.7	4.3	4.1	3.1	3.4	3.5	3.5
Haiti[e]	1.9	3.1	-5.5	5.5	2.9	4.2	2.8	1.2	1.4	1.3	1.3	2.1
Honduras	2.8	-2.4	3.7	3.8	4.1	2.8	3.1	3.6	3.6	3.7	3.7	3.3
Mexico	2.1	-4.7	5.2	3.9	4.0	1.4	2.3	2.6	2.3	2.2	2.4	2.3
Nicaragua	3.9	-2.8	3.2	6.2	5.9	5.0	4.6	4.9	4.7	4.5	4.5	4.1
Panama	6.4	1.6	5.8	11.8	9.2	6.6	6.1	5.8	4.9	5.5	5.4	5.0

Table A.3
Developing economies: rates of growth of real GDP, 2009–2019 (*continued*)

Annual percentage change

	2009–2016[a]	2009	2010	2011	2012	2013	2014	2015	2016	2017[b]	2018[c]	2019[c]
Caribbean	0.4	-1.5	0.2	1.6	1.6	1.8	0.3	0.2	-0.8	0.2	1.8	2.0
Bahamas	-0.2	-4.2	1.5	0.6	3.1	0.0	-0.5	-1.7	0.0	1.4	2.2	1.8
Barbados	0.0	-4.0	0.3	0.8	0.3	-0.1	0.1	0.9	1.7	1.5	1.8	1.7
Belize	2.2	0.7	3.3	2.1	3.8	1.5	4.1	2.9	-0.8	3.2	2.5	2.5
Guyana	4.2	3.3	4.4	5.4	4.8	5.2	3.8	3.1	3.3	2.9	3.6	3.7
Jamaica	-0.2	-4.3	-1.5	1.7	-0.6	0.5	0.5	0.9	1.4	1.6	2.4	2.3
Suriname	0.7	3.0	5.2	5.8	2.7	2.9	0.4	-2.7	-10.4	-0.2	0.8	2.2
Trinidad and Tobago	0.0	-0.5	0.2	-0.3	1.3	2.3	-1.0	0.2	-2.3	-2.3	1.0	1.5
Latin America and the Caribbean - net fuel exporters	1.0	-1.0	1.0	5.3	4.9	3.1	0.2	-1.6	-3.6	-2.4	-0.2	1.3
Latin America and the Caribbean - net fuel importers	1.8	-1.8	6.9	4.3	2.6	2.8	1.0	-0.4	-0.9	1.6	2.4	2.7
Memorandum items:												
Least Developed Countries	5.2	4.9	6.7	4.9	6.1	5.2	5.1	4.2	4.3	4.8	5.4	5.5
Africa (excluding Libya)	3.7	3.3	5.3	4.1	4.0	4.1	4.3	3.3	1.7	2.6	3.3	3.5
North Africa (excluding Libya)	3.2	3.6	3.5	2.7	2.7	2.9	3.2	3.8	2.9	3.4	3.5	3.6
East Asia (excluding China)	4.0	0.9	7.7	4.4	4.2	4.0	4.0	3.5	3.6	4.0	4.0	4.0
South Asia (excluding India)	3.8	2.8	5.0	4.7	0.4	1.0	4.2	3.4	8.9	5.8	5.2	5.6
Western Asia (excluding Israel and Turkey)	3.6	-0.4	4.6	7.3	4.9	4.8	2.3	2.4	2.8	1.0	2.4	2.5
Arab States[g]	3.0	0.8	4.4	3.4	5.9	2.5	2.2	2.6	2.8	2.1	2.9	3.0
Landlocked developing economies	5.3	4.5	7.6	6.4	5.8	6.6	5.4	3.4	3.0	4.1	4.3	4.3
Small island developing economies	3.6	0.1	9.1	4.4	3.3	4.0	3.2	3.0	2.0	2.6	2.7	2.8

Source: UN/DESA, based on data of the United Nations Statistics Division and individual national sources.

Note: Regional aggregates calculated at 2010 prices and exchange rates.

a Average percentage change.

b Partly estimated.

c Baseline scenario forecasts, based in part on Project LINK and the UN/DESA World Economic Forecasting Model.

d Covering countries that account for 98 per cent of the population of all developing countries.

e Fiscal year basis.

f Special Administrative Region of China.

g Currently includes data for Algeria, Bahrain, Comoros, Djibouti, Egypt, Iraq, Jordan, Kuwait, Lebanon, Libya, Mauritania, Morocco, Oman, Qatar, Saudi Arabia, Somalia, Sudan, Syrian Arab Republic, Tunisia, United Arab Emirates, and Yemen.

Table A.4
Developed economies: consumer price inflation, 2009–2019

Annual percentage change[a]

	2009	2010	2011	2012	2013	2014	2015	2016	2017[b]	2018[c]	2019[c]
Developed economies	0.1	1.5	2.6	1.9	1.3	1.4	0.2	0.7	1.5	1.9	2.1
United States	-0.3	1.6	3.2	2.0	1.4	1.7	0.1	1.3	1.7	2.1	2.1
Canada	0.3	1.8	2.9	1.5	0.9	1.9	1.1	1.4	1.5	2.1	2.0
Japan	-1.4	-0.7	-0.3	-0.1	0.4	2.8	0.8	-0.1	0.3	1.4	1.8
Australia	1.8	2.9	3.3	1.8	2.5	2.5	1.5	1.3	1.7	2.3	2.0
New Zealand	2.1	2.3	4.0	1.1	1.1	1.2	0.3	0.6	1.8	2.0	2.5
European Union	0.9	1.9	3.0	2.6	1.5	0.6	0.0	0.3	1.6	1.8	2.1
EU-15	0.7	1.9	2.9	2.5	1.5	0.6	0.1	0.3	1.6	1.8	2.1
Austria	0.5	1.8	3.3	2.5	2.0	1.6	0.9	0.9	2.1	1.8	2.2
Belgium	0.0	2.3	3.4	2.6	1.2	0.5	0.6	1.8	2.1	2.2	2.3
Denmark	1.0	2.2	2.7	2.4	0.5	0.4	0.2	0.0	1.1	2.0	2.3
Finland	1.6	1.7	3.3	3.2	2.2	1.2	-0.2	0.4	0.8	1.9	2.3
France	0.1	1.7	2.3	2.2	1.0	0.6	0.1	0.3	1.0	1.5	2.0
Germany	0.2	1.2	2.5	2.1	1.6	0.8	0.1	0.4	1.6	1.8	2.2
Greece	1.3	4.7	3.1	1.0	-0.9	-1.4	-1.1	0.0	1.3	1.4	2.3
Ireland	-1.7	-1.6	1.2	1.8	0.5	0.3	0.0	-0.2	0.3	1.8	2.2
Italy	0.8	1.6	2.9	3.2	1.3	0.2	0.1	-0.1	1.4	1.2	1.4
Luxembourg	0.0	2.8	3.7	2.9	1.7	0.7	0.1	0.0	1.7	1.8	2.7
Netherlands	1.0	0.9	2.5	2.8	2.6	0.3	0.2	0.1	1.4	1.7	2.0
Portugal	-0.9	1.4	3.6	2.8	0.4	-0.1	0.5	0.6	1.3	1.9	2.2
Spain	-0.2	2.1	3.0	2.4	1.5	-0.2	-0.6	-0.3	1.6	1.6	1.8
Sweden	1.9	1.9	1.4	0.9	0.4	0.2	0.7	1.1	1.6	2.0	2.2
United Kingdom	2.2	3.2	4.5	2.9	2.5	1.5	0.0	0.7	2.8	2.7	2.9
EU-13	3.1	2.7	3.8	3.7	1.5	0.2	-0.4	-0.2	1.9	2.2	2.4
Bulgaria	2.8	2.4	4.2	3.0	0.9	-1.4	-0.1	-0.8	2.0	2.5	2.3
Croatia	2.4	1.0	2.3	3.4	2.2	-0.2	-0.5	-1.1	1.0	1.5	2.3
Cyprus	0.4	2.4	3.3	2.4	-0.4	-1.4	-2.1	-1.4	0.8	1.6	2.0
Czech Republic	0.5	1.2	2.2	3.6	1.3	0.5	0.2	0.7	2.3	2.1	2.1
Estonia	0.2	2.7	5.1	4.2	3.2	0.5	0.1	0.8	3.1	2.8	2.6
Hungary	4.0	4.7	3.9	5.7	1.7	0.0	0.1	0.4	2.7	2.7	2.8
Latvia	3.5	-1.1	4.4	2.3	0.0	0.6	0.2	0.1	3.0	2.4	2.8
Lithuania	4.5	1.3	4.1	3.1	1.0	0.1	-0.9	0.9	3.2	2.6	2.9
Malta	2.1	1.5	2.7	2.4	1.4	0.3	1.1	0.6	1.7	2.9	2.8
Poland	4.0	2.7	3.9	3.6	0.8	0.1	-0.7	-0.2	2.0	2.3	2.7
Romania	5.6	6.1	5.8	3.3	4.0	1.1	-0.6	-1.5	1.0	1.7	2.1
Slovakia	0.9	0.7	4.1	3.7	1.5	-0.1	-0.3	-0.5	1.3	1.9	2.1
Slovenia	0.9	2.1	2.1	2.8	1.9	0.4	-0.8	-0.2	2.0	2.5	2.1
Other European countries	0.7	1.4	0.6	-0.2	0.9	0.8	0.4	1.3	1.2	1.4	1.4
Iceland	16.3	7.5	4.2	6.0	4.1	1.0	0.3	0.8	1.8	3.2	3.2
Norway	2.3	2.3	1.3	0.3	2.0	1.9	2.0	3.9	2.1	2.1	1.5
Switzerland	-0.7	0.6	0.1	-0.7	0.1	0.0	-0.8	-0.5	0.4	0.8	1.3
Memorandum items:											
North America	-0.2	1.6	3.2	2.0	1.4	1.7	0.2	1.3	1.7	2.1	2.1
Developed Asia and Pacific	-0.7	0.0	0.4	0.3	0.7	2.7	0.9	0.1	0.6	1.6	1.9
Europe	0.8	1.9	2.8	2.4	1.5	0.6	0.0	0.4	1.6	1.8	2.1
Major developed economies	-0.1	1.3	2.5	1.8	1.3	1.6	0.3	0.7	1.4	1.9	2.1
Euro area	0.3	1.6	2.7	2.5	1.4	0.4	0.0	0.2	1.4	1.6	2.0

Sources: UN/DESA, based on OECD *Main Economic Indicators*; Eurostat; and individual national sources.

a Data for country groups are weighted averages, where weights for each year are based on 2010 GDP in United States dollars.

b Partly estimated.

c Baseline scenario forecasts, based in part on Project LINK and the UN/DESA World Economic Forecasting Model.

Table A.5
Economies in transition: consumer price inflation, 2009–2019

Annual percentage change[a]

	2009	2010	2011	2012	2013	2014	2015	2016	2017[b]	2018[c]	2019[c]
Economies in transition	11.1	7.1	9.7	6.3	6.3	7.9	15.8	7.8	5.3	5.1	4.6
South-Eastern Europe	4.2	4.1	7.2	4.8	4.4	1.0	0.8	0.4	2.3	2.0	2.6
Albania	2.3	3.6	3.5	2.0	1.9	1.6	1.9	1.3	2.2	2.7	2.9
Bosnia and Herzegovina	-0.4	2.2	3.7	2.1	-0.1	-0.9	-0.9	-1.3	1.5	2.0	2.1
Montenegro	3.5	0.7	3.4	4.1	2.2	-0.7	1.5	-0.3	2.0	2.2	2.2
Serbia	8.1	6.1	11.1	7.3	7.7	2.1	1.4	1.1	3.1	2.0	3.0
The former Yugoslav Republic of Macedonia	-0.7	1.5	3.9	3.3	2.8	-0.3	-0.3	-0.2	0.9	1.5	1.9
Commonwealth of Independent States and Georgia[d]	11.4	7.2	9.8	6.3	6.4	8.2	16.4	8.1	5.4	5.2	4.7
Net fuel exporters	**11.1**	**7.0**	**8.6**	**5.2**	**6.6**	**7.6**	**14.2**	**7.6**	**4.6**	**4.7**	**4.3**
Azerbaijan	1.4	5.7	7.9	1.0	2.4	1.4	4.2	4.2	12.0	5.9	7.5
Kazakhstan	7.3	7.1	8.3	5.1	5.8	6.7	6.6	14.5	7.6	6.1	5.7
Russian Federation	11.7	6.8	8.4	5.1	6.8	7.9	15.5	7.1	3.9	4.4	3.9
Turkmenistan	9.8	2.3	12.9	8.3	1.2	0.6	-1.0	6.7	5.6	6.0	4.6
Uzbekistan	17.2	16.5	16.6	14.9	12.5	12.6	13.7	9.0	10.5	8.1	7.6
Net fuel importers	**13.2**	**8.7**	**18.9**	**14.7**	**4.7**	**12.3**	**33.4**	**11.5**	**11.4**	**9.3**	**7.9**
Armenia	3.4	8.2	7.7	2.6	5.8	3.0	3.7	-1.3	2.1	2.9	3.3
Belarus	12.9	7.7	53.2	59.2	18.3	18.1	13.5	11.8	7.1	6.8	6.5
Georgia[d]	1.7	7.1	8.5	-0.9	-0.5	3.1	4.0	2.1	5.8	3.0	3.0
Kyrgyzstan	6.9	8.0	16.5	2.7	6.6	7.5	6.5	0.4	4.0	3.0	3.0
Republic of Moldova	-0.1	7.4	7.6	4.6	4.6	5.1	9.7	6.4	6.9	5.8	5.3
Tajikistan	6.4	6.4	12.4	5.8	5.0	6.1	5.7	6.0	7.6	5.6	4.8
Ukraine[e]	15.9	9.4	8.0	0.6	-0.3	12.2	48.7	13.9	14.8	11.7	9.5

Source: UN/DESA, based on data of the Economic Commission for Europe.

a Data for country groups are weighted averages, where weights for each year are based on 2010 GDP in United States dollars.

b Partly estimated.

c Baseline scenario forecasts, based in part on Project LINK and the UN/DESA World Economic Forecasting Model.

d Georgia officially left the Commonwealth of Independent States on 18 August 2009. However, its performance is discussed in the context of this group of countries for reasons of geographic proximity and similarities in economic structure.

e Starting in 2010, data for the Ukraine excludes the temporarily occupied territory of the Autonomous Republic of Crimea and Sevastopol.

Table A.6
Developing economies: consumer price inflation, 2009–2019

Annual percentage change[a]

	2009	2010	2011	2012	2013	2014	2015	2016	2017[b]	2018[c]	2019[c]
Developing countries by region[d]	**3.8**	**5.3**	**6.5**	**5.5**	**5.9**	**5.1**	**4.4**	**5.2**	**4.4**	**4.3**	**4.2**
Africa	**8.1**	**7.6**	**8.7**	**8.8**	**6.8**	**6.8**	**7.0**	**11.3**	**13.0**	**9.5**	**8.1**
North Africa	**7.0**	**6.7**	**8.6**	**8.8**	**7.3**	**7.8**	**7.8**	**11.3**	**17.6**	**8.3**	**7.1**
Algeria	5.7	3.9	4.5	8.9	3.3	2.9	4.8	6.4	5.4	3.8	3.2
Egypt	11.8	11.3	10.1	7.1	9.4	10.1	10.4	13.8	30.5	12.2	10.8
Libya	2.5	2.8	15.5	6.1	2.6	2.4	9.8	25.9	27.0	14.0	10.0
Mauritania	2.2	6.3	5.6	4.9	4.1	3.5	0.5	1.5	2.3	4.3	5.3
Morocco	1.0	1.0	0.9	1.3	1.9	0.4	1.6	1.6	0.7	2.8	2.7
Sudan	11.2	13.2	22.1	37.4	30.0	36.9	16.9	17.6	26.8	10.0	9.5
Tunisia	3.5	4.4	3.5	5.1	5.8	4.9	4.9	3.7	4.9	3.6	3.5
East Africa	**9.5**	**5.8**	**17.4**	**13.4**	**5.8**	**5.4**	**6.0**	**6.0**	**7.3**	**6.0**	**5.5**
Burundi	11.0	6.4	9.7	18.0	8.0	4.4	5.6	5.5	17.0	14.0	4.7
Comoros	4.4	3.4	1.8	1.8	2.3	0.6	2.0	2.0	2.2	0.4	0.8
Democratic Republic of the Congo	2.8	7.1	15.3	9.7	1.6	1.0	1.0	4.9	5.0	3.9	3.4
Djibouti	1.7	4.0	5.1	3.7	2.4	1.3	-0.8	2.7	3.5	4.0	2.7
Eritrea	32.4	15.2	25.3	20.7	7.3	15.2	9.0	11.5	7.5	5.9	4.3
Ethiopia	8.5	8.1	33.2	22.8	8.1	7.4	10.1	7.3	9.0	8.2	8.3
Kenya	9.2	4.0	14.0	9.4	5.7	6.9	6.6	6.3	9.0	6.0	5.0
Madagascar	9.0	9.2	9.5	5.7	5.8	6.1	7.4	6.7	7.0	6.5	6.2
Rwanda	10.4	2.3	5.7	6.3	4.2	1.8	2.5	5.7	7.0	5.1	5.1
Somalia	2.7	-15.3	-3.0	-2.0	-3.2	9.0	-2.9	2.0	2.2	0.8	1.3
Uganda	13.0	4.0	18.7	12.7	4.9	3.1	5.4	5.5	6.4	5.6	5.5
United Republic of Tanzania	12.1	6.2	12.7	16.0	7.9	6.1	5.6	5.2	5.3	5.4	5.3
Central Africa	**4.8**	**2.1**	**1.9**	**5.0**	**2.3**	**3.2**	**3.3**	**2.2**	**2.6**	**2.9**	**2.8**
Cameroon	3.0	1.3	2.9	2.9	1.9	1.9	2.7	0.9	2.3	2.3	2.2
Central African Republic	3.5	1.5	1.3	5.8	1.5	25.3	37.1	41.8	21.8	11.1	8.0
Chad	10.0	-2.1	-3.7	14.0	0.1	1.7	3.7	-3.1	-0.8	1.6	2.5
Congo	7.5	0.4	0.8	6.1	6.0	0.1	4.5	3.7	4.2	4.0	3.3
Equatorial Guinea	4.7	7.8	4.8	3.7	2.9	4.3	1.7	1.4	1.6	2.6	3.0
Gabon	1.9	1.5	1.3	2.7	0.5	4.7	-0.3	2.1	2.5	2.8	2.7
Sao Tome and Principe	17.0	13.3	14.3	10.6	8.1	7.0	5.2	5.4	4.5	3.9	2.7
West Africa	**10.3**	**11.6**	**9.7**	**10.5**	**7.6**	**7.3**	**8.3**	**13.2**	**14.3**	**15.4**	**12.8**
Benin	2.2	2.3	2.7	6.8	1.0	-1.1	0.3	-0.9	3.2	3.5	2.9
Burkina Faso	2.6	-0.8	2.8	3.8	0.5	-0.3	1.0	-0.2	1.6	2.2	2.2
Cabo Verde	1.0	2.1	4.5	2.5	1.5	-0.2	0.1	-1.5	0.4	1.6	2.1
Côte D'Ivoire	1.0	1.2	4.9	1.3	2.6	0.5	1.2	0.7	0.7	4.0	4.0
Gambia (Islamic Republic of the)	4.6	5.0	4.8	4.3	5.7	5.9	6.8	7.2	4.6	4.1	3.9
Ghana	19.3	10.7	8.7	9.2	11.6	15.5	17.1	17.5	12.5	10.2	9.2
Guinea	4.7	15.5	21.4	15.2	11.9	9.7	8.2	8.1	9.6	8.1	6.6
Guinea Bissau	-1.7	2.5	5.0	2.1	1.2	-1.5	1.4	1.7	2.5	3.1	2.9
Liberia	7.4	7.3	8.5	6.8	7.6	9.8	7.8	8.8	6.2	5.3	4.0
Mali	2.5	1.1	2.9	5.4	-0.6	0.9	1.4	-1.8	1.3	2.7	2.8
Niger	0.6	0.8	2.9	0.5	2.3	-0.9	1.0	0.2	1.9	2.0	2.4
Nigeria	11.5	13.7	10.8	12.2	8.5	8.1	9.0	15.7	17.2	18.7	15.3
Senegal	-2.2	1.2	3.4	1.4	0.7	-1.1	0.1	0.8	1.8	2.7	2.6
Sierra Leone	9.3	16.6	6.8	6.6	5.5	4.6	6.7	10.9	9.2	8.6	7.5
Togo	3.3	1.8	3.6	2.6	1.8	0.2	1.8	0.9	2.3	2.2	2.1

Table A.6
Developing economies: consumer price inflation, 2009–2019 (*continued*)

Annual percentage change

	2009	2010	2011	2012	2013	2014	2015	2016	2017[b]	2018[c]	2019[c]
Southern Africa	7.7	6.4	6.3	6.6	6.4	6.3	5.9	12.5	9.4	7.9	6.8
Angola	13.7	14.5	13.5	10.3	8.8	7.3	12.1	41.2	28.0	19.4	16.7
Botswana	8.0	6.9	8.5	7.5	5.9	4.4	3.1	3.7	3.6	3.9	4.2
Lesotho	7.4	3.6	5.0	6.1	4.9	5.3	3.2	6.6	5.5	6.2	5.4
Malawi	8.4	7.4	7.6	21.3	27.3	23.8	21.9	21.7	14.0	11.9	8.7
Mauritius	2.5	2.9	6.5	3.9	3.5	3.2	1.3	1.0	3.5	3.2	3.5
Mozambique	3.8	28.2	-2.5	2.6	4.3	2.6	3.6	19.9	7.0	6.0	6.5
Namibia	9.5	4.9	5.0	6.7	5.6	5.3	3.4	6.7	6.2	5.6	5.1
South Africa	7.3	4.1	5.0	5.7	5.8	6.1	4.6	6.6	5.6	5.7	4.9
Swaziland	7.4	4.5	6.1	8.9	5.6	5.7	5.0	7.8	6.7	5.9	5.1
Zambia	13.4	8.5	6.4	6.6	7.0	7.8	10.1	17.9	14.5	9.7	7.8
Zimbabwe	-34.9	3.0	3.3	3.9	1.6	-0.2	-2.4	-1.6	1.7	2.1	2.5
Africa - net fuel exporters	9.5	9.8	10.0	10.4	7.9	8.0	8.7	15.4	18.8	12.9	10.8
Africa - net fuel importers	6.5	4.7	7.0	6.9	5.4	5.3	5.0	6.2	5.7	5.4	4.8
East and South Asia	2.5	4.9	6.4	4.7	5.3	3.5	2.6	2.6	2.4	3.1	3.4
East Asia	0.4	3.3	5.2	2.8	2.8	2.3	1.6	1.9	1.8	2.5	2.7
Brunei Darussalam	1.0	0.4	2.0	0.5	0.4	-0.2	-0.4	-0.7	-0.1	0.5	1.0
Cambodia	-0.7	4.0	5.5	2.9	2.9	3.9	1.2	3.0	3.5	3.6	3.4
China	-0.7	3.2	5.6	2.6	2.7	1.9	1.4	2.0	1.5	2.5	2.8
Fiji	3.2	3.7	7.3	3.4	2.9	0.5	1.4	3.9	2.8	3.0	3.2
Hong Kong SAR[e]	0.6	2.3	5.3	4.1	4.4	4.5	3.0	2.4	1.5	2.0	2.2
Indonesia	4.4	5.2	5.4	4.3	6.4	6.4	6.4	3.6	3.8	3.8	4.0
Kiribati	0.6	1.5	2.3	0.5	0.9	4.0	0.9	1.3	1.7	2.0	2.2
Lao People's Democratic Republic	0.0	6.0	7.6	4.3	6.4	4.1	1.3	1.5	1.1	1.8	2.2
Malaysia	0.6	1.7	3.2	1.6	2.1	3.2	2.1	2.1	3.9	2.5	2.9
Mongolia	6.3	10.1	9.5	15.0	8.6	13.0	5.8	0.6	3.7	3.9	4.5
Myanmar	1.5	7.7	5.0	1.5	5.5	5.5	9.5	7.0	6.8	7.5	6.6
Papua New Guinea	6.9	6.0	4.4	4.5	5.0	5.2	6.0	6.7	7.5	7.2	5.1
Philippines	4.2	3.8	4.6	3.2	3.0	4.1	1.4	1.8	3.1	3.2	3.0
Republic of Korea	2.8	2.9	4.0	2.2	1.3	1.3	0.7	1.0	2.1	2.0	2.2
Samoa	6.3	0.8	5.2	2.0	0.6	-0.4	0.7	1.3	1.6	2.1	2.4
Singapore	0.6	2.8	5.3	4.5	2.4	1.0	-0.5	-0.5	0.6	1.5	1.8
Solomon Islands	7.1	1.1	7.3	5.9	5.4	5.2	-0.6	1.1	1.8	2.2	2.5
Taiwan Province of China	-1.0	1.1	1.1	1.1	0.6	0.3	-0.7	0.8	1.0	1.1	1.3
Thailand	-0.8	3.2	3.8	3.0	2.2	1.9	-0.9	0.2	0.6	1.4	2.0
Timor-Leste	0.7	6.8	13.5	11.8	11.2	0.4	0.6	-1.2	1.9	3.3	3.3
Vanuatu	4.3	2.8	0.9	1.4	1.4	0.8	2.5	0.9	2.6	3.0	3.2
Viet Nam	7.1	8.9	18.7	9.1	6.6	4.1	0.9	3.2	3.7	4.2	4.8
South Asia	11.0	11.4	11.3	12.5	15.6	8.4	6.9	5.5	4.9	5.8	5.9
Afghanistan	-8.3	0.9	10.2	7.2	7.7	4.6	-1.5	2.2	5.5	6.0	6.4
Bangladesh	5.4	8.1	10.7	6.2	7.5	7.0	6.2	5.5	5.4	5.4	5.5
Bhutan	4.4	7.0	8.8	10.9	7.0	8.2	4.5	4.4	4.6	5.1	4.8
India	10.9	12.0	8.9	9.3	10.9	6.3	5.9	4.9	3.5	4.5	4.8
Iran (Islamic Republic of)	13.5	10.1	20.6	27.4	39.3	17.2	13.7	8.6	9.6	10.9	10.2
Maldives	4.0	6.6	12.9	10.9	3.8	2.1	1.0	0.5	2.9	3.7	3.9

Table A.6
Developing economies: consumer price inflation, 2009–2019 (*continued*)

Annual percentage change

	2009	2010	2011	2012	2013	2014	2015	2016	2017[b]	2018[c]	2019[c]
Nepal	11.1	9.3	9.3	9.5	9.0	8.4	7.9	8.8	4.5	7.8	6.8
Pakistan	13.6	13.9	11.9	9.7	7.7	7.2	2.5	3.8	4.2	4.9	5.2
Sri Lanka	3.5	6.2	6.7	7.5	6.9	2.8	2.2	4.0	6.1	5.2	5.0
East and South Asia - net fuel exporters	7.7	7.1	11.6	12.4	17.4	9.8	8.3	5.2	5.7	6.2	6.1
East and South Asia - net fuel importers	1.8	4.6	5.8	3.7	3.9	2.7	2.0	2.3	2.0	2.8	3.0
Western Asia	4.1	4.9	4.9	5.6	6.7	5.1	4.9	5.4	4.8	4.5	3.9
Net fuel exporters	3.3	3.3	4.4	2.8	2.8	2.7	2.9	3.6	1.6	2.5	2.7
Bahrain	2.8	2.0	-0.4	2.8	3.3	2.7	1.8	2.8	1.3	2.5	3.0
Iraq	6.9	2.9	5.8	6.1	1.9	2.2	1.4	2.8	2.0	3.0	3.4
Kuwait	4.6	4.5	4.9	3.2	2.7	2.9	3.3	3.2	3.4	3.8	3.4
Oman	3.9	3.2	4.1	2.9	1.2	1.0	0.1	1.1	1.7	2.9	2.6
Qatar	-4.9	-2.4	1.9	1.9	3.1	3.1	1.9	2.9	0.8	2.6	3.2
Saudi Arabia	5.0	5.4	5.8	2.9	3.5	2.7	2.2	3.6	-0.3	1.0	1.4
United Arab Emirates	1.6	0.9	0.9	0.7	1.1	2.3	4.1	1.6	2.2	2.5	3.5
Yemen	5.4	11.2	19.5	9.9	11.0	8.1	21.4	35.0	22.5	18.0	9.3
Net fuel importers	5.1	6.8	5.6	8.8	11.2	7.9	7.3	7.5	8.6	7.0	5.4
Israel	3.3	2.7	3.5	1.7	1.6	0.5	-0.6	-0.5	0.2	2.3	2.2
Jordan	-0.7	5.0	4.2	4.5	4.8	2.9	-0.9	-0.8	3.4	2.6	2.3
Lebanon	1.2	4.0	3.8	7.8	5.5	0.8	-3.7	-0.8	3.2	2.2	2.3
Syrian Arab Republic	2.9	4.4	4.8	36.7	101.0	31.2	42.5	46.1	21.3	13.9	10.6
Turkey	6.2	8.6	6.5	9.0	7.5	8.9	7.7	7.7	10.8	8.3	6.3
Latin America and the Caribbean[d]	5.5	5.8	6.7	6.3	6.5	8.4	7.7	9.3	5.8	4.9	4.7
South America[d]	5.8	6.5	7.7	7.1	7.6	10.3	9.8	11.9	5.9	5.4	5.2
Argentina	15.0	21.8	20.0	21.8	23.7	42.5	23.4	40.5	24.0	17.9	14.4
Bolivia (Plurinational State of)	3.3	2.5	9.8	4.6	5.7	5.8	4.1	3.6	2.6	4.5	3.6
Brazil	4.8	5.0	6.6	5.4	6.2	6.3	9.1	8.7	3.4	3.7	4.1
Chile	1.5	1.5	3.3	3.0	1.8	4.7	4.3	3.8	2.1	2.6	3.0
Colombia	4.2	2.3	3.4	3.2	2.0	2.9	5.0	7.5	4.6	3.7	3.2
Ecuador	5.2	3.6	4.5	5.1	2.7	3.6	4.0	1.7	0.6	1.7	2.3
Paraguay	2.6	4.7	8.3	3.7	2.7	5.0	3.1	4.1	3.4	3.6	3.7
Peru	2.9	1.5	3.4	3.7	2.8	3.2	3.6	3.6	3.1	2.8	2.9
Uruguay	7.1	6.7	8.1	8.1	8.6	8.9	8.7	9.6	6.2	6.8	6.5
Venezuela (Bolivarian Republic of)	27.1	28.2	26.1	21.1	40.6	62.2	109.7	400.0	448.8	346.3	79.5
Mexico and Central America	4.6	4.1	4.3	4.2	3.7	3.8	2.5	2.8	5.4	3.8	3.4
Costa Rica	7.8	5.7	4.9	4.5	5.2	4.5	0.8	0.0	1.6	2.9	3.1
Cuba	-0.8	0.5	11.1	5.6	0.2	1.4	1.8	4.5	4.6	4.3	3.9
Dominican Republic	1.4	6.3	8.5	3.7	4.8	3.0	0.8	1.6	3.1	3.9	3.6
El Salvador	1.1	0.9	5.1	1.7	0.8	1.7	-1.3	0.6	1.1	1.6	1.8
Guatemala	1.9	3.9	6.2	3.8	4.3	3.4	2.4	4.4	4.3	4.2	3.9
Haiti	0.0	5.7	8.4	6.3	5.9	4.6	9.0	13.8	15.2	14.0	12.0
Honduras	5.5	4.7	6.8	5.2	5.2	6.1	3.2	2.7	3.8	4.1	4.2
Mexico	5.3	4.2	3.4	4.1	3.8	4.0	2.7	2.8	5.9	3.8	3.4
Nicaragua	3.7	5.5	8.1	7.2	7.1	6.0	4.0	3.5	3.7	4.5	4.1

Table A.6
Developing economies: consumer price inflation, 2009–2019 (*continued*)

Annual percentage change

	2009	2010	2011	2012	2013	2014	2015	2016	2017[b]	2018[c]	2019[c]
Panama	2.4	3.5	5.9	5.7	4.0	2.6	0.1	0.7	1.0	1.5	1.9
Caribbean	5.7	8.5	6.6	6.5	4.7	4.9	3.4	6.1	4.1	3.5	3.8
Bahamas	2.1	1.3	3.2	2.0	0.3	1.5	1.9	-0.3	1.6	2.0	2.3
Barbados	3.6	5.8	9.4	4.5	1.8	1.9	-1.1	-0.7	1.2	1.5	1.8
Belize	-1.1	0.9	1.6	1.3	0.5	1.2	-0.9	1.1	1.2	1.7	1.8
Guyana	2.9	2.1	5.0	2.4	1.8	0.9	-1.0	0.7	1.7	2.1	1.8
Jamaica	9.6	12.6	7.5	6.9	9.3	8.3	3.7	2.3	4.3	4.0	4.0
Suriname	-0.2	6.9	17.7	5.0	1.9	3.4	6.9	55.5	23.8	10.5	9.0
Trinidad and Tobago	7.0	10.5	5.1	9.3	5.2	5.7	4.7	3.1	2.0	3.1	4.0
Latin America and the Caribbean - net fuel exporters	4.5	3.0	4.0	3.9	2.5	3.3	4.7	6.1	3.6	3.3	3.1
Latin America and the Caribbean - net fuel importers	5.6	6.1	7.0	6.5	6.8	8.9	8.0	9.6	6.0	5.1	4.8
Memorandum items:											
Least developed countries	7.1	8.5	12.2	11.0	8.6	8.3	8.3	13.1	11.4	8.6	7.5
East Asia (excluding China)	2.1	3.4	4.6	3.1	3.0	2.9	1.8	1.7	2.3	2.4	2.6
South Asia (excluding India)	11.2	10.2	15.9	18.2	24.1	12.1	8.9	6.6	7.3	8.2	7.9
Western Asia (excluding Israel and Turkey)	3.2	3.4	4.4	4.4	7.1	3.8	4.4	5.2	2.5	2.9	3.0
Arab States[f]	4.4	4.4	5.7	5.8	7.2	5.1	5.5	7.2	7.3	4.6	4.3
Landlocked developing economies	6.1	6.4	10.3	7.5	5.8	5.7	5.9	8.0	7.1	5.8	5.6
Small island developing States	1.5	3.7	6.4	4.8	2.9	2.0	0.9	1.8	2.4	2.9	2.9

Source: UN/DESA

a Data for country groups are weighted averages, where weights are based on GDP in 2010 prices and exchange rates.

b Partly estimated.

c Baseline scenario forecasts, based in part on Project LINK and the UN/DESA World Economic Forecasting Model.

d Regional aggregates exclude Venezuela (Bolivarian Republic of), due to the potential distortionary impacts of very high inflation in a single country.

e Special Administrative Region of China.

f Currently includes data for Algeria, Bahrain, Comoros, Djibouti, Egypt, Iraq, Jordan, Kuwait, Lebanon, Libya, Mauritania, Morocco, Oman, Qatar, Saudi Arabia, Somalia, Sudan, Syrian Arab Republic, Tunisia, United Arab Emirates and Yemen..

Table A.7
Developed economies: unemployment rates,[a,b] 2009–2019

Percentage of labour force

	2009	2010	2011	2012	2013	2014	2015	2016	2017[b]	2018[c]	2019[c]
Developed economies	8.4	8.8	8.5	8.6	8.5	7.8	7.1	6.5	5.9	5.6	5.4
United States	9.3	9.6	8.9	8.1	7.4	6.2	5.3	4.9	4.4	4.0	3.7
Canada	8.4	8.0	7.5	7.3	7.1	6.9	6.9	7.0	6.4	6.0	5.8
Japan	5.1	5.1	4.6	4.3	4.0	3.6	3.4	3.1	2.8	3.0	3.0
Australia	5.6	5.2	5.1	5.2	5.7	6.1	6.1	5.7	5.7	5.4	5.2
New Zealand	5.8	6.1	6.0	6.4	5.8	5.4	5.4	5.1	4.7	4.9	5.0
European Union	9.0	9.6	9.7	10.5	10.9	10.2	9.4	8.6	7.7	7.4	7.2
EU-15	9.1	9.5	9.6	10.6	11.1	10.5	9.8	9.0	8.2	8.0	7.7
Austria	5.3	4.8	4.6	4.9	5.4	5.6	5.7	6.0	5.6	5.6	5.6
Belgium	7.9	8.3	7.1	7.5	8.5	8.5	8.5	7.9	7.3	7.2	7.1
Denmark	6.0	7.5	7.6	7.5	7.0	6.5	6.2	6.2	5.8	5.4	5.0
Finland	8.1	8.3	7.8	7.8	8.2	8.7	9.3	8.9	8.7	8.6	8.3
France	9.1	9.3	9.2	9.8	10.3	10.3	10.4	10.0	9.6	9.5	9.2
Germany	7.7	6.9	5.9	5.4	5.2	5.0	4.6	4.2	3.7	3.5	3.2
Greece	9.6	12.7	17.9	24.5	27.5	26.6	25.0	23.6	21.4	20.9	20.5
Ireland	12.1	13.9	14.7	14.7	13.1	11.3	9.5	7.9	6.3	6.9	6.9
Italy	7.7	8.3	8.4	10.7	12.1	12.6	11.9	11.7	11.3	11.0	10.7
Luxembourg	5.2	4.6	4.8	5.1	5.8	6.0	6.5	6.3	6.0	6.1	6.1
Netherlands	4.4	5.0	5.0	5.8	7.3	7.4	6.9	6.0	4.9	4.7	4.5
Portugal	10.7	12.0	12.9	15.8	16.4	14.1	12.6	11.2	9.1	8.9	8.8
Spain	17.9	19.9	21.4	24.8	26.1	24.5	22.1	19.6	17.3	16.5	16.1
Sweden	8.3	8.6	7.8	8.0	8.0	7.9	7.4	6.9	6.7	6.4	6.0
United Kingdom	7.6	7.8	8.1	7.9	7.6	6.1	5.3	4.8	4.3	4.2	4.0
EU-13	8.4	9.9	9.8	10.0	10.1	9.0	7.9	6.6	5.4	5.1	4.8
Bulgaria	6.9	10.3	11.3	12.3	12.9	11.5	9.1	7.6	6.2	5.9	5.7
Croatia	9.3	11.8	13.7	15.8	17.4	17.2	16.1	13.3	11.0	10.6	10.2
Cyprus	5.4	6.3	7.9	11.9	15.9	16.2	15.0	13.0	11.1	10.9	10.8
Czech Republic	6.7	7.3	6.7	7.0	7.0	6.1	5.1	4.0	3.0	2.7	2.5
Estonia	13.6	16.7	12.4	9.9	8.6	7.4	6.2	6.7	5.8	5.1	4.8
Hungary	10.0	11.2	11.1	11.0	10.1	7.8	6.8	5.1	4.3	3.9	3.9
Latvia	17.6	19.5	16.2	15.0	11.8	10.8	9.9	9.6	8.5	8.0	7.7
Lithuania	13.8	17.8	15.4	13.4	11.8	10.7	9.2	7.9	7.6	7.2	6.9
Malta	6.9	6.8	6.4	6.4	6.3	5.8	5.4	4.8	4.1	4.1	4.0
Poland	8.1	9.6	9.7	10.2	10.4	9.0	7.5	6.2	4.9	4.6	4.4
Romania	6.5	7.0	7.2	6.9	7.1	6.8	6.8	5.9	5.1	4.9	4.7
Slovakia	12.1	14.5	13.7	14.0	14.2	13.2	11.5	9.7	7.9	7.0	6.6
Slovenia	5.9	7.3	8.2	8.9	10.2	9.7	9.0	8.0	6.7	6.8	6.0
Other Europe	4.0	4.2	3.8	3.8	4.1	4.1	4.4	4.6	4.3	4.2	4.0[c]
Iceland	7.1	7.5	7.1	6.0	5.5	4.9	3.9	3.0	2.9	2.9	2.7
Norway	3.2	3.6	3.3	3.2	3.5	3.5	4.4	4.7	4.2	4.1	4.0
Switzerland	4.3	4.5	4.0	4.1	4.3	4.5	4.5	4.6	4.5	4.4	4.1
Memorandum items:											
Major developed economies	8.0	8.1	7.6	7.3	7.1	6.4	5.8	5.5	5.1	4.7	4.4
Euro area	9.6	10.2	10.2	11.4	12.0	11.6	10.9	10.0	9.1	8.8	8.6

Source: UN/DESA, based on data of the OECD and Eurostat.

a Unemployment data are standardized by the OECD and Eurostat for comparability among countries and over time, in conformity with the definitions of the International Labour Organization (see OECD, Standardized Unemployment Rates: Sources and Methods (Paris, 1985)).

b Data for country groups are weighted averages, where labour force is used for weights.

c Partly estimated.

d Baseline scenario forecasts, based in part on Project LINK and the UN/DESA World Economic Forecasting Model.

Table A.8
Economies in transition and developing economies: unemployment rates,[a] 2008–2017

Percentage of labour force

	2008	2009	2010	2011	2012	2013	2014	2015	2016[b]	2017[b]
South-Eastern Europe[c]										
Albania	13.0	13.8	14.2	14.0	13.4	15.6	17.5	17.1	16.3	15.8
Bosnia and Herzegovina	23.4	24.1	27.2	27.6	28.0	27.5	27.5	27.7	25.4	25.4
Montenegro	16.8	19.1	19.7	19.7	19.6	19.5	18.0	17.5	17.5	17.4
Serbia	13.6	16.1	19.2	23.0	23.9	22.1	19.2	17.7	15.3	15.5
The former Yugoslav Republic of Macedonia	33.8	32.2	32.0	31.4	31.0	29.0	28.0	26.1	26.7	27.3
Commonwealth of Independent States and Georgia[c, d]										
Armenia	16.4	18.7	19.0	18.4	17.3	16.2	17.6	17.0	16.8	16.6
Azerbaijan	5.9	5.7	5.6	5.4	5.2	5.0	4.9	5.0	5.1	5.2
Belarus	0.7	0.9	0.7	0.7	0.6	0.5	0.5	0.9	1.0	1.0
Georgia[d]	16.5	16.8	16.3	15.1	15.0	14.6	12.4	12.0	11.6	11.4
Kazakhstan	6.6	6.6	5.8	5.4	5.3	5.2	5.1	5.0	5.0	5.4
Kyrgyzstan	8.2	8.4	8.6	8.5	8.4	8.3	8.1	7.6	7.7	7.7
Republic of Moldova	4.0	6.4	7.5	6.7	5.6	5.1	3.9	4.9	4.2	4.4
Russian Federation	6.2	8.3	7.3	6.5	5.5	5.5	5.2	5.6	5.7	5.8
Tajikistan	2.2	2.0	2.1	2.3	2.4	2.3	2.4	2.3	2.3	2.3
Turkmenistan[e]	9.2	9.2	9.2	9.2	9.1	9.0	9.0	8.7	8.6	8.6
Ukraine[f]	6.4	8.8	8.1	7.9	7.5	7.2	9.3	9.1	8.9	8.8
Uzbekistan	4.9	5.0	5.4	5.0	4.9	4.9	5.1	5.0	5.0	5.0
Africa[f]										
Algeria	11.3	10.2	10.0	10.0	11.0	9.8	10.6	11.0	11.2	11.4
Botswana	12.9	15.4	17.9	17.6	17.4	17.4	17.1	17.9	18.4	18.6
Egypt	8.7	9.4	9.0	12.0	12.7	13.2	13.2	12.8	12.0	11.5
Mauritius	7.2	7.3	7.7	7.9	8.7	7.6	7.7	7.9	7.8	7.6
Morocco	9.6	9.1	9.1	8.9	9.0	9.2	9.9	9.7	10.0	10.4
South Africa	22.4	23.5	24.7	24.6	24.7	24.6	24.9	25.2	25.9	26.0
Tunisia	12.4	13.3	13.1	18.3	17.6	15.9	15.8	15.2	14.8	14.6
Developing America[g]										
Argentina	7.9	8.7	7.7	7.2	7.2	7.1	7.3	6.5	6.6	6.5
Barbados	8.1	10.0	10.8	11.2	11.6	11.6	12.3	11.3	9.3	9.3
Bolivia (Plurinational State of)	4.4	4.9	4.3	3.8	3.2	4.0	3.5	4.5	4.5	4.5
Brazil	7.9	8.1	6.7	6.0	8.2	8.0	7.8	9.3	12.0	12.7
Chile	7.8	9.7	8.2	7.1	6.4	5.9	6.4	6.2	6.6	6.8
Colombia	11.0	12.3	11.8	10.9	10.6	10.1	9.5	9.2	9.9	10.5
Costa Rica	4.8	8.5	7.1	7.7	9.8	9.1	9.5	9.7	9.0	8.6
Dominican Republic	5.3	5.8	5.7	6.7	7.2	7.9	7.2	6.9	6.9	6.9
Ecuador	6.9	8.5	7.6	6.0	4.9	4.7	5.1	5.4	6.4	6.0
El Salvador	5.5	7.1	6.8	6.6	6.2	5.6	6.7	6.2	6.3	6.4
Guatemala	..	..	4.8	3.1	4.0	3.8	4.0	2.8	2.4	2.4
Honduras	4.1	4.9	6.4	6.8	5.6	6.0	7.5	8.8	6.3	5.6
Jamaica	10.6	11.4	12.4	12.7	13.7	15.3	13.7	13.3	13.3	13.1
Mexico[h]	3.9	5.4	5.3	5.2	4.9	4.9	4.8	4.3	4.0	4.1
Nicaragua	6.1	7.9	7.8	5.9	5.9	5.6	6.6	6.6	6.7	6.7

Table A.8
Economies in transition and developing economies: unemployment rates,[a] 2008–2017 (*continued*)

Percentage of labour force

	2008	2009	2010	2011	2012	2013	2014	2015	2016	2017[b]
Developing America (*continued*)										
Panama	5.0	6.3	5.8	3.6	3.6	3.7	4.1	4.5	5.5	5.5
Paraguay	7.4	8.2	7.2	7.1	8.1	8.1	8.0	6.8	7.7	7.8
Peru	8.4	8.4	7.9	7.7	6.8	5.9	5.9	6.5	6.6	7.2
Trinidad and Tobago	4.6	5.3	5.9	5.1	5.0	3.7	3.3	3.5	3.9	4.2
Uruguay	8.3	8.2	7.5	6.6	6.7	6.7	6.9	7.8	8.2	8.8
Venezuela Bolivarian Republic of	7.3	7.9	8.7	8.3	8.1	7.8	7.2	7.0	16.4	18.6
Developing Asia[e]										
China	4.4	4.3	4.2	4.3	4.5	4.5	4.6	4.6	4.6	4.6
Hong Kong SAR[i]	3.6	5.3	4.3	3.4	3.3	3.4	3.3	3.3	3.4	3.5
India	4.2	3.9	3.6	3.5	3.6	3.6	3.5	3.5	3.5	3.4
Indonesia	8.4	7.9	7.1	7.5	6.1	6.2	5.9	6.0	5.6	5.8
Iran, Islamic Republic of	10.5	12.0	13.5	12.3	12.2	10.4	10.6	11.1	11.3	11.3
Israel	7.7	9.5	8.5	7.1	6.9	6.2	5.9	5.3	5.6	5.9
Jordan	12.7	12.9	12.5	12.9	12.2	12.6	11.9	13.1	13.2	13.4
Korea, Republic of[h]	3.2	3.6	3.7	3.4	3.2	3.1	3.5	3.6	3.7	3.6
Malaysia	3.3	3.7	3.4	3.1	3.0	3.1	2.9	3.1	3.3	3.3
Pakistan	5.0	5.5	5.6	6.0	6.0	6.2	5.6	5.9	5.9	5.9
Philippines	7.3	7.5	7.4	7.0	7.0	7.1	6.6	6.3	5.9	5.9
Saudi Arabia	5.1	5.4	5.6	5.8	5.5	5.6	5.7	5.6	5.5	5.5
Singapore	4.0	4.3	3.1	2.9	2.8	2.8	2.8	1.7	1.8	2.0
Sri Lanka	5.2	5.9	4.9	4.2	4.0	4.4	4.4	4.7	5.0	5.2
Taiwan Province of China	4.1	5.9	5.2	4.4	4.2	4.2	4.0	3.8	4.0	4.1
Thailand	1.2	1.5	1.0	0.7	0.6	0.8	0.8	0.7	0.6	0.6
Turkey[h]	9.7	12.6	10.7	8.8	8.1	8.7	9.9	10.2	10.3	10.8
Viet Nam	2.3	2.6	2.6	2.0	1.8	2.0	1.9	2.1	2.2	2.2

Sources: UN/DESA, based on data of the Economic Commission for Europe (ECE); ILOstat; Economic Commission for Latin America and the Caribbean (ECLAC) and OECD.

a   As a percentage of labour force. Reflects national definitions and coverage. Not comparable across economies.

b   Partly estimated.

c   Sourced from UNECE Statistical Database.

d   Georgia officially left the Commonwealth of Independent States on 18 August 2009. However, its performance is discussed in the context of this group of countries for reasons of geographic proximity and similarities in economic structure.

e   Sourced from ILOstat

f   Starting in 2010, data for the Ukraine excludes the temporarily occupied territory of the Autonomous Republic of Crimea and Sevastopol.

g   Sourced from CEPALSTAT Database, ECLAC.

h   Sourced from OECD Short-Term Labour Market Statistics.

i   Special Administrative Region of China.

Table A.9
Major developed economies: financial indicators, 2008–2017

Percentage

	2008	2009	2010	2011	2012	2013	2014	2015	2016	2017[a]
Short-term interest rates[b]										
Canada	3.31	0.69	0.78	1.17	1.16	1.16	1.17	0.82	0.82	1.00
Euro area[c]	4.63	1.23	0.81	1.39	0.57	0.22	0.21	-0.02	-0.26	-0.33
Japan	0.85	0.58	0.38	0.33	0.33	0.24	0.20	0.17	0.07	0.06
United Kingdom	5.49	1.20	0.69	0.89	0.84	0.49	0.54	0.55	0.49	0.33
United States	2.97	0.56	0.31	0.30	0.28	0.17	0.12	0.23	0.64	1.10
Long-term interest rates[d]										
Canada	3.6	3.2	3.2	2.8	1.9	2.3	2.2	1.5	1.3	1.8
France	4.2	3.7	3.1	3.3	2.5	2.2	1.7	0.8	0.5	0.8
Germany	4.0	3.2	2.7	2.6	1.5	1.6	1.2	0.5	0.1	0.3
Italy	4.7	4.3	4.0	5.4	5.5	4.3	2.9	1.7	1.5	2.2
Japan	1.5	1.3	1.2	1.1	0.8	0.7	0.5	0.4	-0.1	0.1
United Kingdom	4.6	3.7	3.6	3.1	1.9	2.4	2.6	1.9	1.3	1.2
United States	3.7	3.3	3.2	2.8	1.8	2.4	2.5	2.1	1.8	2.3
General government financial balances[e]										
Canada	0.2	-3.9	-4.7	-3.3	-2.5	-1.5	0.0	-1.1	-1.9	-1.7
France	-3.2	-7.2	-6.8	-5.1	-4.8	-4.0	-3.9	-3.6	-3.4	-3.0
Germany	-0.2	-3.2	-4.2	-1.0	0.0	-0.2	0.3	0.7	0.8	0.7
Italy	-2.7	-5.3	-4.3	-3.7	-2.9	-2.9	-3.0	-2.7	-2.4	-2.1
Japan	-4.1	-9.8	-9.1	-9.1	-8.3	-7.6	-5.4	-3.5	-4.6	-5.0
United Kingdom	-4.9	-10.6	-9.6	-7.7	-8.3	-5.7	-5.6	-4.3	-3.3	-3.1
United States	-7.2	-12.8	-12.2	-10.8	-9.0	-5.5	-5.0	-4.4	-5.0	-4.7

Source: UN/DESA, based on OECD, *Economic Outlook*; OECD, *Main Economic Indicators*.

a Average for the first nine months for short- and long-term interest rates.

b Three-month Interbank or money market rate.

c Three-month Euro Interbank Offered Rate (EURIBOR).

d Yield on 10-year government bonds.

e Surplus (+) or deficit (-) as a percentage of nominal GDP. Estimates for 2017.

Table A.10
Selected economies: real effective exchange rates, broad measurement,[a, b] 2008–2017

	2008	2009	2010	2011	2012	2013	2014	2015	2016	2017[c]
Developed economies										
Australia	90.3	87.5	100.0	106.9	108.5	102.9	98.2	89.6	90.3	93.6
Bulgaria	99.5	103.6	100.0	101.7	100.2	100.8	99.8	96.6	96.8	97.7
Canada	96.1	91.6	100.0	101.6	100.9	97.2	91.4	83.2	81.5	82.5
Croatia	102.1	103.1	100.0	97.3	95.2	96.3	95.5	92.2	92.6	93.4
Czech Republic	104.1	99.7	100.0	101.7	97.7	95.9	90.6	88.0	90.3	92.9
Denmark	101.6	104.4	100.0	99.2	96.5	97.3	98.2	94.7	96.0	96.1
Euro area	108.0	108.9	100.0	99.3	94.4	97.7	98.2	89.7	91.5	91.7
Hungary	105.5	99.3	100.0	99.6	96.8	95.9	92.0	88.0	88.6	90.3
Japan	88.5	99.4	100.0	101.3	100.0	79.7	75.1	70.3	79.6	76.3
New Zealand	98.8	92.1	100.0	103.9	106.5	109.5	113.0	104.7	105.3	108.5
Norway	98.7	96.2	100.0	100.3	99.6	97.9	93.4	85.2	85.6	87.0
Poland	112.7	95.0	100.0	98.2	95.2	96.1	96.6	92.1	88.3	90.9
Romania	106.7	98.8	100.0	102.5	96.3	100.9	101.7	98.0	96.3	94.5
Sweden	104.6	94.4	100.0	105.8	105.1	106.3	100.9	93.9	94.5	93.6
Switzerland	92.5	96.2	100.0	109.5	105.1	103.4	104.5	111.2	108.9	107.7
United Kingdom	110.2	99.5	100.0	100.5	104.5	103.1	110.3	115.5	103.4	97.8
United States	100.3	104.5	100.0	95.0	97.2	97.5	99.6	110.5	114.5	114.5
Economies in transition										
Russian Federation	100.0	91.5	100.0	103.7	104.9	106.7	96.2	77.8	76.5	89.7
Ukraine[d]	116.3	97.4	100.0	100.3	102.9	99.7	78.2	73.7	72.6	75.7
Developing economies										
Algeria	102.0	100.0	100.0	99.2	103.9	101.5	102.8	97.8	96.1	98.9
Argentina	110.4	103.1	100.0	95.2	98.2	90.1	73.9	86.4	70.9	74.3
Brazil	87.7	87.5	100.0	104.6	94.4	90.0	88.9	74.0	78.3	85.6
Chile	97.5	94.3	100.0	100.8	102.8	101.6	92.0	90.2	91.5	94.3
China	96.4	100.7	100.0	102.5	108.7	115.6	118.3	129.7	124.4	120.2
Colombia	91.1	87.6	100.0	98.5	103.9	100.1	95.3	77.8	74.9	77.4
Hong Kong SAR[e]	100.6	104.1	100.0	95.9	99.4	103.1	107.4	118.1	121.5	121.6
India	94.9	89.6	100.0	100.1	93.8	89.4	90.8	97.8	98.7	102.8
Indonesia	88.9	88.5	100.0	100.0	96.3	93.0	87.1	88.9	92.5	94.8
Iran, Islamic Republic of	85.6	97.0	100.0	109.3	123.2	122.4	92.0	103.9	106.6	108.3
Israel	97.6	95.5	100.0	100.8	95.9	102.2	103.3	103.0	104.5	109.2
Korea, Republic of	104.4	92.4	100.0	99.9	99.5	103.9	109.9	110.9	109.2	112.4
Malaysia	97.9	95.0	100.0	99.8	99.6	99.7	99.3	91.6	87.8	85.7
Mexico	105.7	92.8	100.0	99.4	96.4	101.9	101.0	90.9	79.1	81.0
Morocco	102.3	104.2	100.0	97.8	95.9	97.6	97.7	98.1	100.4	100.0
Nigeria	99.2	92.0	100.0	100.4	111.5	119.0	127.4	126.5	116.2	105.0
Pakistan	94.6	95.1	100.0	102.9	104.5	102.4	109.9	120.0	122.8	126.6

Table A.10

Selected economies: real effective exchange rates, broad measurement,[a, b] 2008–2017 (continued)

	2008	2009	2010	2011	2012	2013	2014	2015	2016	2017[c]
Developing economies (continued)										
Peru	94.4	96.9	100.0	98.2	105.7	104.8	102.8	101.9	99.9	102.1
Philippines	97.7	96.5	100.0	100.4	105.6	109.4	109.5	117.0	113.3	109.0
Saudi Arabia	91.2	99.0	100.0	97.4	100.3	102.9	105.4	116.5	121.1	119.5
Singapore	96.4	96.7	100.0	105.4	110.4	112.5	112.3	110.5	109.7	108.3
South Africa	79.8	86.8	100.0	98.1	92.2	82.0	77.0	75.5	70.1	80.5
Taiwan Province of China	104.2	99.5	100.0	100.2	100.3	101.0	100.2	102.2	101.8	107.3
Thailand	98.3	94.8	100.0	99.1	99.5	104.9	101.8	103.9	100.1	102.9
Turkey	97.0	90.8	100.0	88.4	91.6	90.4	85.4	84.0	82.4	74.3
United Arab Emirates	98.9	104.7	100.0	93.5	95.2	95.4	96.9	108.4	111.2	110.8
Uruguay	87.0	89.3	100.0	102.0	105.2	112.2	110.3	114.4	119.3	128.0
Venezuela, Bolivarian Republic of	122.1	161.5	100.0	117.5	141.9	137.1	208.4	481.2	852.5	1705.1

Source: Bank for International Settlements, IMF International Financial Statistics..

a Year 2010=100.

b CPI-based indices. The real effective exchange rate gauges the effect on international price competitiveness of the country's manufactures owing to currency changes and inflation differentials. A rise in the index implies a fall in competitiveness and vice versa.

c Average for the first ten months.

d Starting in 2010, data for the Ukraine excludes the temporarily occupied territory of the Autonomous Republic of Crimea and Sevastopol.

e Special Administrative Region of China.

Table A.11
Indices of prices of primary commodities, 2008–2017

Index: Year 2000=100

| | Non-fuel commodities | | | | | Combined index | | | | |
	Food	Tropical beverages	Vegetable oilseeds and oils	Agricultural raw materials	Minerals and metals	Dollar	SDR	Manufactured export prices	Real prices of non-fuel commodities[a]	Crude petroleum[b]
2008	234	178	298	198	332	256	213	142	180	342.2
2009	220	181	213	163	232	213	182	134	159	221.2
2010	230	213	262	226	327	256	222	136	188	280.6
2011	265	270	333	289	375	302	253	150	201	389.3
2012	270	212	307	223	322	277	239	146	190	396.6
2013	255	174	269	206	306	258	225	149	173	383.6
2014	240	214	253	186	280	243	211	148	164	348.9
2015	204	197	203	161	218	202	190	133	152	179.3
2016	207	190	226	157	205	200	191	132	152	147.7
2017	202	185	230	170	246	210	202	134	157	183.1
2014										
I	244	198	279	198	289	249	214	151	165	379.6
II	245	220	270	191	281	248	212	150	165	383.6
III	238	220	237	181	285	242	210	149	162	365.2
IV	233	219	227	172	265	232	209	142	164	265.8
2015										
I	218	201	215	164	235	214	201	134	160	182.3
II	204	196	210	166	236	207	196	134	154	217.0
III	200	197	194	160	209	196	185	134	147	174.5
IV	195	194	193	153	193	189	179	132	143	143.9
2016										
I	193	180	204	148	189	186	177	130	143	109.3
II	212	186	230	157	198	200	188	133	151	153.6
III	218	197	231	157	206	206	195	133	155	155.5
IV	205	197	240	165	229	208	202	132	158	172.2
2017										
I	207	191	242	180	250	216	211	132	164	188.3
II	200	180	222	164	235	205	197	134	153	175.7
III	197	182	222	165	255	209	196	...	..	181.1

Source: UNCTAD, *Monthly Commodity Price Bulletin*; United Nations, *Monthly Bulletin of Statistics*; and data from the Organization of the Petroleum Exporting Countries (OPEC) website, available from http://www.opec.org.
a Combined index of non-fuel commodity prices in dollars, deflated by manufactured export price index.
b The new OPEC reference basket, introduced on 16 June 2005, currently has 14 crudes. Indonesian (Minas) and Gabon (Rabi Light) crudes were added.

Table A.12
World oil supply and demand, 2009–2018

	2009	2010	2011	2012	2013	2014	2015	2016	2017[a]	2018[b]
World oil supply[c, d] *(millions of barrels per day)*	83.9	85.6	86.9	89.0	89.3	91.7	94.3	94.7	95.3	97.1
Developed economies	15.7	15.9	16.1	17.0	18.1	20.1	21.4	21.0	21.7	23.1
Economies in transition	13.4	13.7	13.7	13.7	13.9	14.0	14.1	14.2	14.5	14.5
Developing economies	52.8	53.8	55.0	56.2	55.1	55.3	56.6	57.2	56.8	57.2
OPEC	34.2	34.7	35.8	37.5	37.7	37.7	39.1	39.6	39.6	40.0
Non-OPEC	18.6	19.1	19.2	18.7	17.4	17.6	17.6	17.6	17.2	17.2
Processing gains[e]	2.0	2.1	2.1	2.1	2.2	2.2	2.2	2.3	2.3	2.3
Global biofuels[f]	1.6	1.8	1.9	1.9	2.0	2.2	2.3	2.4	2.4	2.5
World total demand[g]	85.5	88.5	89.5	90.7	92.0	93.2	95.0	96.1	97.7	99.1
Oil prices *(dollars per barrel)*										
OPEC basket[h]	61.1	77.5	107.5	109.5	105.9	96.3	49.5	40.8	50.5	...
Brent oil	61.9	79.6	110.9	112.0	108.9	98.9	52.3	43.7	52.5	55.4

Source: UN/DESA, International Energy Agency; U.S. Energy Information Administration; and OPEC.
a Partly estimated.
b Baseline scenario forecasts.
c Including global biofuels, crude oil, condensates, natural gas liquids (NGLs), oil from non-conventional sources and other sources of supply.
d Totals may not add up because of rounding.
e Net volume gains and losses in the refining process (excluding net gain/loss in the economies in transition and China) and marine transportation losses.
f Global biofuels comprise all world biofuel production including fuel ethanol from Brazil and the United States.
g Including deliveries from refineries/primary stocks and marine bunkers, and refinery fuel and non-conventional oils.
h The new OPEC reference basket, introduced on 16 June 2005, currently has 14 crudes.

Table A.13

World trade:[a] changes in value and volume of exports and imports, by major country group, 2009–2019

Annual percentage change

	2009	2010	2011	2012	2013	2014	2015	2016	2017[b]	2018[c]	2019[c]
Dollar value of exports											
World	-19.6	19.3	18.7	1.6	2.7	1.6	-11.0	-0.1	4.3	4.2	6.4
Developed economies	**-19.6**	**14.1**	**15.4**	**-1.5**	**3.3**	**3.1**	**-9.6**	**0.1**	**3.1**	**3.6**	**6.0**
North America	-16.7	17.4	14.3	3.6	3.0	3.9	-6.4	-2.4	4.3	3.6	5.7
Europe	-19.9	10.8	16.4	-3.0	5.0	3.0	-10.4	0.6	2.8	3.7	6.1
Developed Asia and Pacific	-23.1	31.1	11.6	-2.3	-6.6	1.7	-11.9	3.8	1.9	2.4	6.5
Economies in transition	**-32.3**	**27.9**	**30.3**	**3.2**	**-0.3**	**-6.1**	**-28.3**	**-0.3**	**12.3**	**6.2**	**6.9**
South-Eastern Europe	-18.9	13.9	21.2	-6.4	16.3	1.4	-8.3	4.3	3.6	5.1	6.1
Commonwealth of Independent States and Georgia[d]	-32.8	28.5	30.7	3.6	-0.9	-6.4	-29.2	-0.5	12.9	6.2	6.9
Developing economies	**-18.3**	**26.7**	**22.2**	**5.4**	**2.3**	**0.4**	**-11.4**	**-0.5**	**5.4**	**4.9**	**6.3**
Latin America and the Caribbean	-20.7	31.4	17.7	1.7	-0.2	-3.9	-13.0	1.1	6.6	6.1	4.8
Africa	-26.5	28.2	16.2	9.0	-10.7	-5.0	-24.8	-2.0	9.1	6.1	7.8
East Asia	-15.4	27.2	20.5	5.1	5.0	3.3	-6.6	-0.3	3.8	4.2	6.2
South Asia	-6.1	26.0	23.9	-0.7	4.7	-3.6	-7.5	3.0	7.8	6.1	6.2
Western Asia	-25.9	20.0	36.1	11.1	0.6	-2.4	-23.8	-4.0	8.8	6.4	7.8
Dollar value of imports											
World	-19.8	18.7	18.9	1.3	2.6	1.7	-9.7	-2.0	4.5	4.3	6.5
Developed economies	**-21.9**	**14.5**	**16.2**	**-1.9**	**1.6**	**2.8**	**-10.3**	**-0.7**	**4.3**	**4.2**	**6.3**
North America	-22.0	19.7	13.6	3.0	0.1	3.4	-4.5	-2.0	5.8	5.0	5.8
Europe	-21.4	11.1	16.2	-5.0	3.6	2.7	-11.7	0.9	3.4	3.8	6.5
Developed Asia and Pacific	-24.6	23.9	23.0	5.3	-5.4	1.6	-17.1	-6.7	5.9	4.9	7.2
Economies in transition	**-30.4**	**22.3**	**27.1**	**8.5**	**3.3**	**-9.6**	**-27.6**	**-3.2**	**4.6**	**5.1**	**4.8**
South-Eastern Europe	-27.0	2.4	20.0	-6.7	5.4	2.4	-12.5	4.6	5.0	5.8	7.8
Commonwealth of Independent States and Georgia[d]	-30.7	24.3	27.7	9.6	3.2	-10.3	-28.7	-3.9	4.6	5.1	4.5
Developing economies	**-15.0**	**25.7**	**22.4**	**5.3**	**3.9**	**1.2**	**-7.5**	**-3.7**	**5.0**	**4.9**	**7.3**
Latin America and the Caribbean	-20.5	27.8	19.9	5.7	4.9	0.4	2.5	-19.9	3.0	4.5	4.8
Africa	-9.2	12.1	15.9	3.3	3.5	0.9	-15.3	-4.6	3.6	5.0	7.2
East Asia	-16.0	31.5	24.2	5.0	4.8	1.7	-10.0	0.8	5.7	4.6	7.5
South Asia	-2.6	21.7	23.8	5.1	-4.2	-3.3	-3.1	2.9	4.8	7.0	13.2
Western Asia	-15.4	13.6	21.0	7.7	5.0	3.0	-6.2	-5.8	5.5	4.8	5.2
Volume of exports											
World	-10.7	13.0	7.4	2.9	3.1	3.6	2.5	2.1	3.7	3.5	3.7
Developed economies	**-12.0**	**10.7**	**5.0**	**1.0**	**2.0**	**4.3**	**5.1**	**2.9**	**3.7**	**3.3**	**3.6**
North America	-13.5	12.9	5.5	2.5	1.2	4.0	4.2	0.9	3.3	3.0	3.1
Europe	-11.1	9.6	4.5	-0.3	2.3	4.1	6.3	4.4	4.0	3.5	3.8
Developed Asia and Pacific	-14.2	12.1	7.1	5.4	2.1	6.1	0.6	-0.9	3.3	3.0	3.6
Economies in transition	**-26.5**	**16.5**	**16.0**	**9.0**	**2.6**	**-6.7**	**-17.1**	**-2.3**	**9.5**	**5.2**	**4.1**
South-Eastern Europe	-16.2	3.6	6.1	0.9	3.1	5.1	5.2	6.5	6.3	5.9	4.6
Commonwealth of Independent States and Georgia[d]	-27.3	17.7	16.8	9.5	2.6	-7.4	-18.8	-3.1	9.8	5.2	4.1

Table A.13

World trade[a]: changes in value and volume of exports and imports, by major country group, 2009–2019 (*continued*)

Annual percentage change

	2009	2010	2011	2012	2013	2014	2015	2016	2017[b]	2018[c]	2019[c]
Developing economies	-7.6	13.0	9.2	5.0	4.1	4.5	1.5	1.9	2.8	3.1	3.4
Latin America and the Caribbean	-9.3	8.8	6.4	2.5	1.2	1.3	5.1	1.2	1.0	1.9	2.2
Africa	-10.9	10.6	1.2	6.8	-5.9	4.8	3.0	2.4	3.4	3.1	4.0
East Asia	-7.4	16.6	9.6	4.6	6.5	5.8	0.7	2.3	3.3	3.5	3.5
South Asia	-0.1	11.4	12.0	3.2	5.2	5.8	5.1	0.6	1.2	2.3	3.5
Western Asia	-7.8	6.0	13.4	8.7	2.4	1.5	-0.8	1.4	2.5	3.4	3.9
Volume of imports											
World	-10.7	13.0	7.4	2.9	3.1	3.6	2.5	2.1	3.7	3.5	3.7
Developed economies	-12.0	10.7	5.0	1.0	2.0	4.3	5.1	2.9	3.7	3.3	3.6
North America	-13.5	12.9	5.5	2.5	1.2	4.0	4.2	0.9	3.3	3.0	3.1
Europe	-11.1	9.6	4.5	-0.3	2.3	4.1	6.3	4.4	4.0	3.5	3.8
Developed Asia and Pacific	-14.2	12.1	7.1	5.4	2.1	6.1	0.6	-0.9	3.3	3.0	3.6
Economies in transition	-26.5	16.5	16.0	9.0	2.6	-6.7	-17.1	-2.3	9.5	5.2	4.1
South-Eastern Europe	-16.2	3.6	6.1	0.9	3.1	5.1	5.2	6.5	6.3	5.9	4.6
Commonwealth of Independent States and Georgia[d]	-27.3	17.7	16.8	9.5	2.6	-7.4	-18.8	-3.1	9.8	5.2	4.1
Developing economies	-7.0	16.4	10.3	5.0	4.6	3.4	0.5	1.3	3.2	3.6	3.7
Latin America and the Caribbean	-14.4	21.3	11.2	4.6	3.0	0.2	-1.6	-2.7	1.2	2.2	2.4
Africa	-2.4	8.3	2.2	6.5	2.5	1.8	-0.6	0.6	3.8	4.7	4.3
East Asia	-6.1	19.9	11.4	4.8	6.8	5.1	1.2	2.6	3.8	3.7	3.7
South Asia	1.3	8.6	12.3	2.8	-6.0	0.5	1.4	1.0	2.9	4.0	7.6
Western Asia	-10.0	8.1	8.8	7.1	6.0	2.6	-0.6	0.1	2.4	3.4	2.5

Source: UN/DESA.

a Includes goods and non-factor services.

b Partly estimated.

c Baseline forecast, based in part on Project LINK.

d Georgia officially left the Commonwealth of Independent States on 18 August 2009. However, its performance is discussed in the context of this group of countries for reasons of geographic proximity and similarities in economic structure.

Table A.14
Balance of payments on current accounts, by country or country group, summary table, 2008–2016

Billions of dollars

	2008	2009	2010	2011	2012	2013	2014	2015	2016
Developed economies	-765.7	-256.1	-181.6	-219.1	-167.2	16.7	-1.1	54.2	97.8
Japan	142.6	145.3	221.0	129.8	59.7	45.9	36.8	134.1	188.1
United States	-681.4	-372.5	-430.7	-444.6	-426.2	-349.5	-373.8	-434.6	-451.7
Europe[a]	-166.4	60.3	134.2	194.5	336.3	433.9	427.6	471.6	450.3
EU-15	-127.3	21.9	52.0	126.7	233.6	301.1	313.0	356.9	350.6
EU-13	-120.9	-41.8	-49.9	-48.7	-29.8	-0.5	-2.8	3.0	9.1
Economies in transition[b]	90.3	35.4	62.5	98.8	59.1	11.6	50.9	48.6	-4.5
South-Eastern Europe	-18.6	-7.5	-6.0	-8.5	-8.5	-5.7	-6.2	-4.4	-4.3
Commonwealth of Independent States[c]	111.6	44.1	69.7	109.2	69.4	18.2	58.8	54.7	1.7
Developing economies[d]	726.8	366.0	385.3	444.0	453.8	362.5	371.3	170.9	166.1
Net fuel exporters	426.1	64.5	213.5	474.6	465.3	369.2	190.4	-182.5	-140.5
Net fuel importers	300.7	301.5	171.8	-30.5	-11.4	-6.7	180.9	353.4	306.6
Latin America and the Caribbean	-39.0	-33.6	-96.9	-113.9	-134.5	-164.1	-183.8	-172.8	-98.7
Net fuel exporters	37.1	-1.5	0.2	10.5	-3.6	-2.7	-10.7	-37.8	-19.0
Net fuel importers	-1.9	-35.1	-96.7	-103.4	-138.1	-166.7	-194.5	-210.6	-117.7
Africa	21.3	-44.9	-9.9	-12.9	-43.2	-62.5	-95.6	-144.2	-119.6
Net fuel exporters	108.3	1.2	40.4	43.6	54.3	14.3	-42.1	-90.6	-68.4
Net fuel importers	-87.0	-46.1	-50.3	-56.5	-97.6	-76.8	-53.5	-53.6	-51.2
Western Asia	220.8	36.6	99.2	274.1	338.5	278.3	196.2	-77.9	-96.1
Net fuel exporters	264.2	48.1	146.5	351.8	400.6	348.6	242.7	-47.6	-62.0
Net fuel importers	-43.4	-11.5	-47.3	-77.7	-62.1	-70.3	-46.5	-30.3	-34.0
East and South Asia	523.9	407.8	392.9	296.7	293.2	310.8	454.5	565.9	480.5
Net fuel exporters	16.6	16.6	26.4	68.6	13.9	8.9	0.4	-6.5	8.9
Net fuel importers	507.3	391.2	366.5	228.1	279.2	301.8	454.1	572.4	471.6
World residual[e]	51.4	145.3	266.2	323.7	345.7	390.8	421.0	273.8	259.4

Source: International Monetary Fund (IMF), *World Economic Outlook* database, October 2017.

Note: IMF-WEO has adopted the sixth edition of the Balance of Payments Manual (BPM6).

a Europe consists of the EU-15, the EU-13 and Iceland, Norway and Switzerland (Table A).

b Includes Georgia.

c Excludes Georgia, which left the Commonwealth of Independent States on 18 August 2009.

d Libya has been excluded in the calculation due to unavailability of data.

e Statistical discrepancy.

Table A.15
Balance of payments on current accounts, by country or country group, 2008–2016

Billions of dollars

	2008	2009	2010	2011	2012	2013	2014	2015	2016
Developed economies									
Trade balance	-817.8	-410.8	-493.0	-671.0	-628.4	-494.6	-535.7	-413.5	-324.7
Services, net	303.8	278.3	311.0	402.2	411.8	487.1	550.7	521.8	488.1
Primary income	94.3	220.0	354.0	414.5	404.2	401.7	373.2	300.5	289.7
Secondary income	-345.9	-343.4	-353.5	-364.6	-354.8	-377.3	-389.1	-354.3	-355.1
Current-account balance	-765.7	-256.1	-181.6	-219.1	-167.2	16.7	-1.1	54.2	97.8
Japan									
Trade balance	55.6	57.8	108.5	-4.5	-53.9	-90.0	-99.9	-7.4	51.4
Services, net	-38.0	-34.9	-30.3	-35.0	-47.8	-35.7	-28.8	-16.0	-10.8
Primary income	138.1	134.6	155.1	183.1	175.6	181.6	184.6	173.8	167.1
Secondary income	-13.1	-12.3	-12.4	-13.8	-14.2	-10.0	-19.0	-16.3	-19.7
Current-account balance	142.6	145.3	221.0	129.8	59.7	45.9	36.8	134.1	188.1
United States									
Trade balance	-832.5	-509.7	-648.7	-740.6	-741.2	-702.2	-751.5	-761.9	-752.5
Services, net	123.8	125.9	154.0	192.0	204.4	240.4	261.2	261.4	247.7
Primary income	129.7	115.2	168.2	211.1	207.5	206.0	210.8	181.0	173.2
Secondary income	-102.3	-103.9	-104.3	-107.0	-96.9	-93.6	-94.2	-115.1	-120.1
Current-account balance	-681.4	-372.5	-430.7	-444.6	-426.2	-349.5	-373.8	-434.6	-451.7
Europe[a]									
Trade balance	-72.3	51.1	43.4	48.9	188.2	297.3	308.5	394.3	404.0
Services, net	237.0	202.3	212.3	275.9	290.3	318.9	349.1	301.6	267.7
Primary income	-101.8	30.5	110.0	107.4	94.7	85.1	40.8	-5.8	-10.4
Secondary income	-229.3	-223.7	-231.5	-237.7	-236.8	-267.4	-270.7	-218.5	-211.1
Current-account balance	-166.4	60.3	134.2	194.5	336.3	433.9	427.6	471.6	450.3
EU-15									
Trade balance	-45.8	39.7	7.2	3.8	113.6	197.0	220.5	326.9	347.9
Services, net	158.4	140.2	150.9	208.0	224.2	248.0	273.6	230.3	189.7
Primary income	-14.9	57.0	118.0	144.1	121.8	108.0	65.3	1.1	8.2
Secondary income	-224.9	-215.1	-224.1	-229.2	-226.0	-251.9	-246.4	-201.4	-195.3
Current-account balance	-127.3	21.9	52.0	126.7	233.6	301.1	313.0	356.9	350.6
EU-13									
Trade balance	-128.7	-45.7	-47.7	-51.4	-34.7	-14.4	-17.1	-11.4	-9.2
Services, net	45.3	36.0	36.2	45.1	45.6	52.9	58.5	55.6	65.1
Primary income	-46.6	-36.9	-45.7	-49.9	-45.4	-44.5	-47.1	-44.6	-47.5
Secondary income	9.1	4.8	7.4	7.5	4.7	5.4	2.9	3.5	0.8
Current-account balance	-120.9	-41.8	-49.9	-48.7	-29.8	-0.5	-2.8	3.0	9.1
Economies in transition[b]									
Trade balance	176.7	105.6	154.3	221.7	205.9	179.4	203.1	132.3	62.3
Services, net	-27.8	-24.1	-31.0	-36.6	-52.7	-61.4	-62.7	-39.2	-23.6
Primary income	-72.2	-58.9	-72.7	-98.6	-103.9	-113.3	-97.0	-54.4	-54.2
Secondary income	13.6	13.3	11.9	12.3	9.7	6.9	7.4	9.9	11.0
Current-account balance	90.3	35.4	62.5	98.8	59.1	11.6	50.9	48.6	-4.5

Table A.15
Balance of payments on current accounts, by country or country group, 2008–2016 (*continued*)

Billions of dollars

	2008	2009	2010	2011	2012	2013	2014	2015	2016
Economies in transition[b] (*continued*)									
South-Eastern Europe									
Trade balance	-29.8	-19.8	-17.6	-20.8	-19.4	-17.3	-18.2	-14.8	-14.7
Services, net	2.3	2.3	2.5	3.1	2.9	3.4	3.8	3.8	4.4
Primary income	-0.6	-0.3	-0.9	-1.1	-1.5	-1.6	-1.7	-1.8	-2.4
Secondary income	9.6	10.3	10.0	10.3	9.6	9.8	9.9	8.5	8.4
Current-account balance	-18.6	-7.5	-6.0	-8.5	-8.5	-5.7	-6.2	-4.4	-4.3
Commonwealth of Independent States[c]									
Trade balance	210.2	127.8	174.4	246.0	229.6	200.2	225.6	151.1	80.8
Services, net	-30.1	-26.7	-34.0	-40.4	-56.7	-66.2	-67.8	-44.5	-29.6
Primary income	-71.5	-58.6	-71.6	-97.1	-102.2	-111.4	-95.1	-52.2	-51.1
Secondary income	3.0	2.0	0.8	0.7	-1.3	-4.4	-3.9	0.3	1.5
Current-account balance	111.6	44.1	69.7	109.2	69.4	18.2	58.8	54.7	1.7
Developing economies[d]									
Trade balance	859.8	546.4	679.1	850.5	860.2	884.2	859.6	656.5	635.2
Services, net	-190.0	-181.9	-210.2	-242.5	-273.3	-315.4	-414.6	-358.5	-354.0
Primary income	-188.3	-216.5	-308.8	-389.2	-340.3	-400.1	-296.5	-306.0	-290.1
Secondary income	245.3	218.0	225.2	225.2	207.3	193.9	222.8	179.0	175.1
Current-account balance	726.8	366.0	385.3	444.0	453.8	362.5	371.3	170.9	166.1
Net fuel exporters									
Trade balance	659.1	317.4	514.3	859.5	840.1	785.1	629.6	181.5	172.1
Services, net	-207.5	-190.4	-210.6	-242.4	-254.1	-266.1	-290.0	-232.6	-197.5
Primary income	-68.6	-65.0	-85.0	-115.6	-110.5	-105.6	-91.2	-63.1	-47.8
Secondary income	6.0	-6.8	-19.8	-30.1	-33.9	-44.2	-39.0	-58.9	-62.7
Current-account balance	389.0	55.1	198.9	471.4	441.5	369.2	209.4	-173.1	-136.0
Net fuel importers									
Trade balance	200.8	229.0	164.8	-9.0	20.1	99.0	230.0	475.0	463.1
Services, net	17.5	8.5	0.4	-0.1	-19.2	-49.3	-124.6	-125.9	-156.5
Primary income	-119.7	-151.4	-223.7	-273.6	-229.8	-294.6	-205.3	-242.9	-242.3
Secondary income	239.3	224.8	245.0	255.3	241.2	238.1	261.8	237.9	237.8
Current-account balance	337.8	310.9	186.4	-27.4	12.4	-6.7	161.9	344.1	302.0
Latin America and the Caribbean									
Trade balance	40.4	51.2	45.5	67.1	38.2	2.8	-16.3	-52.4	2.9
Services, net	-33.9	-36.2	-51.5	-68.8	-74.1	-81.2	-79.1	-57.9	-46.2
Primary income	-113.8	-106.9	-153.6	-176.8	-162.2	-150.0	-156.5	-132.1	-131.3
Secondary income	68.3	58.3	62.7	64.6	63.5	64.3	68.0	69.6	76.0
Current-account balance	-39.0	-33.6	-96.9	-113.9	-134.5	-164.1	-183.8	-172.8	-98.7
Africa									
Trade balance	65.3	-15.6	27.2	51.5	12.7	-5.9	-54.4	-130.2	-115.8
Services, net	-52.1	-43.9	-51.4	-66.1	-61.7	-62.3	-73.8	-49.2	-39.7
Primary income	-59.1	-48.2	-56.3	-73.5	-75.7	-77.9	-66.7	-50.1	-41.7

Table A.15

Balance of payments on current accounts, by country or country group, 2007–2015 (*continued*)

Billions of dollars

	2008	2009	2010	2011	2012	2013	2014	2015	2016
Africa (*continued*)									
Secondary income	67.1	62.8	70.6	75.3	81.4	83.6	99.2	85.2	77.6
Current-account balance	21.3	-44.9	-9.9	-12.9	-43.2	-62.5	-95.6	-144.2	-119.6
Western Asia									
Trade balance	343.6	164.5	264.0	459.4	537.6	491.0	421.8	128.0	91.2
Services, net	-85.4	-75.3	-90.8	-99.7	-109.8	-116.7	-132.4	-106.4	-93.3
Primary income	-6.1	-12.0	-16.2	-15.5	-9.0	-6.2	2.1	6.6	11.0
Secondary income	-31.3	-40.5	-57.9	-70.1	-80.4	-89.8	-95.2	-106.0	-104.9
Current-account balance	220.8	36.6	99.2	274.1	338.5	278.3	196.2	-77.9	-96.1
East Asia									
Trade balance	410.6	346.2	342.3	272.5	271.7	396.3	508.4	711.1	656.9
Services, net	-18.6	-26.4	-16.5	-7.9	-27.8	-55.3	-129.3	-145.0	-174.7
Primary income	-9.4	-49.4	-82.7	-123.4	-93.5	-166.0	-75.4	-130.4	-128.1
Secondary income	141.2	137.4	149.8	155.5	142.7	135.8	150.7	130.1	126.4
Current-account balance	523.9	407.8	392.9	296.7	293.2	310.8	454.5	565.9	480.5
South Asia									
Trade balance	218.6	241.1	340.3	401.2	437.8	569.0	527.0	375.3	372.7
Services, net	86.0	72.3	69.8	123.0	85.8	110.2	73.4	124.0	110.5
Primary income	-166.2	-55.5	-27.5	-73.3	-39.9	-111.8	-20.3	-59.9	-54.7
Secondary income	-87.0	-112.2	-116.4	-127.1	-137.8	-176.5	-158.9	-165.5	-169.0
Current-account balance	51.4	145.3	266.2	323.7	345.7	390.8	421.0	273.8	259.4
World residual[e]									
Trade balance	239.4	250.8	239.4	338.1	393.7	435.1	567.3	512.0	357.6
Services, net	124.6	60.4	74.8	70.5	124.0	90.3	117.6	100.9	127.8
Primary income	-21.0	-150.9	-46.0	-26.0	-61.8	-29.7	-101.1	-7.0	-61.7
Secondary income	-105.4	-114.5	-135.0	-140.7	-158.8	-172.8	-212.2	-199.8	-176.3
Current-account balance	237.5	45.7	133.1	241.9	297.1	322.7	371.5	406.0	247.3

Source: International Monetary Fund (IMF), *World Economic Outlook* database, October 2017.

Note: IMF-WEO has adopted the sixth edition of the Balance of Payments Manual (BPM6).

a Europe consists of the EU-15, the EU-13 and Iceland, Norway and Switzerland (Table A).

b Includes Georgia.

c Excludes Georgia, which left the Commonwealth of Independent States on 18 August 2009.

d Libya has been excluded in the calculation due to unavailability of data.

e Statistical discrepancy.

Table A.16

Net ODA from major sources, by type, 1995–2016

Donor group or country	Growth rate of ODA (2015 prices and exchange rates)					ODA as a percentage of GNI	Total ODA (millions of dollars)	Percentage distribution of ODA by type, 2016			
								Bilateral	Multilateral		
	1995-2005	2005-2013	2014	2015	2016	2016	2016	Total	Total (United Nations & Other)	United Nations	Other
Total DAC countries	1.8	1.2	1.0	1.0	1.1	0.32	142619	71.5	28.5	4.1	24.4
Total EU	1.8	1.3	1.1	1.0	1.1	0.51	81308	66.3	33.7	4.2	29.5
Austria	2.5	0.7	1.1	1.1	1.2	0.41	1583	61.3	38.7	2.6	36.1
Belgium	1.9	1.2	1.1	0.8	1.2	0.49	2306	62.1	37.9	5.9	32.0
Denmark	1.3	1.4	1.0	0.9	0.9	0.75	2372	71.7	28.3	9.7	18.6
Finland	2.3	1.6	1.1	0.8	0.8	0.44	1057	60.0	40.0	9.3	30.7
France[a]	1.2	1.1	0.9	0.9	1.1	0.38	9501	57.4	42.6	3.7	39.0
Germany	1.3	1.4	1.2	1.1	1.4	0.70	24670	79.3	20.7	1.7	19.0
Greece	.. ..	0.6	1.0	1.0	1.1	0.14	264	26.9	73.1	2.7	70.5
Ireland	4.7	1.2	1.0	0.9	1.1	0.33	802	53.0	47.0	16.4	30.6
Italy	3.1	0.7	1.2	1.0	1.2	0.26	4856	48.1	51.9	3.5	48.5
Luxembourg	3.9	1.7	1.0	0.9	1.1	1.00	384	70.7	29.3	9.9	19.5
Netherlands	1.6	1.1	1.0	1.0	0.9	0.65	4988	63.7	36.3	8.5	27.7
Portugal	1.5	1.3	0.9	0.7	1.1	0.17	340	37.5	62.5	3.5	59.0
Spain	2.2	0.8	0.8	0.7	2.9	0.33	4096	60.8	39.2	1.5	37.7
Sweden	2.0	1.7	1.1	1.1	0.7	0.94	4870	71.1	28.9	9.9	19.0
United Kingdom	3.4	1.7	1.1	1.0	1.0	0.70	18013	63.9	36.1	4.4	31.7
Australia	0.7	2.9	0.9	0.8	0.9	0.25	3025	73.2	26.8	8.7	18.1
Canada	1.8	1.3	0.9	1.0	0.9	0.26	3962	68.5	31.5	6.2	25.3
Japan	0.9	2.2	0.8	1.0	1.1	0.20	10368	68.0	32.0	4.2	27.7
New Zealand	2.2	1.7	1.1	0.9	1.0	0.25	438	81.7	18.3	9.0	9.3
Norway	2.2	2.0	0.9	0.8	1.0	1.11	4352	78.7	21.3	8.9	12.4
Switzerland	1.6	1.8	1.1	1.0	1.0	0.54	3563	78.1	21.9	6.6	15.3
United States	3.8	1.1	1.1	0.9	1.1	0.18	33589	83.2	16.8	2.1	14.7

Source: UN/DESA, based on OECD/DAC online database, available from http://www.oecd-ilibrary.org/statistics.

a Excluding flows from France to the Overseas Departments, namely Guadeloupe, French Guiana, Martinique and Réunion.

Table A.17

Total net ODA flows from OECD Development Assistance Committee countries, by type, 2007–2016

	Net disbursements at current prices and exchange rates (billions of dollars)									
	2007	2008	2009	2010	2011	2012	2013	2014	2015	2016
Official Development Assistance	105.0	122.9	120.7	128.5	135.1	127.0	134.8	137.6	131.6	142.6
Bilateral official development assistance	73.7	87.1	84.0	90.6	94.8	88.5	93.5	94.8	94.2	102.0
in the form of:										
Technical cooperation	15.1	17.3	17.6	18.6	18.0	18.2	16.9	17.3	14.9	…
Humanitarian aid	6.5	8.8	8.6	9.3	9.7	8.5	10.5	13.1	13.4	…
Debt forgiveness	9.7	11.1	2.0	4.2	6.3	3.3	6.1	1.4	0.3	…
Bilateral loans	-2.2	-1.1	2.5	3.8	1.9	2.6	1.4	5.3	6.1	…
Contributions to multilateral institutions[a]	31.3	35.8	36.7	37.8	40.3	38.6	41.4	42.8	37.3	40.6
of which are:										
UN agencies	5.9	5.9	6.2	6.5	6.5	6.6	6.9	6.8	6.1	5.9
EU institutions	12.1	13.6	14.3	13.7	13.8	12.0	12.8	13.4	11.9	13.7
World Bank	6.2	8.6	7.6	8.8	10.2	8.6	9.4	9.8	8.6	8.9
Regional development banks	2.4	3.2	3.1	3.2	4.1	3.9	3.9	4.0	3.2	3.2
Others	4.7	4.4	5.4	5.7	5.8	7.5	8.4	8.8	7.6	…
Memorandum item										
Bilateral ODA to least developed countries	19.7	23.5	24.3	28.2	30.7	27.4	30.0	26.4	25.0	…

Source: UN/DESA, based on OECD/DAC online database, available from http://www.oecd.org/dac/stats/idsonline.
a Grants and capital subscriptions. Does not include concessional lending to multilateral agencies.

Table A.18
Commitments and net flows of financial resources, by selected multilateral institutions, 2007–2016

Billions of dollars

	2007	2008	2009	2010	2011	2012	2013	2014	2015	2016
Resource commitments[a]	74.5	135.2	193.7	245.4	163.8	189.8	130.8	185.0	119.9	245.4
Financial institutions, excluding International Monetary Fund (IMF)	66.6	76.1	114.5	119.6	106.8	96.5	98.8	99.2	99.9	106.9
Regional development banks[b]	31.9	36.7	55.1	46.2	46.9	43.0	45.8	41.1	46.9	49.8
World Bank Group[c]	34.7	39.4	59.4	73.4	59.9	53.5	53.0	58.1	53.0	57.0
International Bank for Reconstruction and Development (IBRD)	12.8	13.5	32.9	44.2	26.7	20.6	15.2	18.6	23.5	29.7
International Development Association (IDA)	11.9	11.2	14.0	14.6	16.3	14.8	16.3	22.2	19.0	16.2
International Financial Corporation (IFC)[d]	10.0	14.6	12.4	14.6	16.9	9.2	11.0	10.0	10.5	11.1
International Fund for Agricultural Development (IFAD)	0.6	0.6	0.7	0.8	1.0	1.0	0.8	0.7	1.3	0.8
International Monetary Fund (IMF)	2.0	48.7	68.2	114.1	45.7	82.5	19.6	72.7	6.2	123.9
United Nations operational agencies[e]	6.3	10.5	11.0	11.6	11.3	10.8	12.4	13.1	13.7	14.7
Net flows	-4.4	43.4	54.6	64.6	78.7	35.1	8.8	-5.1	17.7	32.2
Financial institutions, excluding IMF	13.6	24.5	22.6	27.2	38.0	26.3	22.2	25.0	35.5	33.8
Regional development banks[b]	6.2	21.4	15.7	9.9	10.5	8.6	5.7	11.2	15.4	14.2
World Bank Group[c]	7.4	3.1	6.9	17.2	27.6	17.7	16.5	13.8	20.1	19.6
International Bank for Reconstruction and Development (IBRD)	-1.8	-6.2	-2.1	8.3	17.2	8.0	7.8	6.4	9.0	10.0
International Development Association (IDA)	7.2	6.8	7.0	7.0	9.1	7.8	7.0	7.4	9.9	8.8
International Financial Corporation (IFC)	1.9	2.4	2.1	1.9	1.2	1.9	1.6	0.1	1.3	0.8
International Fund for Agricultural Development (IFAD)	0.2	0.2	0.2	0.2	0.3	0.3	0.2	0.2	0.2	0.2
International Monetary Fund (IMF)	-18.0	18.9	32.0	37.4	40.7	8.9	-13.4	-30.1	-17.9	-1.5

Source: Annual reports of the relevant multilateral institutions, various issues.

a Loans, grants, technical assistance and equity participation, as appropriate; all data are on a calendar-year basis.

b African Development Bank (AfDB), Asian Development Bank (ADB), Caribbean Development Bank (CDB), European Bank for Reconstruction and Development (EBRD), Inter-American Development Bank (IaDB) and the International Fund for Agricultural Development (IFAD).

c Data is for fiscal year.

d Effective 2012, data does not include short-term finance.

e United Nations Development Programme (UNDP), United Nations Population Fund (UNFPA), United Nations Children's Fund (UNICEF), and the World Food Programme (WFP).

Bibliography

Abed, George, and Hamid Davoodi (2003). Challenges of growth and globalization in the Middle East and North Africa. Washington, D. C: International Monetary Fund.

Adler, Gustavo, et al. (2017). Gone with the headwinds: Global productivity. IMF Staff Discussion Note, No. SDN/17/04. Washington, D.C.: International Monetary Fund. April.

Alschner, Wolfgang, Julia Seiermann and Dimitriy Skougarevskiy (2017). Text-as-data analysis of preferential trade agreements: Mapping the PTA landscape. UNCTAD Research Paper, No. 5. UNCTAD/SER.RP/2017/5. Geneva.

Anand, Rahul, Saurabh Mishra and Shanaka J. Peiris (2013). Inclusive Growth: Measurement and Determinants, IMF Working Paper, WP/13/135. Washington, D. C.: International Monetary Fund. .

Arregui, Nicolas (2016). Operationalizing macroprudential policies. Presentation at the Institute for Capacity Development, International Monetary Fund, 9 July.

Asian Infrastructure Investment Bank (2017). Annual Report 2016: Connecting Asia for the future. Available from https://www.aiib.org/en/news-events/news/2016/annual-report/index.html

Auboin, Marc, and Floriana Borino (2017). The falling elasticity of global trade to economic activity: Testing the demand channel. WTO Staff Working Papers, No ERSD-2017-09. Geneva: World Trade Organization, Economic Research and Statistics Division.

Bank for International Settlements (BIS) (2017a). International banking and financial market development, *BIS Quarterly Review*. Basel, Switzerland. September.

Bank for International Settlements (BIS) (2017b). Basel Committee on Banking Supervision, Basel III Monitoring Report, September 2017.

Bank for International Settlements (BIS) (2017c). International debt security statistics. Available from http://www.bis.org/statistics/secstats_to1509.htm

Blanchard, Olivier, et al. (2016). Capital flows: Expansionary or contractionary? *American Economic Review: Papers & Proceedings 2016*, v. 106, No. 5, pp. 565–569.

Bussière, Matthieu, et al. (2013). Estimating trade elasticities: Demand composition and the trade collapse of 2008–2009. *American Economic Journal: Macroeconomics*, vol, 5, No. 3: pp. 118–151.

Cernat, Lucian, and Zornitsa Kutlina-Dimitrova (2014). Thinking in a box: A "mode 5" approach to services trade. Chief Economist Note, Issue 1. European Commission. March.

Cerutti, Eugenio, Stijn Claessens and Luc Laeven (2015). The use and effectiveness of macroprudential policies. IMF Working Paper, WP/15/61. Washington, D. C.: International Monetary Fund. March.

Corbett, James J., and James J. Winebrake (2016). Shipping Can Deliver. Health impacts by country. Energy and Environmental Research Associates, LLC. Available from http://www.shippingcandeliver.com/ (accessed 22 October 2017).

Corbett, James J., et al. (2007). Mortality from ship emissions: A global assessment. *Environmental Science & Technology*, vol. 41, No. 24, pp. 8512–8518.

Dabla-Norris, Era, et al. (2015). The new normal: A sector-level perspective on productivity trends in advanced economies. IMF Staff Discussion Note, No. SDN/15/03. Washington, D.C.: International Monetary Fund. March.

De Groot, Olaf, and Miguel Perez Ludeña (2014). Foreign direct investment in the Caribbean: Trends, determinants and policies. ECLAC Studies and Perspectives Series: The Caribbean, No. 35. Santiago, Chile: United Nations Economic Commission for Latin America and the Caribbean.

Didier, Tatiana, and Magali Pinat (2017). The nature of trade and growth linkages. Policy Research Working Paper, No. 8168. Washington, D. C.: World Bank. Available from https://openknowledge.worldbank.org/handle/10986/27975

Diebold, Francis X., Laura Liu and Kamil Yilmaz (2017). Commodity connectedness. PIER Working Paper, No. 17-003. Philadelphia, Pennsylvania: Penn Institute of Economic Research, University of Pennsylvania.

Economic and Social Commission for Western Asia (ESCWA) (2017). *Survey of Economic and Social Developments in the Arab Region 2016-2017.* Beirut.

Economic Commission for Latin America and the Caribbean (ECLAC) (2017). *Foreign Direct Investment Report.* Santiago.

Eichengreen, Barry, and Poonam Gupta (2016). Managing sudden stops. Policy Research Working Paper, No. 7639. Washington, D. C.: World Bank.

Evenett, Simon, and Johannes Fritz (2015). Throwing sand in the wheels: How trade distortions slowed LDC export-led growth. A report prepared for the Government of Sweden. London: CEPR Press.

Food and Agriculture Organization of the United Nations (FAO) (2017). *The State of Food Security and Nutrition in the World 2017: Building Resilience for Peace and Food Security.* Rome.

Frankfurt School-UNEP Collaborating Centre for Climate & Sustainable Energy Finance and Bloomberg New Energy Finance (2017). *Global Trends in Renewable Energy Investment 2017.* Available from http://fs-unep-centre.org/sites/default/files/publications/globaltrendsinrenewableenergyinvestment2017.pdf.

Galati, Gabriele, and Richhild Moessner (2017). What do we know about the effects of macroprudential policy? *Economica*, doi:10.1111/ecca.12229. March.

Ghosh, Swati, Ines Gonzalez del Mazo and Inci Ötker-Robe (2012). Chasing the shadows: How significant is shadow banking in emerging markets? Economic Premise, No. 88. Washington, D. C.: World Bank. September.

Global Carbon Project (2017). Carbon budget and trends 2017. Available from www.globalcarbonproject.org/carbonbudget (accessed 13 November 2017).

Hansda, Sanjay K. (2006). Sustainability of services-led growth: An input output analysis of the Indian economy. Available from http://econwpa.repec.org/eps/ge/papers/0512/0512009.pdf

Hoekman, Bernard, and Dirk Willem te Velde, eds. (2017). *Trade in Services and Economic Transformation: A New Development Policy Priority.* London: Overseas Development Institute.

Hurley, Gail (2015). Financing for Development and Small Island Developing States: A Snapshot and Ways Forward. UNDP and UN-OHRLLS Discussion Paper. June.

Hussein, K., A. Mukungu and Y. Awel (2017). Drivers of inclusive growth in Africa. ECA Working Paper. Addis Ababa: Economic Commission for Africa.

Institute of International Finance (IIF) (2017). *Capital Flows to Emerging Markets: A Brighter Outlook* (5 June 2017).

International Civil Aviation Organization (ICAO) (2016). *ICAO Environmental Report 2016: Aviation and Climate Change*. Montreal, QC, Canada.

International Energy Agency (IEA) (2016). CO_2 emissions from fuel combustion: Highlights. Paris: International Energy Agency/Organisation for Economic Co-operation and Development. Available from https://www.iea.org/publications/freepublications/publication/CO2EmissionsfromFuelCombustion_Highlights_2016.pdf (accessed 22 October 2017).

International Energy Agency (IEA) (2017). CO_2 emissions from fuel combustion: Highlights. Paris: International Energy Agency/Organisation for Economic Co-operation and Development. Available from https://www.iea.org/publications/freepublications/publication/CO2EmissionsfromFuelCombustionHighlights2017.pdf (accessed 15 November 2017)

International Labour Organization (ILO) (2015). ILO Global estimates on migrant workers: Results and methodology. Geneva.

International Labour Organization (ILO) (2016). *Assessment of Labour Provisions in Trade and Investment Arrangements. Studies on Growth with Equity*. Paris.

International Labour Organization (ILO) (2017a). *World Employment and Social Outlook: Trends for Women 2017*. Geneva.

International Labour Organization (2017b). *World Employment and Social Outlook: Sustainable Enterprises and Jobs – Formal Enterprises and Decent Work*. Geneva.

International Labour Organization (ILO) (2017c). *Global Wage Report 2016/17*. Geneva.

International Maritime Organization (IMO) (2015). *Third IMO Greenhouse Gas Study 2014: Executive Summary and Final Report*. London.

International Maritime Organization (IMO) (2017). IMO Secretary-General speaks out against regional emission trading system. IMO Press briefing, 9 January 2017. Available from http://www.imo.org/en/MediaCentre/PressBriefings/Pages/3-SG-emissions.aspx (accessed 20 October 2017).

International Monetary Fund (IMF) (2016). Global trade: What's behind the slowdown? In *World Employment and Social Outlook, October 2016*. Washington, D.C.

International Monetary Fund (IMF) (2017a). *Global Financial Stability Report: Is Growth at Risk? October 2017*. Washington, D.C.

International Monetary Fund (IMF) (2017b). World Economic Outlook database. October 2017.

International Monetary Fund (IMF) (2017c). Currency composition of official foreign exchange reserves (COFER). Available from http://data.imf. org/?sk=E6A5F467-C14B-4AA8-9F6D-5A09EC4E62A4

International Monetary Fund (IMF) (2017d). *IMF Fiscal Monitor: Tackling Inequality. October 2017*. Washington, D. C.

International Monetary Fund (IMF), Financial Stability Board (FSB), and Bank for International Settlements (BIS) (2016). Elements of effective macroprudential policies: Lessons from international experience. 31 August.

Kindleberger, Richard (1978). *Manias, Panics and Crashes. A History of Financial Crisis*. New York: Basic Books.

Louw, Abraham (2017). Clean energy investment trends, 3Q 2017. Bloomberg New Energy Finance. 5 October.

Lund, Susan, et al. (2017). The new dynamics of financial globalization. McKinsey Global Institute, August. Available from https://www.mckinsey.com/industries/financial-services/our-insights/the-new-dynamics-of-financial-globalization

Mashayekhi, Mina (2017). Preferential treatment in services for developing countries. In *Trade in Services and Economic Transformation: A New Development Policy Priority*, Bernard Hoekman and Dirk Willem te Velde, eds. London: Overseas Development Institute.

Mashayekhi, Mina, and Bruno Antunes, eds. (2017). Services and structural transformation for development. Geneva: United Nations Conference on Trade and Development.

Mashayekhi, Mina, Marcelo Olarreaga and Guido Porto (2011). Services, trade and development. Geneva. United Nations Conference on Trade and Development.

McMillan, Margaret, Dani Rodrik and Íñigo Verduzco-Gallo (2014). Globalization, structural change, and productivity growth, with an update on Africa. *World Development*, vol.63, pp. 11–32.

Miroudot, Sébastien, and Charles Cadestin (2017). Services in global value chains: From inputs to value-creating activities. OECD Trade Policy Papers, No. 197. Paris: Organisation for Economic Co-operation and Development. March.

Morin, Jean-Frédéric, and Myriam Rochette (2017). Transatlantic convergence of preferential trade agreements environmental clauses. *Business and Politics*, vol. 19, Issue 4.

Morin, Jean-Frédéric, Joost Pauwelyn and James Hollway (2017): The trade regime as a complex adaptive system: Exploration and exploitation of environmental norms in trade agreements. *Journal of International Economic Law*, vol. 20, Issue 2, pp. 365–390.

New Development Bank (2017). Projects database. Available from www.ndb.int/projects/list-of-all-projects

Nicita, Alessandro, and Julia Seiermann (2016). G20 policies and export performance of least developed countries. Policy Issues in International Trade and Commodities Study Series, No. 75. Geneva: United Nations Conference on Trade and Development.

Olmer, Naya, and Dan Rutherford (2017). International Civil Aviation Organization's

Carbon Offset and Reduction Scheme for International Aviation (CORSIA). ICCT Policy Update. Washington, D. C.: International Council on Clean Transportation. February.

Organisation for Economic Co-operation and Development (OECD) (2011). *Divided We Stand: Why Inequality Keeps Rising.* Paris: OECD Publishing.

Organisation for Economic Co-operation and Development (OECD) (2017a). Development finance of countries beyond the DAC. Available from www.oecd.org/development/stats/non-dac-reporting.htm.

Organisation for Economic Co-operation and Development (OECD) (2017b). Development aid rises again in 2016 but flows to poorest countries dip. Available from http://www.oecd.org/dac/development-aid-rises-again-in-2016-but-flows-to-poorest-countries-dip.htm

Organisation for Economic Co-operation and Development (OECD) (2017c). How to make trade work for all. OECD Economic Outlook, vol. 2017, Issue 1. Paris.

Rey, Hélène (2015). Dilemma not trilemma: The global financial cycle and the monetary policy independence. NBER Working Paper, No. 21162. Massachusetts: National Bureau for Economic Research. May.

Rodrik, Dani (2016). Premature deindustrialization. *Journal of Economic Growth*, vol. 21, No. 1, pp. 1–33.

Schoenmaker, Dirk (2017). Investing for a common good: A sustainable finance framework. Bruegel Essay and Lecture Series. Brussels, Belgium.

Sims, Ralph, Roberto Schaeffer, et al. (2014). Transport. In *Climate Change 2014: Mitigation of Climate Change. Contribution of Working Group III to the Fifth Assessment Report of the Intergovernmental Panel on Climate Change*, Edenhofer et al., eds. Cambridge, United Kingdom and New York, USA: Cambridge University Press.

Tax Policy Center Urban Institute and Brookings Institution (2017). T17-0225 Unified framework; Distribution of federal tax change by expanded cash income percentile 2018. Available from http://www.taxpolicycenter.org/model-estimates/unified-framework-september-2017/t17-0225-unified-framework-distribution-federal-tax

te Velde, Dirk Willem (forthcoming). Services trade and economic transformation: Services economy and trade for structural transformation and inclusive development. Geneva: United Nations Conference on Trade and Development.

Thornton, Joel A., et al. (2017). Lightning enhancement over major oceanic shipping lanes. Geophysical Research Letters, vol. 44, pp. 9102–9111.

UN News Centre (2016). Ban welcomes steps by UN maritime agency to limit carbon emissions from international shipping. 28 October. Available from http://www.un.org/apps/news/story.asp?NewsID=55434#.WeoNuVtSxph (accessed 20 October 2017).

United Nations (2016a). Commending civil aviation proposal, Secretary-General says 'eyes' of world on airlines to significantly reduce emissions. SG/SM/17536-SAG/478. 12 February. Available from https://www.un.org/press/en/2016/sgsm17536.doc.htm (accessed 20 October 2017).

United Nations (2016b). Trends and Progress in International Development Cooperation. E/2016/65, 10 May.

United Nations (2017). *World Economic Situation and Prospects 2017*. Sales No. E.17.II.C.2.

United Nations Conference on Trade and Development (UNCTAD) (2014). *World Investment Report 2014: Investing in the SDGs–An Action Plan*. United Nations publication, Sales No. E.14.II.D.1.

United Nations Conference on Trade and Development (UNCTAD) (2016a). *World Investment Report 2016: Investor Nationality: Policy Challenges*. United Nations publication, Sales No. E.16.II.D.4.

United Nations Conference on Trade and Development (UNCTAD) (2016b). *Review of Maritime Transport 2016*. United Nations publication, Sales No. E.16.II.D.7.

United Nations Conference on Trade and Development (UNCTAD) (2017a). *The State of Commodity Dependence 2016*. United Nations publication, Sales No. E.17.II.D.9. Geneva.

United Nations Conference on Trade and Development (UNCTAD) (2017b). *Review of Maritime Transport 2017*. United Nations publication, Sales No. E.17.II.D.10.

United Nations Conference on Trade and Development (UNCTAD) (2017c). *World Investment Report 2017: Investment and the Digital Economy*. United Nations publication, Sales No. E.17.II.D.3.

United Nations Conference on Trade and Development (UNCTAD) (2017d). The role of the services economy and trade in structural transformation and inclusive development. TD/B/C.I/MEM.4/14. Geneva.

United Nations Office of the High Representative for the Least Developed Countries, Landlocked Developing Countries and Small Island Developing States (UN-OHRLLS) (2017). *State of the Least Developed Countries 2017: Follow up of the implementation of the Istanbul Programme of Action for the Least Developed Countries*. United Nations publication. Available from http://unohrlls.org/custom-content/uploads/2017/09/Flagship_Report_FINAL_V2.pdf

United Nations World Tourism Organization (UNWTO) (2017). UNWTO Tourism Highlights 2017 edition. Available at http://www.e-unwto.org/doi/pdf/10.18111/9789284419029 (accessed 22 October 2017).

United Nations, Economic and Social Council (2017). Report of the Secretary-General on Progress towards the Sustainable Development Goals. E/2017/66.

United Nations, General Assembly (2015). International trade and development. Report of the Secretary-General. A/70/277. 4 August.

United Nations, General Assembly (2016). International trade and development. Report of the Secretary-General. A/71/275. 2 August.

Vazquez, Francisco (2016). Recent country experiences with macroprudential instrument implementation. Presentation at the Institute for Capacity Development, International Monetary Fund. 10 July.

Winebrake, James, et al. (2009). Mitigating the health impacts of pollution from oceangoing shipping: An assessment of low-sulfur fuel mandates. *Environmental Science & Technology*, vol. 43, No. 13, pp. 4776–4782.

World Bank (2016a). Annual Report. Available from https://openknowledge. worldbank.org/handle/10986/24985

World Bank (2016b). *Poverty and Shared Prosperity 2016: Taking on Inequality.* Washington, D. C.

World Bank (2017a). Migration and Remittances Data, updated as of October 2017. Available from http://www.worldbank.org/en/topic/ migrationremittancesdiasporaissues/brief/migration-remittances-data

World Bank (2017b). Macro poverty outlook for Zambia. Washington, D. C.

World Bank (2017c). Migration and Remittances: Recent Developments and Outlook Special Topic: Global Compact on Migration. Washington, D. C. April.

World Trade Organization (WTO) (2016). Overview of developments in the international trading environment. Annual report by the Director General, mid-October 2015 to mid-October 2016. Available from https://docs.wto.org/dol2fe/Pages/SS/directdoc.aspx?filename=q:/ WT/TPR/OV19.pdf

World Trade Organization (WTO) (2017). Report to the TPRB from the Director-General on trade-related developments, mid-October 2016 to mid-May 2017. Available from https://docs.wto.org/dol2fe/Pages/ SS/directdoc.aspx?filename=q:/WT/TPR/OVW11.pdf